POLITICAL AESTHETICS

POLITICAL
AESTHETICS

CRISPIN SARTWELL

CORNELL UNIVERSITY PRESS
Ithaca and London

First published 2010 by Cornell University Press

Printed in the United States of America

Library of Congress Cataloging-in-Publication Data
Sartwell, Crispin, 1958–
    Political aesthetics / Crispin Sartwell.
        p. cm.
    Includes bibliographical references and index.
    ISBN 978-0-8014-4890-4 (cloth : alk. paper)
    1. Aesthetics—Political aspects.   2. Arts—Political
aspects.   I. Title.
    BH301.P64S27   2010
    111'.85—dc22   2009051498

Cornell University Press strives to use environmentally
responsible suppliers and materials to the fullest extent
possible in the publishing of its books. Such materials
include vegetable-based, low-VOC inks and acid-free
papers that are recycled, totally chlorine-free, or partly
composed of nonwood fibers. For further information, visit
our website at www.cornellpress.cornell.edu.

Cloth printing   10 9 8 7 6 5 4 3 2 1

Contents

ACKNOWLEDGMENTS

This book arose as I waffled through the political science, art, and philosophy departments at Dickinson College. I thank my colleagues and students in these departments who kept feeding in information to be integrated. I might mention Melinda Schlitt, Ward Devanny, Elizabeth Lee, Harry Pohlman, John Ransom, Susan Feldman, Phil Grier, Tom Nadelhoffer, Jessica Wahman, and Neil Weissman. Early versions of the basic ideas were presented at the Mississippi State University School of Architecture, the School of Visual Arts in New York, the University of Virginia philosophy colloquium, the Summer Institute in American Philosophy at the University of Colorado, C. W. Post College, and, probably, elsewhere. Many good ideas arose from exchanges with people at these places, including Rachel McCann, Judith Schaechter, Jim Cargile, Cora Diamond, Arthur Lothstein, and Marc Lombardo. Glen Mazis and Marion Winik processed many early formulations of the basic ideas. Roger Haydon at Cornell University Press steered this manuscript through a number of deep revisions, and two anonymous reviewers provided extremely useful, detailed guidelines for those revisions. Though no errors remain, I hope you will blame whatever shortcomings you are under the delusion you detect in this book on these people and not the author.

POLITICAL AESTHETICS

Introduction
The Idea of Political Aesthetics

There are, of course, many connections between art and politics. Regimes of all sorts—democratic, monarchical, communist, and all the rest—use and repress the arts in various ways for propagandistic purposes, to control or deflect public opinion. And much of what we take as fine art has explicitly political themes; this is truer now than ever, or was truer twenty years ago than ever, as artists expressed feminist, antiracist, animal rights, or AIDS activist ideology in their work, for example. These are important areas for investigation. But what I am calling the program or inquiry of political aesthetics begins with a claim that I think is stronger and more interesting.

Not all art is political, but all politics is aesthetic; at their heart political ideologies, systems, and constitutions are aesthetic systems, multimedia artistic environments. The political "content" of an ideology can be understood in large measure actually to be—to be identical with—its formal and stylistic aspects. It's not that a political ideology or movement gets tricked out in a manipulative set of symbols or design tropes; it's that an ideology *is* an aesthetic system, and this is what moves or fails to move people, attracts their loyalty or repugnance, moves them to action or to apathy. But the political function of the arts—including various crafts and design practices—is not merely a matter of manipulation and affect: the aesthetic expressions of a regime or of the resistance to a regime are central also to the cognitive content and concrete effects of political systems. Whether a political ideology is true or false, admirable or repugnant: answering these questions is not exclusively a matter of understanding its texts or speeches or assertions, but also requires seeing these as part of a multisensory aesthetic surround or context. The aesthetic embodiments of political positions are material transformations and interventions, with concrete effects.

I think of the project of political aesthetics as attending to the aesthetic features of what is usually taken to be the material of political science, and I assert that such descriptions can yield insight into political systems, ideologies, and constitutions which is available by no other method, and which is fundamental to an understanding of these items. This book is intended to constitute an argument for that position, and to make that argument, I oscillate between case studies (Nazism, punk, Black Nationalism, and American republicanism) and theoretical excurses on central concepts (beauty and sublimity, language and form, representation and the state, and so on).

Text and Architecture

We tend to think of political ideologies and constitutions as being essentially texts: paradigmatic cases might be the *Republic* of Plato, the United States Constitution, and the *Communist Manifesto.* But political ideologies and constitutions are aesthetic systems of which texts form a portion, in the precise sense that political systems appear in different media, none of which is fundamental and all of which are related; the ideology or system in part simply is the design style. (Indeed, in the term's old acceptation, as in Aristotle or Blackstone, a "constitution" is the structure of political arrangements, an institutional shape, or as Aristotle puts it, an arrangement of offices; it may be embodied in a text, or it may simply be a tradition of political design.) A politics is an aesthetic environment, whatever else it may be. Political systems are no more centrally textual than they are centrally systems of imagery, architecture, music, styles of embodiment and movement, clothing and fibers, furnishings, graphic arts. It's not that systems use these things as tools to gain loyalty, for propaganda; it's that a military junta, sharia law, and anarchism, for example, constitute artpolitical environments in all media.

In the *Critique of Judgment*—the originary text of modern aesthetics— Kant writes, "By an aesthetic idea, I understand that representation of the imagination which occasions much thought, without however any definite thought whatever, i.e. any *concept,* being capable of being adequate to it; it consequently cannot be completely compassed and made intelligible by language" (Kant 1, p. 157). I would quibble with various bits of this, especially the association of definiteness with discursive concept. But the excess of the aesthetic to the linguistic, remarked here by Kant, is proverbial. And the notion that the "aesthetic" (nonlinguistic) "induces much thought" is enough to mark out nonlinguistic items as potential sources of political content. Of course, texts themselves have aspects in excess of their content conceived conceptually: the poetry or lack thereof of the sound of the spoken word, and the arrangements of shapes that constitute or convey the written text: calligraphy or typography, paper and bound volume. That is, the thoughts expressed in the text or received from it, the content of the text, are embodied in more-than-conceptual—in particular, aesthetic—material objects.

Texts, of course, are potentially among the data of political aesthetics. I discuss the aesthetic aspects of political documents—potentially anything from charters and constitutions to statutes to the words employed in political advertising to the lyrics of songs. This project is a political rhetoric not in the sense of a treatment of the craft of persuasion but rather as an elucidation of the poetics of politics, a characterization of the various styles, eras, expressive modes, forms, and so on of political texts. We could treat political rhetoric in terms of schools and movements, arrange speechwriters into metaphysical poets and Beats. This might appear to be a somewhat precious idea or of limited use, but that would be true only if the style of a political document were separable from its content, or if form were not important in explaining the content and effects of political texts, or if the form of something were not its material arrangement.

I am trying to say, on the one hand, that the uses of aesthetics in politics run deeper than propaganda or public relations, but on the other hand, the dichotomy between rhetoric as a craft of persuasion and poetics or aesthetics as a condition on identity for political systems needs itself to be broken down.[1] Take a text such as *The Federalist Papers,* which were written flatly for the purpose of affecting public opinion in New York toward the ratification of the Constitution. The way the texts accomplish this embodies something of a collaborative and persuasive work of art, a systematic and multifarious poetry of republicanism. The language is beautiful and persuasive, but it is the content reflected in the language that compels, the sense of reasonable men reasoning about a balanced and rational construction of institutions. Art, craft, and the technique of truth-telling are one multivalent, interdimensional being.

Drawing from the same tradition, which is the subject of the last chapter of this book, a good example of what I'm calling an "interdimensional

---

1. I am grateful to a reviewer of the manuscript for Cornell University Press who suggested that this point should be made explicit.

being" is the neoclassical political aesthetics of Thomas Jefferson. When John Adams was asked to compose the Declaration of Independence, he suggested Jefferson be assigned the task, on the grounds that Jefferson's prose style was more beautiful, and perhaps specifically more classical, than his own. And this despite the fact that Adams was a strong writer who was immersed throughout his life in the classics. Now, Jefferson's neoclassicism is embodied not only in his prose but also in his architecture and in the influence his architecture (for example the Virginia State House) has had on American public buildings, including the U.S. Capitol; it is embodied in the form of government he devised for the state of Virginia, one of the models for the United States Constitution. All of these aspects are equally central to understanding Jefferson's politics and the transformative effect it had on the American republic. To understand the meaning of the Declaration of Independence, it is necessary to have a sense of its poetry and the sources and significances of its poetry. The text is not a transparent window through which we see Lockean liberalism (as though Lockean liberalism were not itself a style as well as a set of concepts, or as though these were separable); its poetry connects it to centuries of political and nonpolitical discourse, and to centuries of nondiscursive images and objects.

In other words, one effect of political aesthetics is to widen contexts of interpretation of political texts, to make the history of political thought a history of political literature as well. But given the emphasis on texts within political theory, political aesthetics faces a more urgent task than delivering aesthetic descriptions of political texts: refocusing political theory on the nondiscursive modes of political formulation. Even in cases where imagery or architecture or music has figured centrally in accounts of political communication, the governing metaphor has been linguistic. We develop a rhetoric of images, deploy persuasive tactics with discursive effects that draw people toward certain beliefs, principles, ideologies, dogmas formulated as statements. These beliefs, in turn, are conceived of as propositional attitudes—attitudes toward a textual or linguistic item. That is, to believe is to endorse a certain sentence or proposition. This is treated as the cognitive dimension of politics, whereas what I am calling political aesthetics is supposed to be its affect. The distinction is invidious. Political aesthetics as I try to practice it in this book focuses on the nondiscursive features of an ideology, a system, and so on, and then presses back toward an aesthetic understanding of the texts.

The Aesthetic

Let me say briefly something about how I intend to use the word "aesthetic" and its cognates. First of all, aesthetics is a subdiscipline of philosophy that is concerned, in my view, with four main questions (as well as many ancillary ones): the nature of art; aesthetic values, especially beauty and sublimity; standards of taste and aesthetic assessment; and mimesis or representation. All of these are importantly related to political matters, and though the definition of "art" is only tangentially connected to the main lines of argument in this book, the other three themes are central to it.

What to count as an aesthetic property or aspect of a political system or anything else is an extremely vexed issue that I want to hold in abeyance for now as a full-fledged theoretical task. The approach of this book is to open rather than close the range of properties profitably regarded as aesthetic. It seems to me that a rough idea of aesthetic properties as properties of a thing's design or configuration (conceived as an arrangement of materials) under an interpretation will suffice. We might gesture toward the relevant properties thus: a thing's aesthetic features are the features of a thing that could be relevant to assessment of its beauty. Beauty itself is of course not the only aesthetic value (elegance, wildness, ease, intensity, sublimity, for example); indeed ugliness has many legitimate applications in the making of things, including works of art, as we shall see when we come to the artpolitics of punk. Nevertheless, the scale of beauty, or the judgment of Paris, is the most ancient subject matter of aesthetics. Some of the aesthetic properties are formal properties, or properties of appearance or material surface in some sense: something's being longer than it is wide, or being asymmetrical, for example. Others are physical or structural properties: of what a thing is made (stone, code), and by what it is made (pedal steel guitars versus synthesizers; hand as against machine lathe). Yet others are historically emergent properties, properties of the object under a cultural or disciplinary interpretation, as in the assignment of an oeuvre to a movement: to say Gauguin's work is postimpressionist, for example.

We deal with tools and materials with regard to culturally circulating meanings, while the physical features of tools and materials massively shape those very meanings. For instance, the stone slabs that form the floor and counter of an old-fashioned small-town bank convey stability and quiet wealth. But the stone is fitted in virtue of its physical features to express such things. Its semiotics is not a mere stipulation; it was selected for the task because it was physically suited to convey such meanings. Stone is more stable, enduring, and heavy than Bakelite or linoleum, for example. The meaning is neither only out there among things themselves nor only in the head or the language but is an interaction of persons and environments, physical or virtual, stone or televised image. The attribution of an aesthetic feature to a thing involves a language and a culture, but if it's true, it picks out a real feature of that thing in its context. Attributions of aesthetic properties to things are not merely objective, not merely subjective, and not merely culturally fixed: the aesthetic features of a thing are features of it in a situation that implicates all of these, in every case.

Stone slabs are perfectly concrete physical objects, whereas words, for example, do not seem to be. And as information technologies expand, we operate within an environment in which we do not encounter objects in the same way, or in which banks and money are made of code rather than physical materials. Of course, like language in general, code still relies on material interventions; we have not floated into a wholly abstract world. Nevertheless, the same observations apply at least to some extent to objects such as websites, and the design features of a banking site, for example, are in part developments out of the stone slab bank: the site is going to look stable, relatively simple, dignified, sober. No bank in its right mind has a whimsical or idiosyncratic or wildly "artistic" website, any more than it wants these qualities in the architecture of its headquarters. The design decisions shape the screen, and the screen shapes the experience; the aesthetic features of the site are features of it in a situation, and they are real features. And they are features that emerge in a set of design traditions, multifarious aesthetic histories.

A building or a city section might resolve roughly into a triangle, be symmetrical or balanced; it might be made of local stone, or concrete and steel, or whatever can be salvaged from the local dump. And it will have what we might think of as art historical properties, which are also underlain by formal properties and other design features, for example, stylistic properties: Gothic, classical, baroque, rococo, neoclassical, modernist, eclectic. It may be bold or timid, traditional or innovative, inspiring or depressing. I use all of these terms to pick out aesthetic features, at least on some occasions of their use. And to an aesthetic experience or judgment of a façade as Gothic, for example, the actual date at which it was built, information about the design process and the people who participated in it, and its location are as relevant as the shape of the windows. Notice that, although we might refer to a contemporary building made of glass and steel as "Gothic," we might also refer to it as "pseudo-Gothic" or "contemporary Gothic" and so on, terms for aesthetic features that no fourteenth-century building could display. That is, a thing's various relations or relational properties—its histories and historically emergent properties—are potentially aesthetic features of it, depending on the purpose and context of interpretation.

The aesthetic features of a thing are often considered to be qualities not of that thing but of the experience of that thing: beauty in the eye of the beholder and so on. But again, in my view, aesthetic features of an object—its shape, let's say, and the ways that shape means within a culture—are no more subjective than any other qualities of an object, for example, its weight; indeed it is not hard to imagine cases in which weight itself is an aesthetic feature of an object. People can be simply wrong about the aesthetic features of an object. Aesthetic features become evident in interpretations of an object, but these interpretations are constrained massively by the character of the object, its origin, its material, as well as by real and recalcitrant features of the culture from which it emerges and the discourses in which it appears. To say of the universe that it is beautiful or well ordered (and I do not assert that it is beautiful or well ordered) would be to talk about its character, not one's own (though it might display or betray something about one's character); and if we wanted to figure out whether the universe is in fact beautiful or well ordered, we would have to look at it, not at our looking at it, except insofar as our looking at it is itself a part of it. We wouldn't justify the assertion that it is beautiful merely by examining our own swoon. We'd start rhapsodizing about the stars or something. And yet, in assessing whether the universe is well ordered, we would do well to figure out what we might mean by such a term, and the material to be elucidated in a treatment of the subject would include our vocabulary and related verbal, perceptual, and other cognitive and social structures.

That a couch weighs 150 pounds is a fact about the couch; to know what it means, you'd have to know what a pound is, more or less, and understand a decimal notation. That a pound or kilogram is a standard measure of weight has to do with the conditions of human life and of the cultures where the measures arose, and if we'd been a thousand seventeen times as strong as we are, we'd have a completely different system. But that doesn't make the weight of things subjective or a mere cultural construction, and it doesn't make an assertion about the weight of something an assertion about our language. The aesthetic features of a situation are potentially as external to us and to our practices and as epistemically available as any other aspects of the world, though there are special problems of subtlety or ambiguity in the case of ascriptions of some aesthetic features, notoriously "beauty." Well, there are special problems in a lot of areas: think about how complex a matter it might be in a vexed case to show that a particular economic system is capitalist or socialist, for example. Political and aesthetic descriptions are similarly vexed, but they also have similar shorthand or conventional uses, and it is often not at all hard to say in a general way in virtue of what some website is elegant or some system democratic. To talk about the aesthetic features of a political system is not to move from hard objective assessments of its real features to a subjective response to its ornamentation; it is, in the framework of this book, to expand the (potentially) concrete descriptions, to broaden the sense of the causes and the causal outcomes of political systems, their material ramifications.

The Political

The other definitional question is about the nature of "the political," and here I'm going to rest content with the vaguest gestures. Politics is the place where systematic or enduring power relations or public identities are negotiated or constituted in a group of people. Power, in turn, we might think of as the ability to annex persons or their energies, actions, and resources to one's own purposes, or to the purposes of a group, or as the articulation of these interests in relation to one another, the space in which they are distinguished, merged, or articulated. In doing that, and perhaps in doing other things, the political creates or reflects some identity or principle of cohesion: a culture or several cultures, a structure of roles, and so on.

With regard to the first of these themes, Sheldon Wolin has it that

> the system of political institutions in a given society represents an arrangement of power and authority. At some point within the system, certain institutions are recognized as having the authority to make decisions applicable to the whole community. The exercise of this function naturally attracts the attention of groups and individuals who feel that their interests and purposes will be affected by the decisions taken. When this awareness takes the form of action, the activities become "political" and a part of political nature.... Although one could multiply the ways in which human activities become "political," the main point lies in the "relating" function performed by political institutions.... They serve to define, so to speak, "political space" or the locus where the tensional forces of society are related. (Wolin, pp. 7–8)

Primordially, the political is a place or polis, an actual capitol or arena: the Pnyx, meeting place of the Athenian citizenry. In a given case the Pnyx might be a single person (such as a tribal chieftain), or it might be a tremendously complex set of institutions. It is the center of power and hence of contestation between interests—classes, professions, races, religions—the place you have to occupy to secure or expand the purposes or resources of a given group. (It might also be possible for someone to transcend mere self- or group interest and represent the polis as a whole, or such concrete abstractions as justice or happiness, or to weld a whole polis into a single interest, multiply articulated; in a classical conception the polis exists to make that possible.) It is also a place where these interests, in their competition and cooperation, become conscious in a certain way, in which people *deliberate* as to their adjudication, in which the polis takes shape as an object of consciousness, something that could be designed. That is, with the emergence of the political emerges the politically aesthetic: questions about design features, constitutions, balance, flow, and so on. Within each of the groups meeting in the Pnyx is a Pnyx, wherein its internal division into interests is negotiated or resolved, and this might be shaved finer and finer, so that there is even a politics of a family or couple, or even possibly within a single individual: a procedure or place where the power is transacted and shaped. So the political is not distinct from various other activities and institutions but is an aspect of them. But as well, the political has formed up into a quasi-autonomous sphere: the state or multistate institutions: the places where powers are distributed on the widest scope current.

Now, the idea of politics as a place where interests negotiate or adjudicate claims to power seems too particular, or too jaundiced. Various philosophers—Habermas or Arendt, for example, or even Rousseau—might characterize it more positively (at least under decent circumstances) as the place wherein our social nature is expressed, or as a public sphere in which collective identities, and hence also individual identities, are forged. Such views provide an important corrective to the idea that people have pre-political identities and interests which they use political activity, instrumentally, to achieve. The latter might be thought of as a peculiarly modern idea, and peculiarly attuned to a classical liberal conception of individuals as atoms that precede, rather than being constituted within, political or social activity; whereas the constitutive conception might be termed republican or Aristotelian, and often finds expression in the contemporary trend in political philosophy termed "communitarianism," associated with thinkers such as Alasdair MacIntyre and Michael Sandel. And this much is certainly true: the creation of interests and the character of individuals occur within various already constituted political contexts, so that the interests that are negotiated in the Pnyx are incomprehensible except in their already articulated context within the Pnyx. And in some sense the Pnyx extends to the whole of the polis, including into the person of each person it encompasses (though human identity is not, I believe, exhaustively political).

I think that whatever I say about the political in what follows is compatible either with a narrower (power- or interest-oriented) or with a broader conception of the political (as identity-formation). And indeed, if the political is where the identities and interests that constitute the political are themselves forged, then political aesthetics will yield a richer and more specific sense of how this occurs, of the ways that identities and interests are actually formed and expressed. Whatever the scope of political activity and identity, I suggest, they are centrally aesthetic.

There is also politics within what we might think of as aesthetic institutions: workshops and schools, museums and galleries, craft shops and recording studios. That is, these are sites where power is negotiated and distributed, and public or social identities are constituted or articulated. Michelangelo, to issue his visual theology, has to work his way through the institutional politics of the Vatican. There is a hierarchy of galleries in New York and elsewhere, and who shows where or is dealt by whom is the basis of a pecking order. Power is transacted, albeit in fairly small dollops, and the available roles and personae are in part constituted in the institutional context. The history of patronage is central to the history of art. But these are not what I'm regarding as primary data of political aesthetics. Issues of politics within art and design practices and institutions could become questions for political aesthetics as I've characterized it, but only by putting the art institutions into a context of power wielded over a culture or society, and of resistance to that power. For example, state patronage of the arts could become an issue or an example within an artpolitical interpretation of a particular political system. But I'm fundamentally concerned with the design aspects of political systems, not the political aspects of design systems. I want, again, to focus on what would normally be thought of as the subject matter of political science: political systems, constitutions, philosophies; state institutions and resistance to them; revolutions and parties; policies and powers.

Even the vague characterization of the political as the space where interests contest or negotiate power suggests the centrality of the aesthetic aspects of politics. For the question insistently presents itself in terms of coordinations, in terms of shape or form. In this light we might also consider more radical or realist conceptions of the political, as for example that of Carl Schmitt, who defines it in terms of the construction of the dichotomy friend/enemy. Here, to define what a system excludes is to define that system, and what makes a political system itself is its form, its shape defined by its conceptual (and geographic) borders and contours (see, for example, Schmitt, p. 26). There are procedures for negotiating power. But there is also the institutional/societal form that emerges from these procedures: the actual state of play of power relations and social functions at a given moment. Politics—even as understood in this way—is a design discipline. That is a useful first remark, at any rate, even if it suggests too much intentionality: the real shape of a society is not anyone's design but a complex and unstable result of the decisions of many people in interaction with their material and informational environments. Nevertheless what emerges is something like a shape, and when we

withdraw to the most general characterizations of a polity, we are withdraw-
ing to the question of its form and the constituents of that form in relation
to the whole.

The basic treatment of the relation of the aesthetic and the political in this
book is conceived as follows. Aesthetic values and political values are not
identical. There is a difference, for example, between beauty and justice. But
first of all, they are inseparable in every particular application: they inform
each other fundamentally. The dimensions of value cut across each other,
infest each other, and exceed each other in every case. There can be an aesthetic critique of political institutions and a political critique of art styles.
The relation is not identity, but it is intimate: complex, coincident, contradictory. The values are orthogonal, but this entails that they are always correlated. These are vague remarks. But I think we can give them considerable
precise content as we move forward.
    In short, political aesthetics

1. Treats political systems (constitutions, ideologies) as aesthetic environments rather than as primarily composed of (textually expressed)
   doctrines.
2. Considers textual materials themselves in their aesthetic aspects.
3. Strategically, starts by questioning and exploring the distinctions
   between fundamental dimensions of value: truth (epistemic value);
   goodness (moral value); justice (political value); and beauty (aesthetic value).
4. Concerns the design of political systems, not the politics of design
   systems.
5. Asserts not that all art is political, but that all politics is aesthetic.
6. Asserts that aesthetic and other values (epistemic and ethical, for
   example) intersect at each actual political site.
7. Suggests a token identity between aesthetic and political systems at
   a given time and place, but rejects a type identity between style and
   ideology (for example, between classicism and republicanism). This
   cryptic remark is clarified in the book's conclusion.

The chapters that follow alternate case studies with theoretical excurses.
Each of the theoretical chapters deploys some of the resources of a particular
discipline: philosophical aesthetics (chapter 2), political philosophy (chapter 4),
and art history (chapter 6), in order to display some of the connections
among and between these domains, and between them and the domain of

the political. The case studies are meant both to illustrate and to underpin, to provide the data for and to spell out the implications of, the theoretical chapters.

Chapter 1 discusses the first case that, for many, shows the relation of politics and aesthetics: Nazi Germany. The centrality of the arts for the Nazis, both ways around—as creators and destroyers, idolaters and iconoclasts—has led to the objection that the aestheticization of politics is inherently totalitarian. While treating the Nazi state as both paradigmatic and unique, I suggest that this is not so, and that aesthetics is central to many sorts of regimes, or indeed to all of them. The chapter also broaches "the question of the classical," which recurs throughout the book. Nazism as an aesthetic is described as a synthesis of romanticism and classicism, a sublimization of the classical, and to trace the development of this idea would be to trace the prehistory of Nazi politics in a complex and politically ambi-valent aesthetic history.

Chapter 2 lays out the basic conceptual framework of the book. It attempts to elucidate the relation of political, aesthetic, epistemic, and ethical values in a general way, arguing that such values are both distinct from and inextricable from one another. Specifically, it argues that although not all art is best understood as directly political expression, all political expression contains, centrally, an aesthetic element, without taking cognizance of which it remains not fully comprehensible. It then explores the political origins, dimensions, and implications of some key terms in the discipline of aesthetics: beauty, sublimity, and representation. All of these concepts are simultaneously aesthetic and political, though not always in the same respect at a given moment. The political and aesthetic terrains coincide but are not reducible in either direction. Indeed all three are central dimensions, strategies, and structures of political expression and the exercise of political power—essential, among other things, for developing an understanding of the modern state. The chapter embodies a case for the idea that politics cannot be understood except as an aesthetic environment. The descriptive vocabulary of "political science" cannot be stripped of aesthetic categories, which entails limitations on how scientific the description of political phenomena can possibly be, depending on how we conceive the art/science dualism.

Chapter 3 explores a second case study: punk, in its relation to all the arts, including music and images, film and costume, dance and festival. I argue that although punk music is occasionally appropriated by neo-Nazis, and very frequently by anarchists, its basic stance is defiance or opposition, and I connect it finally to a history of anarchist arts that is at least as old as Shelley or Courbet. To some extent the ideas of punk fashion and performance were supplied by thinkers of the previous cohort of dissidents, such as Guy

Debord and the Situationists. The multiple influences and complex histories are paradigmatic of the shifts and ambiguities inherent in the arts as politics: the forms cannot be held constant as to meanings. This has to be dealt with carefully, as punk has been continuously appropriated as a commercial design style. And in fact this displays the reversal that might befall any set of art-political forms or gestures. The punk tropes, however, are potent, and a new generation of angst-ridden or angry teenagers discovers them every, say, five years and breathes new life into them.

Chapter 4 is parallel to chapter 2, this time considering the role of aesthetics within political philosophy and the development, in British philosophy of the eighteenth century and German idealism, of a recognizable discourse in political aesthetics proper. I examine the centrality of aesthetics, briefly, in some classics of political philosophy, including Plato and Confucius. And I consider some apparently anti-aesthetic political philosophies, such as Aristotle's and Mozi's, as well as similar strands in the Reformation and Marxism. And I suggest that two figures are central in setting out the theoretical bases for the inquiry of political aesthetics: Shaftesbury and Schiller. The former argues for a Neoplatonic unification of the categories of value and explicitly tries to systematize the stylistic aspects of politics. Schiller could be described as the founder of the discourse that this book takes up, picturing a political/public use of the arts and an aesthetic/artistic vocabulary for describing the political.

Chapter 5, like chapter 3, develops a case study in oppositional politics: Black Nationalism in its aesthetic expressions. The chapter can be read as a stand-alone essay, and if this book makes any independent, properly historiographic (as opposed to more overtly theoretical) contribution, it is here. I try to draw out a series of connections that have emerged piecemeal in the research of various historians and ethnomusicologists between the Garvey movement, Rastafarianism, the Nation of Islam, reggae music, and hip hop. These connections are far more elaborate than they might appear to be, and reggae and hip hop constitute (in part) a central Black Nationalist political discourse that cannot be understood except as also essentially musical. In other words, Black Nationalism does not have its Constitution, its *Communist Manifesto*. Though there are important texts, including early Garveyite scriptures and the writings and speeches of Garvey and Malcolm X, Black Nationalism is also an elaborate series of musical developments that have changed world music and also world liberation movements, and that have reconfigured the concept of race and color. Contemporary graffiti, which emerges from the same milieu, is an important form of political expression and the site of new aesthetic uses of language.

Chapter 6 explores concepts drawn from art history. It begins with a discussion of the disciplinary relation between art history and political science, and the various distinctions and rapprochements between art and science generally. It deploys the artpolitical conception derived from the work of Jacques Rancière: "the distribution of the sensible" in relation to broadening conceptions of art historical data such as the notion of "material culture." Many political traditions appear to have aesthetic origins, such as in various national (or nationalist) epics, or in the use of drama in the Athenian polis, or in the role of sculpture in idolatry and political monarchy. I take up the question of periodization, which sheds light on the relation of aesthetic and political concepts; an artpolitical periodization would fail to coincide with the familiar periodizations in art history or in political theory. I try to give some justification for my basic taxonomy—reflected in the case studies— between dominant and resistant aesthetic systems. And I return here, as at a number of times throughout the book, to the question of the classical.

That theme is taken up yet again in the last case study. Chapter 7 concerns the relation of neoclassicism of the eighteenth century to Revolutionary and Constitution-era America. I hope that this case clinches the detachment of aesthetic politics from fascism, and also shows quite specifically why aesthetic categories are necessary to understand the politics of the founding period. Central cases here include John Adams—a man of great classical learning who tried to codify all classical sources on republicanism—and Thomas Jefferson, whose architecture and political ideas are something like identical. Here as well I return to the theme of a constitution as an arrangement or form, an attempt to arrange populations and environments aesthetically.

The conclusion suggests a structure for understanding the relation of stylistic/aesthetic properties to political categories: classicism to republicanism or sublimity to fascism, for example. I suggest that although at any given place and moment the aesthetic expressions of a political system just are that political system, the concepts are separable. Typically, aesthetic aspects of political systems shift in their meaning over time, or even are inverted or redeployed with an entirely transformed effect. You cannot understand politics without understanding the aesthetics of politics, but you cannot understand aesthetics as politics. The point is precisely to show the concrete nodes at which two distinct discourses coincide or connive, come apart or coalesce.

CHAPTER 1

Leni Riefenstahl Meets Charlie Chaplin

Aesthetics of the Third Reich

In "The Work of Art in the Age of Mechanical Reproduction," Walter Benjamin writes, "All efforts to render politics aesthetic culminate in one thing: war" (Benjamin, p. 241). And in 1922 Mussolini said, "The task of fascism is to make [the masses] an organic whole with the Nation, much as an artist needs raw material to forge his masterpieces" (quoted in Falasca-Zamponi, p. 21). In political aesthetics, the case of fascism in general and the Nazis in particular must be considered central, for two reasons. First, few regimes have ever developed an aesthetic more explicitly and self-consciously, or made it more central to their program. And second, perhaps the most and the best work on political aesthetics has been done with regard to the Nazi regime: by Hellmut Lehmann-Haupt, Eric Michaud, Frederick Spotts, Susan Sontag, Benjamin, and many others. Nevertheless, the Nazi regime is by any standard unusual, and we must beware of too easily drawing universal conclusions from such an extraordinary case.

The Benjamin quotation expresses the oft-argued position that one source of the evil of fascism is the aestheticization of politics, or that fascism just is the aestheticization of politics, that every aestheticization of politics is ipso facto fascist. I reject that conclusion. Such a notion would be a fundamental objection to the whole inquiry in which we are engaged. I take the assertion that centralizing the aesthetic aspects of political systems is totalitarian as the fundamental objection to political aesthetics, and thus something that must be dealt with seriously from the outset.

A few preliminary points. First of all, the aesthetics of Italian fascism and German National Socialism was eclectic, encompassing everything from the avant-garde art of the Italian futurists to Speer's imperial, neoclassical architecture. At its height I would emphasize two elements that were apparently in tension, but in the best Nazi art reconciled coherently: German romantic nationalism (which we should associate with the thought of Herder, the work of the Grimm brothers, and the music of Wagner, for example), and the neoclassicism from which romanticism emerged and to which it provided a response. (The notions of the classical and the romantic, in relation to the categories of beauty and sublimity, will be central throughout this book.) The classical makes a claim to universal validity, rationality, composure, or even serenity. The romantic, by contrast, is particularist, emotional, potentially irrational, and grandiose. In its banal forms, Nazi art was indeed comically incoherent. But in its moments of sublimity—and I choose the word advisedly—it constituted a remarkably powerful synthesis. I see this synthesis above all in the films of Leni Riefenstahl, where it is perfectly conscious and perfectly crafted. One way to formulate the effect of a Nazi romantic classicism is that it articulates German national culture—its language, its arts, and its "Aryan" bodies—as the particular repository of universal values: an aesthetics of German world conquest.

As a set of doctrines or texts, Nazism was a mess: a grab bag of extreme nationalism, race theory, militarism, state capitalism, socialism, autocratic bureaucracy, and quasi-paganism. It presented itself, however, not as a political text but as a system of the arts, one of the reasons why the case is both central and peculiar. Hitler himself was an artist, of course, and throughout his career he devoted more attention to aesthetics than to clearly military or political matters. That is an extraordinary and counterintuitive claim, but it is the consensus of the historians who have focused on Hitler's engagements with the arts. Hitler paid obsessive attention to the architecture of cities: in Nuremberg and Berlin he and Albert Speer embarked on the creation of a monumental world of architectural spectacle. But he also devoted enormous energy to stagecraft in his speeches, to symbol systems for flags and uniforms, to insignia, to film and music and painting and sculpture. There was nothing he cared about more than opera, and he was still planning opera houses as German cities were being leveled by Allied bombs.

The most practical aesthetic measures taken by the Nazis, aside from their hugely ambitious building projects, constituted a complete, directly totalitarian control over the arts. This effort was coordinated by Goebbels's propaganda ministry, which established the Reichskulturkammer in 1933. The Reich Chamber of Culture attempted fully to organize and control not only painters, sculptors, and architects but also interior decorators, landscape gardeners, crafters, graphic artists, and antique dealers.[1] The organization grew to 42,000 members, and if one lacked membership, one was prohibited from practicing the art in question, even in the privacy of one's own home. In the "Strength through Joy" organization, the Nazis introduced the most thorough arts "education" programs that any regime has ever attempted, reaching into the redesign of homes and factories: design pictured as the central activity of the people and fully regimented.

In one remarkable moment in 1936 Goebbels issued a blanket ban on all art criticism, which Hitler promptly violated as follows:

> From now on—of that you can be certain—all those mutually supporting and thereby sustaining cliques of chatterers, dilettantes, and art forgers will be picked up and liquidated. For all we care, those prehistoric stone-age culture bearers and art stutterers can return to the caves of their ancestors and there they can apply their primitive international scratchings. (July 18, 1937; quoted in Lehmann-Haupt, p. 77)

I rather like the complexity of "primitive international scratchings." Hitler was speaking of his effort to confiscate all "degenerate" art, which would include the expressionism of such figures as Munch and Nolde (despite the fact that Nolde was a party member), anything by Jews or leftists or showing leftist themes, all abstract works, and so on. Many of these works were displayed in the gigantic show of "degenerate" art of 1937, which the Nazis twinned with a show of approved forms at the new House of German Art, designed with stripped-down giganticized classicism by Paul Ludwig Troost.

Holocaust Aesthetics

Addressing a party rally in 1937, Hitler said about the redesign of the Königsplatz in Munich, which he drafted with Speer:

> It is precisely these buildings which will help unify our people politically more closely than ever and strengthen them; these buildings will inspire German society with a proud consciousness that each and all belong together; they will prove how ridiculous in our social life are

---

1. See Lehmann-Haupt, pp. 68–73.

all social differences in the face of these mighty, gigantic witnesses to
the life which we share as a community. They will fill our people with a
limitless confidence as they remember they are German. These mighty
works will at the same time prove the most sublime evidence of the
political strength of the German Nation. (Spotts, pp. 99–100)

This passage asserts, among other things, the affective qualities of an aesthetic
environment, or what we might think of as aesthetic tactics: rhetorical or
persuasive effects. But Hitler dealt with the bureaucratic structure, or with
military planning, or with genocide, from the point of view of an aesthetic
sensibility and for the sake of an aesthetic effect. What Hitler hated about
the Jews, above all, was their supposed influence on German culture and the
German arts: as much as any crime, he held them responsible for modernism, and specifically expressionism. The idea of "purity" is at its heart an
aesthetic ideal, in the best Nazi design and in the Final Solution: for example,
in the monumental simplicity of the architecture of Troost and Speer. The
Nazi conception of order—the very center of Nazism's commitment and
strategy—is at its heart an aesthetic concept.

One response to this is, again, to decry precisely its aestheticism, because
among other things it seems to leave the moral world blank, to make over
human suffering into a formal feature of design, or even worse, to revel in
cruelty as artistry. The "aestheticization" of politics in Nazism is indeed monstrous, but not because of the sheer fact that it treats politics as an aesthetic
matter. Rather, I suggest, we should focus on specific features of Nazism as an
artpolitical system (for example, its very emphasis on "purity"). If Nazism is
an aesthetic system, then answers to Nazism consist not in de-aestheticizing
politics—which is not a possibility—but in addressing it as an aesthetic system. This would of course include the familiar criticism of Nazi kitsch, or
the answer on behalf of modernism as the shape of artistic destiny, with Nazi
philistines trying tastelessly to return to Wagner or whatever. But a far deeper
and more emotional response—a response that fully humanizes the victims of
Nazism—also avails itself of a set of aesthetic ideals, as I hope to show.

The other fundamental question in political aesthetics that arises from
Nazism is the question of "propaganda." In my view, the relation of the arts
to political power is not exhausted by this notion; we ought not—at least in
many cases—to think of the aesthetic embodiments of political power as a
set of manipulative or affective tropes overlaying/expressing/falsifying a set
of political ideas construed as texts or sheer power or economic relations. Of
course, conscious propaganda in this sense is possible: Marxist regimes, which
purport to have little interest in aesthetic matters, or on principle regard them as

epiphenomenal, typically manipulate imagery with total consciousness. They treat aesthetics as primarily tactical. Yet even in this case, the account is difficult and rich: that way of regarding aesthetics is itself an aesthetic, or entails an aesthetic, which conveys or is part of the essence of that particular form of political power. But as Frederic Spotts observes in his book *Hitler and the Power of Aesthetics,* the Nazis took the thing in precisely the opposite direction: "Unlike Lenin, who never set foot in an art gallery, or Stalin, whose art collection was pictures torn out of an illustrated magazine, or Mussolini, who despised the arts, [Hitler] held a deep and genuine interest in music, painting, sculpture, and architecture. He regarded politics not art as a means to an end, the end of which was art" (Spotts, p. 20). (This seems wrong about Mussolini.) Now, the idea that a dictator conceives art as the end and politics as a means seems merely bizarre. We might connect our sense of its strangeness to a Machiavellian conception of politics, for example, in which the reality and telos is power and all else mere means or camouflage. That sort of "realism" (which we might point out corresponds with the invention of realism in European painting, and with the rise of modern science) is a necessary cure for the mystified politics of church and state, in which the motives of the people running the show, and even their mere humanity, are buried under layers of ornamental gobbledygook.

Nevertheless, the "Hitlerian" inversion of means and ends is in itself sensible, and is a feature of many sorts and exercises of political power. The idea is to reshape the world, and conceived in this way, the effort is aesthetic. *Literally* to reshape the world: whether in Hitler's obsessive desire to redesign Berlin as the capital of Europe (itself a reshaping of the political map, a shift of form in the way Europe is pictured) or in the high-rise housing projects of the American welfare state, or the Gothic cathedral. Spotts begins his book with a picture of Hitler, hunkered down in his bunker beneath the Reich chancellery, staring at a model of his Austrian hometown, Linz. As the Allied armies closed in on Berlin, Hitler stared at the thing for hours. He had had lighting installed so that he could see the effects of shadows at different times of the day, or examine the city in moonlight. This is, of course, the portrait of a sick man bizarrely detached from the realities he shaped and faced. But it is also a final portrait of the dictatorship of an aesthetic.

Hitler's German nationalism and anti-Semitism are, again, fundamentally to be understood in aesthetic terms. Indeed the German nationalism from which he emerged was articulated almost exclusively in aesthetic terms: in terms of poetry, folktale, myth cycle, blackletter typography, music, vernacular language, clothing styles, all of which were on display, for example, in the presentation of Wagner's operas, in which Hitler was so thoroughly immersed.

Hitler argued that the basic function of a nationalist polity is to nurture the characteristic arts in which national culture consists. As early as 1920 he said:

> [Art] flowers above all where a great political movement gives it the opportunity. We know that the arts in Greece reached their pinnacle after the young state triumphed over the Persian army....Rome first became a city of culture after the Punic wars. We know that art, as reflected, for example, in the beauty of our German cities, was always dependent on the political development of those cities. (quoted in Spotts, p. 17)

He then goes on to attack cosmopolitan modernism as the art of Jews, whose identity floats across national borders, who are geographically and aesthetically rootless. Such claims were always at the heart of Hitler's particular anti-Semitism. He condemns international modernism as "kitsch."

Actually, the idea of kitsch provides one of the more amusing little motifs in Nazi political aesthetics. For of course figures such as Clement Greenberg described Nazi art itself as kitsch. Greenberg writes:

> If kitsch is the official tendency of culture in Germany, Italy and Russia, it is not because their respective governments are controlled by philistines, but because kitsch is the culture of the masses in these countries, as it is everywhere else....As a matter of fact, the main trouble with avant-garde art and literature, from the point of view of fascists and Stalinists, is not that they are too critical, but that they are too "innocent," that it is too difficult to inject effective propaganda into them, that kitsch is more pliable to this end. Kitsch keeps a dictator in closer contact with the "soul" of the people. Should the official culture be one superior to the general mass-level, there would be a danger of isolation. (Greenberg, p. 19)

Even as Greenberg condemns the popular arts and their transfiguration into totalitarian tools, he calls for "international socialism," just what Hitler would predict. Greenberg understood that calling Hitler an idiot or a maniac, would have left him merely sneering. But saying that the art Hitler loved and produced was kitsch would insult him where he lived. And the idea that people are swapping political barbs when they call one another's art kitsch shows just how aestheticized the political understanding of both Hitler and Greenberg was. Hitler and Greenberg had no more total and emotional way to condemn a political system they despised than to say it gave rise to kitsch.

I'm not sure, finally, what the content of the term is, besides a shorthand for almost any form of aesthetic condemnation: it seems mostly to mean "tasteless." In the hands of Greenberg, as in those of Hitler, it marks the contrast between popular and avant-garde art. The art of the Third Reich was of necessity a popular art, both for its propagandistic function and in its origin in nationalism, a (reified) "art of the people." For Hitler, kitsch is art without context, art floating outside the culture that is the source of all beauty. For Greenberg, as also for such figures as Adorno, kitsch is "Volk" art, art emerging from and aimed at "the people" or a people, especially within a capitalist context in which such art is embodied in mass-produced commodities. But for all of these figures, politics is finally a matter of taste.

The aesthetic critique of Judaism carries an enormous ethical/political charge; it is the very content of hatred. Art criticism is a dangerous business, and "the Jews" and "the expressionists" are liable, through their arts, to remake your physical environment and destroy your culture: to kill its language and rebuild your cities ugly. The effect of "the Jews" is aesthetic, and so their slaughter is also . . . aesthetic. Art interpretation is life and death, genocide and survival, German nationalism and Zionism—the currency in which political power is distributed and exchanged and contested. When Hitler and Greenberg start hurling "kitsch" at each other, they are throwing bombs, making rockets, constructing concentration camps. (Of course this is not to equate Greenberg's style of criticism morally with genocide! We may nevertheless be provisionally grateful that Clement Greenberg wasn't the dictator of the United States of International Socialism. The works of Norman Rockwell would now be lost; we wouldn't have Hank Williams, or Bugs Bunny cartoons.) What constitutes kitsch is a matter of human survival as well as the survival of artifacts, and Hitler lost the aesthetic war: while the expressionists are forever preserved in climate-controlled MOMAs, the statues of Thorak get smashed to smithereens. These are not symbolic surrogates, not mere effigies; they are the very bodies of war, the strange oversaturated artifacts from which power really radiates.

In his seminal work *Art under a Dictatorship,* Lehmann-Haupt argued as follows:

> In order to survive, the totalitarian state must draw the individual away from himself, absorb him into a communal scheme of life that tolerates growth and development of the personality only along narrowly prescribed lines. Art that is the expression of individual search, of experiment, of intuitive play, art that penetrates the surface of the visual world, that is prophetic, sensitive, apprehensive, art that challenges

the individual, that demands concentration, effort, art that heightens perception, sharpens the eye, nourishes thought—that art cannot be tolerated by the dictator. He must eliminate it. In its place he must put art that requires no visual effort, that is easily read by all, easy on the eye and on the mind, unproblematic. He must demand art that creates the illusion of a secure, serene world, that hides the sinister motives and the terror. (Lehmann-Haupt, pp. xviii–xix)

There is much truth in these claims, which try to cut to the heart of what the aesthetics of Nazism and Stalinism have in common. Nevertheless, the passage—like the contemporaneous "critical theory" of Adorno, for example—redeploys the very dualisms on which Holocaust aesthetics rests: modernism as providing a challenging, difficult art as against art of totalitarian regimes as kitsch. This is an assessment easily flipped around in its value valence: art that connects with people in their everyday lives, art emerging organically from the loam of a culture, as against rootless art, useless art, elitist art, art disconnected from the social.

But I think from this moment in or after postmodernism we know enough to see that the "avant-garde and kitsch" opposition of Greenberg, and even the opposition between Nazi art and high modernism, is simplistic. For one thing we should think of the role of modernism in the creation of political identities; there is no neat distinction between an art that challenges you as an individual and art that leaves you in complacent group membership. Both perform exclusions, and both constitute elite social affiliations; both are forms of self-congratulation and contempt for others; both mark or constitute class memberships and even ethnicities. Modernism, like totalitarian art, was partly imposed, and our big art institutions with their huge marble or glass edifices perform authorizations and eliminate dissenting voices. Furthermore, it would be wrong to say that the arts of Hitler or of Stalinism did not challenge the individual, or alter ways of seeing, or even that they had no element of individual or eccentric expression.

One connection between Holocaust aesthetics and high modernism is seen in their anti-commercialism, in their contrast between art and commerce. In *Mein Kampf* Hitler said, "If the fate of Rome should strike Berlin, future generations would someday admire the department stores of a few Jews as the mightiest works of our era and the hotels of a few corporations as characteristic examples of our times" (quoted in Spotts, p. 18). The supposedly miserable effects of capitalism on art was a constant theme in Hitler's speeches and writings, always connected to "the Jews." Now, someone like Adorno also wants art detached from capitalism; indeed the "commercialization" of art is the source and acme of kitsch for figures such as Adorno and Green-berg. Of course Hitler's alternative (like the Romans') is monumental state architecture, state patronage of gigantic spectacle, and so on. But we might note that for "post-Marxists" and "international socialists" such as Adorno and Greenberg, the state also lurks behind the de-commercialization of art, makes it possible, though obviously for less expressly or explicitly oppressive ends. And we might even place in this light struggles over state funding of avant-garde art, as in the controversy over National Endowment for the Arts support for artists such as Karen Finley and Andres Serrano. A lot of critics and some of the artists themselves seemed to regard state funding as their due, not to speak of their liberation from the kitsch requirements of the mar-ketplace, exactly the way Speer and Riefenstahl no doubt understood their relation to Hitler.

At any rate, in *Mein Kampf* Hitler made the full identification of the politi-cal and the aesthetic: "I am convinced that the work of great statesmen and military leaders always lies in the field of art" (quoted in Spotts, p. 28). That statement is crystal clear precisely in its apparent confusion. It *identifies* the work of the politician or the general as the work of an artist, and the destruc-tion implicit in the inclusion of military leadership is represented as a form of creation, a theme we might term Nietzschean. And it suggests that leader-ship brings with it *aesthetic obligations:* the true statesman remakes the culture by remaking the arts. The application that Hitler made of this was insane, monstrous. But the principle is unexceptionable and traditional since Plato. It finally applies no more to Hitler than to Confucius, Jefferson, Marcus Garvey, Joe Strummer.

The Case of Speer

The very most compelling aesthetic embodiments of the Third Reich were made by Albert Speer and Leni Riefenstahl in tandem; they developed related syntheses of the romantic and classical. We might call Speer's aesthetic a romantic classicism and Riefenstahl's a classical romanticism, both made pos-sible at least on the scale on which they were conceived by unlimited budget-ing thanks to Hitler. At Nuremberg in 1934, Speer created the architectural context of the party rally, even as Riefenstahl's film of the rally, *Triumph of the Will,* began with ravishing scenes of the old Gothic/medieval city center. Speer designed the "sea of flags" and the "cathedral of light," conceptions of astonishing political beauty, and obviously worked them out in collaboration with Riefenstahl, who filmed them as the aesthetic climax of her film. They are conceived as cinematic effects, and the film technique is manufactured to capture them, is conceived as a way to represent and preserve them. The "cathedral of light," 130 huge spotlights in a symmetrical façade, consisted precisely of light, as does the art of film, and it reconceived architecture as producing dynamic and ephemeral objects, as a sequential or filmic art, the classical column stabbing into the sky and disintegrating into infinity. Speer writes of this work:

> The actual effect surpassed anything I had imagined. The hundred and thirty sharply defined beams, placed around the field at intervals of forty feet, were visible to a height of twenty or twenty-five thousand feet, after which they merged into the general glow. The feeling was of a vast room, with the beams serving as mighty pillars of infinitely high outer walls. Now and then a cloud moved through this wreath of lights, bringing an element of surrealistic surprise to the mirage. I imagine that this "cathedral of light" was the first luminescent architecture of this type, and for me it remains not only my most beautiful architectural concept but, after its fashion, the only one which has survived the passage of time. (Speer, p. 59)

In these new architectures and the technology for recording them, the human body in movement, uniform, emblem, architecture, music, film are all conceived as a single work of art, an unfolding still life depicting infinity: a remarkable innovation of art and of political spectacle. One can't, to put it mildly, understand the political message or effect without understanding the sublimity. The Nazis and Hitler himself produced and celebrated many works that were actually amusing in their badness, but there's no denying the aesthetic excellence of the best of Speer and Riefenstahl. Indeed it would be a happy thought that all Nazi art sucked, as many critics have hoped more than shown (Theodor Adorno: "The Third Reich failed to produce a single work of art" [Adorno, p. 106]), but that would not capture the profound and profoundly disturbing beauty at its heart, key to how everyone from Hitler to Speer to the Aryan peasant grasped it.

Speer was no mere propagandist; he came from a family of architects in Mannheim. He writes, "My father's buildings were influenced by the neo-Renaissance: they had bypassed Jugendstil" (Speer, p. 6). He says of his teacher Heinrich Tessenow that "he believed in architectonic expressiveness by severely delimited means" (Speer, p. 11). He quotes Tessenow from 1931 as saying: "Someone will have to come along who thinks very simply. Thinking today has become too complicated. An uncultured man, a peasant as it were, would solve everything much more easily merely because he would be unspoiled. He would also have the strength to carry out his simple ideas"

(Speer, p. 15). This hardly describes Hitler, but it does describe to perfection the political aesthetics developed by Speer and Riefenstahl in bringing the "primitive" or "natural" national identity into relation with classical dignity and simplicity, a nice little cocktail that we find also in the poetics, philosophy, and politics of Heidegger. Indeed in Hegel, the romantic is the culmination, not the negation, of the classical, and we can see premonitions of Speer/Riefenstahl in the arts associated with Hegel's "history on horseback"—Napoleon—as Speer fully understood in retrospect. In fact, Goethe also is a classical romantic. We might connect such a notion even to Jefferson, in his classicism and agrarianism, his cult of the Greeks and the American yeoman. The effect in Speer and Riefenstahl is the sublimity of Caspar David Friedrich reconceived as lying at the heart of universal truth, German nationalism as a synecdoche for the universal condition of mankind.

Indeed this is an interesting dynamic at the heart of nationalism: possessing a national identity is considered essential to what it means, universally, to be human. Human beings are parts of nations in their essence: the "organic" conception of the national state we find in German idealism. Nations—rather than individuals or the species as a whole—are the agents of human history, but the destination of all is the Absolute. Hitler actually tried to develop a crypto-historiography; he traced the Athenians and Spartans to German origins. Famously he always said he had nothing against Greeks, and tried to hold off destroying their cities "until he had no choice."

Speer even designed flatware and furniture for the Reich and ended up as Minister of Armaments and Building, essentially trying both to destroy and to rebuild Europe. No architect has ever had Speer's opportunity to remake the world, a tribute to Hitler's obsession with architecture and design. He represents the transition to Minister of Armaments as fairly smooth, drawing on the same organizational skills he'd used for the astonishingly rapid transformation of Nuremberg, for example.

Speer was unique among the Nazis in actually reflecting deeply on his own actions, and regretting them in detail; he was the only major Nazi figure who pleaded guilty at the Nuremberg trials. One of the most remarkable things about Speer's expression of his regrets for having participated in a genocidal and totalitarian regime is that they are connected with or are identical to his reflections on the development of his artistic style:

I did not call [my style] neo-classicist, but neo-classical, for I thought I had derived it from the Dorian style. I was deluding myself, deliberately forgetting that these buildings had to provide a monumental backdrop such as had already been attempted on the Champs de Mars in Paris during the French Revolution, although the resources at that time were more modest. Terms like "classical" and "simple" were scarcely consonant with the gigantic proportions I employed in [the redesign of] Nuremberg. Yet, to this day, I like my Nuremberg sketches best of all. . . .

Because of my fondness for the Doric, when I went on my first trip abroad in May 1935, I did not go to Italy to see the Renaissance palaces and the colossal buildings of Rome, although these might have served me better as prototypes for what I wanted. Instead, I turned to Greece—a sign of where I considered my architectural allegiance to lie. . . .

In Delphi I thought I discerned how the purity of Greek artistic creativeness was speedily contaminated by the wealth won in the Ionian colonies in Asia. Didn't this prove how sensitive a high artistic consciousness was and how little it took to distort the ideal conception to the point of unrecognizability? I happily played with such theories; it never occurred to me that my own works might be subject to these same laws. (Speer, p. 63)

Speer's Nuremberg stadium "would have been 1815 feet long and 1518 wide and could have enclosed a volume of over 11,100,000 cubic yards, some three times more than the pyramid at Cheops" (Speer, p. 68). Of the dome for Berlin which Speer and Hitler designed, he says:

The round interior was to have the almost inconceivable diameter of eight hundred and twenty-five feet. The huge dome was to begin a slightly parabolic curve at a height of three hundred and twenty three feet and rise to a height of seven hundred and twenty-six feet. . . . [It] was also to contain a round opening for light, but this opening alone would be . . . larger than the dome of the Pantheon and St. Peter's. . . . [T]he Capitol in Washington could have been contained many times in such a mass." (Speer, pp. 153–54).

Speer insists that the design was practical, to which one might reply that it depends on what he means by practical.

After his years in prison, Speer was magnificently aware of the aesthetic tensions within and the political implications of his gigantism: "The love for vast proportions was not only tied up with the totalitarianism of Hitler's regime. . . . Thus we find the largest buildings in Greek antiquity in Sicily and Asia Minor. It is an interesting corollary that those cities were generally ruled by despots" (Speer, p. 69). The distinction between "classicist" and "classical," for Speer, is the distinction between Rome and Greece. Speer conceived of himself as stripping rational architecture to its primordial and pure form, its origin. But as he sees easily in hindsight, even merely the sheer gigantism of the plans connects him with classicist Rome, and was then expanded even far beyond that. The size of Speer's conceptions is antithetical to the classical, even as it yields a huge reading of classical tropes. First of all, it has lost its relation to the body for good and all. And the rationality of the proportions—which are quite perfect in Speer's models—is contradicted by the disproportion to the environment. Even if the classical design is perfect, Speer's work expresses perversity, self-parodic distortion, an edge of insanity, values flatly antithetical to the architectural style it seeks to exemplify. In a way this is where Speer's classicism becomes romantic as well as where it becomes totalitarian: the sheer size is emotionally charged, and humongousness is an aspect of the sublime.

The Case of Riefenstahl

The life and career of Leni Riefenstahl are among the most astonishing of the twentieth century. She started as an "interpretive" dancer (as opposed to a classically trained ballerina) in a rather sexy romanticist vein, and achieved remarkable success, touring Europe as a young woman. Then she was a movie star in "mountain films," and perhaps the world's best female mountaineer; she climbed exposed Alpine spires without ropes—or shoes—and was buried on film under real avalanches. She was called "the most beautiful woman in Germany," an assessment that seems, at least by contemporary notions of female beauty, to be somewhat exaggerated. She subsequently took up directing. Her first feature was the wildly romantic *The Blue Light,* in which she constructed the persona that attracted Hitler: mysterious misunderstood Alpine witch with access to the powers of nature. Then she was Hitler's greatest image-maker and filmmaker and one of the most important film innovators and documentarians of the century, directing films of the 1934 Nazi Party rally in Nuremberg (*Triumph of the Will*) and of the 1936 Berlin Olympics (*Olympia*). She was for a time in the thirties one of the closest friends and associates of Hitler and Goebbels, possibly also the lover of one or the other or both. (She denied this; but she denied many things that were true.) After her official "de-Nazification," in the 1960s she photographically documented the magnificent hypermasculine wrestlers and the beautiful topless women of the Nuba people of the Sudan. She lived in tribal isolation for weeks at a time, meanwhile surviving a horrific series of car and plane crashes. She fetched up in her nineties as the world's oldest scuba diver and underwater cinematographer. It truly appeared that, having sold her soul to the devil for art, she was immune to death, but she checked out finally in 2003, aged 101.

The most famous and reproduced images from *Triumph of the Will* are the stunning spectacles of collective presence and discipline, the gigantic scale, order, and movement of crowds. The order and movement are based on military aesthetics, but the spectacle on film was something the like of which the world had never seen, and Riefenstahl achieved these effects through innovations in lenses and film stock, and, for example, by moving a camera up and down a lift affixed to a huge flagpole. (Later, at the Olympics, she lifted cameras using balloons.) The crowd designs are abstract works of art, but one never loses the sense that one is seeing human beings in an almost inconceivable perfect unity in which individuality is wholly lost, the individual body treated only as a dot in the pointillist composition unfolding in time, a fantasy of community detectable in Plato, Catholicism, Rousseau, Marxism, and of course in National Socialism.

But these images are one end of a complete aesthetics of the German/Aryan body that was as central to Nazi aesthetics as to the Nazis' genocidal policies. The Nazis constructed an aesthetic of the perfect body, especially male, as seen in the sculpture of Hitler's favorites, Arno Breker and Josef Thorak. This too finds its most perfect and least ridiculous expression in Riefenstahl, not only in *Olympia,* which is an amazing embodiment of the cult of the perfect body, but also in her postwar work with the magnificent bodies of the Nuba. Susan Sontag simply dismissed all of Riefenstahl's work as fascist precisely for this construction of the body, which is also, of course, an aesthetic extrusion of non-perfect bodies, a hint that perhaps we should execute the handicapped, as was actually done. In defense of Riefenstahl, I want to say that many artists have been obsessed by the perfect body: the Greeks, of course, Michelangelo, Ingres, Degas, Mapplethorpe, but even in the "ephebism" of the arts of many African tribes, for example. Even if the sexual and supra-sexual transcendental construction of the perfect body is implicitly a rejection of the eccentric and imperfect body, it is not by itself Nazi art until it comes to be used for Nazi purposes, until the round-up actually starts. Of course the depiction of nonnormative bodies could also be a Nazi expression, and was, in caricatures of Jews and others.

Triumph of the Will, however, deploys the cult of the individual body (especially the normative "German" face) as a segment of a continuous scope of bodies from the individual to the vast mass. It shows the individual German young man as a monumental object, an emblem, but then it pulls back and reveals that the individual body is fundamentally a tiny segment of a huge collective body; it asserts that the individual has his dignity in relation to the singleness and integrity of a gargantuan whole. At each moment at each scale, the depiction is made into a norm specifically by being aestheticized. The value of perfect human bodies might be spiritual (as in the Renaissance), or it might be represented in terms of health or hygiene. But its most powerful valence of value is aesthetic. To make the perfect body a perfect aesthetic object—Riefenstahl's great theme—is to attribute to it a value that bleeds into every dimension of value: political, moral, medical, and every other. Its beauty is its value in all dimensions, and Riefenstahl's demonstration of that value is essentially unanswerable; it is not an assertion but a moving image, a demonstration, an enactment of all values right before your very eyes, inside your own sensorium.

That particular beauty is the political center, as it is the aesthetic center, of Riefenstahl's art, which is why her own excuse—that she was only trying to make beautiful things, not have any political effects—is true, disingenuous, and fundamentally confused.

> I can simply say that I feel spontaneously attracted by everything that is beautiful. Yes: beauty, harmony. And perhaps this care for composition, this aspiration to form is in effect something very German. But I don't know these things myself, exactly. It comes from the unconscious and not from my knowledge.... Whatever is purely realistic, slice-of-life, which is average, quotidian, doesn't interest me.... I am fascinated by what is beautiful, strong, healthy, what is living. I seek harmony. When harmony is produced I am happy. (quoted in Sontag, p. 85, from an interview in *Cahiers du Cinéma*)

In *Olympia,* Riefenstahl had essentially unlimited resources and approached the project with a ferocious perfectionism and an extreme commitment to beauty. Beauty was literally her moral excuse for having pushed forward the Third Reich, which if nothing else would confirm everyone's ethical suspicions about beauty, which we will explore in the next chapter. That such a transcendent artistic stance was itself politically disgusting—that in fact this distance was what allowed her to serve Hitler and become his greatest propagandist—itself is enough to refute the formalism and aestheticism of her artistic persona.

Susan Sontag wrote a famous essay about Riefenstahl called "Fascinating Fascism," in which in a way she (Sontag) sacrifices the whole Western history of beauty on the altar of politics. For Sontag, Riefenstahl's aesthetic fascism consists, to repeat, of the cult of the beautiful human body, a kind of artistic eugenics, implicitly a doctrine of purity. She condemns Riefenstahl's later photographic work with the Nuba on this basis. But if we attack the idealization of the human body as reactionary or a premonition of genocide, we are of course condemning the West in art in the Greeks and the Renaissance, everything from Praxiteles to Michelangelo to Velázquez. The nude is the very center of beauty in the Western artistic tradition, and much else that is beautiful in our tradition is a ramification of the idealized nude. Hence in Sontag's essay we see more or less the whole of the Western tradition with regard to beauty declared to be fascist. Even the romantic celebrations of nature in Riefenstahl's early "mountain" movies are condemned by Sontag as nationalistic mythologies of purity. Neither the human nor the natural, that is, escapes the Nazi taint of Riefenstahl, and beauty as a whole becomes a fascist movement.

Indeed, by the 1960s, when Sontag writes, the fact that she is asserting that the idealized body is a basically fascist trope seems almost a commonplace. She says it as though it's obvious to everyone. By the time you can do that, beauty has, for better or worse, been lost to art. "Those who say fascism say first of all beauty," taught Mussolini (Falasca-Zamponi, p. 16), but ridiculously of course. The beauty of Riefenstahl's films is connected with but is not identical to their political content. Beauty has rhetorical or persuasive effects, but we ought to be happier to say that it convinces by what it is, not by what it appears to be. It is modernist in this sense; it is not primarily the construal or misconstrual of an antecedent reality (such as "the German people"); it is its own reality that reconstructs that to which it apparently refers; it *makes* the German body beautiful, as it shows, beyond anyone's real ability to doubt, that it is beautiful. It should go without saying, in reply to Benjamin, Sontag, and Mussolini, that fascism is not always beautiful and beautiful things are not always fascist. But we cannot possibly separate Riefenstahl's "formalism," her infinite dedication to capturing the perfect shape by every possible means, from her rhetoric or her political effects.

I don't think Riefenstahl actually killed anybody (though she used internment camp prisoners as extras in her film *Tiefland*), and even though the moral effect of adding beautiful things to the world is often profound one way or another, as oppression or liberation, it is not murder; it is not genocide. There is a difference between designing film stock and designing gas chambers. The right answer to the films of Leni Riefenstahl is not detention or even de-Nazification; it is art and world criticism. We need constantly to focus on the omissions, the exclusions, the absences, the holes. The Greek/Renaissance tradition of viewing the human body as the most beautiful object, and of celebrating it by representing physical perfection, is potentially oppressive; it can be turned to fascist ends, for example. It is also the aesthetic of humanism. We cannot understand Riefenstahl's fascist art without connecting it to the cult of the perfect body. But we also can't read her politics directly from her participation in this cult. Nor is the difference between Michelangelo and Riefenstahl merely that Michelangelo is the better artist; the differences cannot be fully captured in aesthetic terms, either. The aesthetic and political values are intrinsically connected, and if we are to understand either fully, they must be placed into correlation. But they are orthogonally connected, and merely identifying them, collapsing either into the other—merely condemning Riefenstahl as kitsch—leads to incomprehension on both sides. The point would be to connect the dimensions of value in their complexity, in detail.

Sontag, again, connects every era and body of Riefenstahl's work to Nazism. She punctures holes in various arguments and falsifications that Riefenstahl resorted to in order to exonerate herself; this has continued apace since Sontag's essay as more and more of Riefenstahl's prevarications have been exposed, notably in Jürgen Trimborn's biography. Yet Sontag's attack, it seems to me, is far too general and tendentious. "Here is a book of 126 splendid color photographs by Leni Riefenstahl," Sontag writes,

> certainly the most ravishing book of photographs published anywhere in recent years. In the intractable mountains of the southern Sudan live about eight thousand aloof, godlike Nuba, emblems of physical perfection, with large, well-shaped, partly shaven heads, expressive faces, and muscular bodies that are depilated and decorated with scars; smeared with sacred gray-white ash, the men prance, squat, brood, wrestle on the arid slopes. And here is a fascinating layout of twelve black-and-white photographs of Riefenstahl on the back cover of *The Last of the Nuba,* also ravishing, a chronological sequence of expressions (from sultry inwardness to the grin of a Texas matron on safari) vanquishing the intractable march of aging. (Sontag, pp. 73–74)

This is a remarkable response in that it begins precisely by finding the photographs beautiful, and then reviles the work and the woman on precisely that ground. Sontag operates within an art-critical framework in which beauty is profoundly suspicious. Demonstrably, to repeat, focusing obsessively on the beautiful body is not enough in itself to constitute an oeuvre as fascist, problematic though it may be in many respects in every case. One surely must speculate that Riefenstahl was drawn to the Nuba precisely in that a celebration of the beauty of black people would show that she was not still (if she had ever been) in thrall to Hitler's particular racial constructions. Her later work constituted her apology, even as she refused to apologize, or even said: "I apologize for having been born. But I won't apologize for my films."[2] But nothing she could have done could fail to be interpreted as Nazi art, unless she were to forswear beauty. And one might point out that, in *Olympia,* Jesse Owens's victories at the 1936 Olympics are depicted in just the same way Riefenstahl depicted all the other triumphs, possibly over party objections. Sontag writes:

> Admittedly, if the book [*The Last of the Nuba*] were not signed by Riefenstahl one would not necessarily suspect that these photographs had been taken by the most interesting, talented, and effective artist of the Nazi era. . . . [B]ut if the photographs are examined carefully, in conjunction with the lengthy text written by Riefenstahl, it becomes clear that they are continuous with her Nazi work. Riefenstahl's particular slant is revealed by her choice of this tribe and not another: a people she describes as acutely artistic (everyone owns a lyre) and beautiful (Nuba men, Riefenstahl notes, "have an athletic build rare in any other African tribe"); endowed as they are with "a much stronger sense of spiritual and religious relations than of worldly and material matters," their principal activity, she insists, is ceremonial. *The Last of the Nuba* is about a primitivist ideal: a portrait of a people subsisting in a pure harmony with their environment, untouched by "civilization." (Sontag, p. 86)

The romance with the primitive or even the cult of nature and natural man that is a characteristic of Riefenstahl's work from her dancing to her underwater film might be better associated with the political philosophy of Rousseau, or for that matter Thoreau, than with that of Hitler. It is an extremely well developed aesthetic but potentially cuts in all sorts of political directions, from direct democracy to environmentalism to colonialism to anticolonialism.

Riefenstahl did not simply engage an antecedent Hitler aesthetic; she guided it, articulated it, gave it form. Riefenstahl is right in a way and to an extent in claiming that she did not merely serve the aesthetic vision of the dictator, that she continued to make movies with her own vision, that her fundamental commitment was to beauty and her engagement with the regime partly an opportunity to explore and expand that vision. She was not fundamentally a propagandist but an artist, as she insisted, and as Sontag ridicules her for insisting. But the truth is in a sense darker. Riefenstahl's work didn't reflect or communicate ideology; it constituted Nazism. Nazism

---

2. In the remarkable film *The Wonderful, Horrible Life of Leni Riefenstahl,* directed by Ray Muller (1993).

became Riefenstahl's art, we might say. She herself in 1941 characterized the purpose of her documentaries not merely as showing what was there but as "bringing to light" the essential idea of the event; and in doing so she showed everyone for the first time the shape that idea had (Trimborn, p. 117). At the same time as Riefenstahl was making her work, Heidegger was arguing in "The Origin of the Work of Art" that the work of art "sets up" a world by bringing Being into the light, and Riefenstahl's work "for" Hitler establishes—is—Nazism. He ended up working for her. We might say she seduced him and used him, bent him to her aesthetic will.

The Case of Chaplin

That Nazi art in its best and worst moments was ripe for satire is an understatement; it was so serious that it was funny. Famously it found its foil in Charlie Chaplin, who in *The Great Dictator* (1940) understood the Nazi movement in terms of a total visual environment, supersaturated with symbols and blown up like a huge balloon. As Chaplin directs himself as Adenoid Hynkel, absolute ruler of Tomainia, he makes all the props flimsy, all the symbols just that little bit off (the "double cross"), displays Nazi sublimity as a flimsy façade. He directly parodies *Triumph of the Will* at a number of points, even constructing the titles as faux stone inscriptions in direct tribute/ ridicule. And of course he waves his arms around, bellows the word "sauerkraut," and crowds of people respond in unison and ecstasy.

Speer says that the great error of the Berlin designs was that "under that vast dome, Hitler dwindled to an optical zero" (Speer, p. 153). Chaplin pits Hynkel's ridiculous little humanity against gigantic machines and ambitions, picking out the burlesque at the heart of Nazism while pointedly criticizing its aesthetic. Meanwhile, Chaplin's other character—a Jewish barber—and the rest of the people in the ghetto live a human life on a human scale and thus have incomparably more dignity.

Chaplin fully grasps Riefenstahl's films, as we might expect. He was an admirer of *The Blue Light* and is said to have based Paulette Goddard's role in *Modern Times* on Riefenstahl's mystery witch, which seems quite evident if you look at the Chaplin film with that in mind; Goddard plays Junta down to the costume (see Trimborn, p. 49). Chaplin embeds Hynkel in giant architecture that would have been far too rococo for Speer. But Chaplin fully understands the persona of Hitler as artistic genius and omnipotent mesmerist and the fundamental ridiculousness of this idea, having him play piano and then seduce his secretary through sheer mind-to-mind communication. "We'll get rid of the Jews first, then we'll concentrate on the brunettes."

Totalitarian aesthetics then reaches nirvana as Chaplin does his famous dance with the globe balloon, beautiful and even poignant until the world pops, showing Riefenstahl how to make a movie: with exquisite lightness of touch. Riefenstahl used a sledgehammer.

Here Chaplin achieves something remarkable: he humanizes Hitler, or attributes his amazing effects finally to the poignantly infinite aspirations of a little man. This at once undercuts Hitler's self-presentation and the fantastic representation of Hitler as a monster with superhuman powers. Chaplin and Hitler were born in the same month in the same year and wore the same funny little mustache, and the greatness of *The Great Dictator* is the connection Chaplin establishes. He finds something beautiful and human even in the character of Hitler; that is his ultimate satire, but also his fundamental insight, one that is related to all of Chaplin's work in film. Chaplin's theme is our shared humanity, the shared humanity of the barber and Hynkel— who after all were both Chaplin himself. This is not an abstraction; the barber and the dictator share a comprehensible aspiration, a need to transcend their circumstances and a sense of their own ridiculous limitations. Chaplin's appropriation of Riefenstahl is anything but a joke; it is a revelation of both the inhumanity and the hidden human heart of Riefenstahl the artist and Riefenstahl the woman. But it is also funny.

At any rate, in its own way, as much as *Triumph of the Will, The Great Dictator* is a propaganda film, and as war approached, Chaplin was urged to continue by Roosevelt. It seems likely that Hitler himself saw *The Great Dictator.*

Totalitarianism and the Aestheticization of Politics

When American troops overran Iraq in 2003, they were engaged in a military operation that was motivated by certain interpretations of global politics, and by a domestic political strategy. Their leaders said they were fighting "the war on terror" and bringing freedom to the Iraqi people. But "Operation Iraqi Freedom" was at least as aesthetic as military. Perhaps the most memorable scenes of the invasion—the scenes that the media focused on obsessively— were the toppling of Saddam Hussein's statues, the defacement of the gigantic images of his face, and the destruction of his palaces. When the media wanted to understand the invasion and its meaning, they turned to its symbolic and its formal content: its styles, its arts, and their destruction.

We might say that the military and the aesthetic aspects of the invasion and the occupation were not distinguishable, that the aesthetic transformation of Iraq was an intrinsic part of the conquest, and the conquest was instrumental in the aesthetic transformation. In many ways, pulling down a statue is trivial in comparison to killing a human being, but the outburst of iconoclasm seems comprehensible or symbolically saturated in a way that the death of a real human body is not. In this case the destruction of symbols was a premonition of the execution of Saddam, a kind of sympathetic magic that proved to be effective. That transformation was also, of course, the destruction of a totalitarian political order and hence of the expressions of the aesthetics of totalitarianism, though we might also examine the ways that the occupying forces themselves tried to use and transform the existing artpolitical emblems. Indeed the American occupation was inflected by Saddam's artpolitics even as the American forces destroyed it: they administered the country precisely from Saddam's palaces and prisons, and caused great resentment and feelings of betrayal. If you fully understood the aesthetic policy of Saddam and the aesthetics of the invasion and occupation, you would have leverage on an interpretation of the event as a whole.

So shall we say that totalitarianism is an aesthetic style? Or a group or history of aesthetic styles? As Lehmann-Haupt put the point at issue in *Art under a Dictatorship:* "The art doctrines of the totalitarian state and the resulting art policies and practices are an inseparable part of its innermost structure" (Lehmann-Haupt, p. xvii). The way things look is an aspect of what they are. Forms of power generate symbols, styles, visible and audible vocabularies. The aesthetic systems of totalitarianism, of which Saddam's is a nice example, are often organized around a single image: the visage of the leader. This appears everywhere in all media all the time, expanded to hundreds of thousands of square feet of stupefyingly repetitive and banal public semiotics. Now, it may be that Saddam himself, like Mao or a hundred other dictators, told himself that reproductions of his own face helped him control the country. Possibly, for example, he believed that seeing his picture all the time everywhere would inspire some sort of loyalty, or give rise to a Saddamist cult. That gives you a sense of the comical and pitiful aspects of totalitarianism, because it should be obvious that people will typically regard the nonstop onslaught of a dictator's face with an indifference that masks a slight but definite irritation. The real purpose is, perhaps, that the dictator wants to see his own face everywhere, wants the whole world to constitute a mirror. To understand why this is a totalitarian strategy, one would have to begin to explore the uses of images in human cultures, the belief, for example, that the object or person depicted in an image is present—perhaps to an attenuated extent—in the image. (An exploration of these themes is found in David Freedberg's book *The Power of Images.*) That Saddam treated his own images this way more or less entailed the destruction of those images as a fulfillment of their purpose.

Another principle of totalitarian aesthetics, and the one that shapes the built environment, is that even as the face of the leader is exposed everywhere, the persons of the leadership must be shrouded and shielded by layers of impregnable stone. When Speer was redesigning Berlin for Hitler, including Hitler's offices, his model was Roman imperial architecture: huge marble edifices and monuments meant to dwarf the human body and convey total invulnerability and inaccessibility (heaviness as an artpolitical property). Washington, D.C., I might gently point out, is not completely free of these concrete mystifications of power. Such embodiments of the state are designed to make resistance seem obviously futile, to juxtapose the tiny human body of the resister with the sheer gargantuan, inanimate, extremely heavy system of the state. One is supposed to forget, faced with an architecture of apparently infinite force and limitless resources, that the people running one's country are human beings too. In fact the architecture, like the portraiture, is a kind of fantastic representation of the leader as something more than human: a massive bionic body, dense as marble.

North Korea is a particularly pointed example of all these trends. The central purpose is to disguise systematically the mediocrity and humanity of the rulers and the degree of resistance or indifference in people's heads. Its form is a grid of apparently rational design dropped over the cruelty and mindlessness of raw power at the state's heart. But though Saddam's palaces were "opulent," to use the preferred term, they also had their chintzy side: huge chandeliers made of plastic beads, paper-thin marble veneers, gold leaf implausibly conveying the impression of solidity. The occupiers took great pleasure both in damaging the palaces and their furnishings and in exposing them to the world as signs of Saddam's ignorance and mediocrity, his grandiosity and tastelessness. "Façade" is the perfect word, and Saddam's façades were conspicuously pathetic, flimsy, and stupid, though also quite typical of classical dictatorships.

Perhaps in Saddam's mind all the images were magical proxies of himself, and the country could be overseen by an army of giant Saddams (then again, perhaps not). But all over the world, such images share the same destiny: to be toppled, tomatoed, ridiculed, shot up. This use of the image in resistance also avails itself of the meanings of images and their forms; and not only do the images embody a certain design style, but so also do the attacks on the images, or the attempt to reimagine or destroy them in a certain way—fire, defacement, storage—and in a certain context. We might say that to use the image of the dictator as an effigy is to interpret it, aesthetically and in other ways. Iconoclasm and vandalism, too, are aesthetic activities, styles of art criticism.

Hitler's absorption in the arts and his political use of the arts were indeed without precedent. From the early days of the Nazi movement he was designing, actually drawing, uniforms and standards, insignia and formations, stagings for rallies, architectural fantasies. He invented a whole vocabulary of political festival—torchlight processions and bonfires; deployment of banners bearing swastikas, iron crosses, lightning bolts—an entire symbol system, incorporating elements of opera, of Italian fascism, of the Roman Empire, and of the Catholic Church, among other bits. And he hopped onto the vision of others, especially Speer, Goebbels, and Riefenstahl, but thousands of artists, to elaborate or ramify these ideas and present them in all available media. Nazism as a political ideology is best understood to be a nontextual or even anti-textual (certainly anti-intellectual) aesthetic system. In comparison to the intellectual edifices of classical liberalism or Marxism, for example, its coherence or elaborateness understood as features of its texts are negligible; as a system of "ideas" it is chaotic or only barely exists at all. But as a style of design and the deployment of design, it is correspondingly replete, and at its most coherent it hangs together as well as Marxism or classical liberalism.

And here I want, explicitly and again, to take up the objection that, far from showing that all politics is aesthetic, fascism and Nazism show that politics and aesthetics must be separated, lest we descend into sheer irrational manipulation and abstraction from concrete human effects. I believe that the range of examples I develop here, both in the case studies and more briefly in the theoretical chapters, shows that to be simplistic. There can be no entirely de-aestheticized politics, and very aestheticized politics can be as antiauthoritarian and decent as you like, as even Chaplin demonstrates. Rather, the Nazi case, and other cases in which the aestheticization of politics creates moral disasters, must be treated specifically and in detail. It is worth saying that, to deploy some sort of provisional distinction between aesthetic and moral matters, it was not primarily in virtue of their arts—sublime or kitschy—that the Nazis were evil. You don't try someone for war crimes because you don't like their interpretation of expressionism; you put them on trial because they kill people.

I often teach the "problem of Riefenstahl" and Hitler on the arts to students, and here is their near-universal conclusion, no matter what I say: Speer's architecture, Riefenstahl's films, Hitler's oratory, and so on *made* the German people follow the Nazis, manipulated them thoroughly, constituted an insidious super-effective mind control. Usually I scribble in the margins of the paper: Do you think a really good billboard or a neoclassical museum could make you start killing people? Attributing the Holocaust to a movie or an ambitious bit of urban planning is asinine. Indeed it is not just teenagers who seem enamored with the idea of a people broken by art. Frederic Spotts writes: "The [party] rallies were a microcosm of Hitler's ideal world: a people reduced to unthinking automatons subject to the control not of the state, not even of the party but of him personally—and that unto death. Never before was there a clearer example of aesthetics used to promote enslavement and heroic death" (Spotts, p. 69).

This idea that a well-designed spectacle reduces people to automata is not merely an "explanation" of Nazi horrors and the otherwise apparently unaccountable phenomenon of Hitler; it is a restatement of Hitler's position and a trace of the twentieth-century cult of propaganda. One function of it is to place all the responsibility for a whole society mobilized into a killing machine on the shoulders of one man: people who see the "cathedral of light" are from that moment on no longer responsible for the murders they perpetrate. The function of the Führer is to guide us, to inspire us, and to take the blame for everything, precisely to relieve us of responsibility, the fantastic appeal of all political leadership. The power of the arts to transform the world and ourselves—a modernist trope seen in as varied a group of thinkers as Heidegger, John Dewey, and Nelson Goodman—is also a basically political idea: a dark fantasy, or a beautiful social-democratic ideal, but also a cooperative resolution to blame the art for the slaughter, or for that matter to credit it for the social welfare. In other words, "the power of aesthetics" is itself a kind of totalitarian fantasy: what is required for the Holocaust, or for the transformation of the class system, is just effective art/propaganda; it's not a matter of real people wanting to kill or achieve justice.

One set of images that is always discussed in treatments of "Nazi aesthetics" is the set of photographs by Heinrich Hoffmann of Hitler practicing the gestures of his oratory, which were distributed in the 1930s as postcards. This is usually accompanied by observations such as the following, from Hitler's secretary Christa Schroeder: Hitler possessed a "sixth sense and a clairvoyant intuition.... [He could] in some mysterious way foretell the subconscious reactions of the masses and in some inexplicable manner mesmerize his interlocutors" (quoted in Spotts, p. 45). And that is merely repeated up through the present as an "explanation" of Hitler's rise and his mobilization of a nation for slaughter. But I suggest that Hitler's supernatural mesmeric power, achieved through art, is as occult an explanation as would be the idea that he was the embodiment of Odin. It relieves people of responsibility even for their mere obedience. Art is central to politics, and propaganda sometimes works to some extent, but the idea that it hypnotizes or breaks the will of millions of people is itself a mere totalitarian fantasy. Greeting Hitler ecstatically and doing what he said were things that actual people did for actual reasons, not mere effects of mesmeric superpowers. Indeed, reading Hoffmann's photographed poses as an explanation for the Holocaust is really ridiculous: comically theatrical arm-waving as the center of infinite effects. This is demonstrated with perfect clarity by Chaplin.

This is in part the other side of the treatment of political ideologies as textual. Texts are supposed to appeal to the rationality of people, to persuade them with the force of ideas and argument, whereas images and oratory merely engage their emotions. Once your emotions are engaged, you can be made to do anything; you're no longer thinking independently at all; you're just emoting like an animal. I do not want to tackle this dualism in any full-fledged way here, but I do assert that it is profoundly confused from both ends, ignoring the aesthetic effects of texts and the cognitive effects of images. I note that genocides can be committed under systems whose ideologies are scientific, rational, and textual (Marxism, for example), and that political systems which avail themselves of aesthetics can be as mellow as any political system can be, given that state power always rest on force. But the position has moral consequences: people are responsible for the products of reason, but not for the products of their passions. Hence the association of text with reason and of the other aesthetic modalities with passion flows into the talk of Hitler's mysterious charismatic universal mind control. Simultaneously with the rise of fascism, Sax Rohmer was writing the Fu Manchu novels, in which the diabolical Chinese embodiment of all evil could hypnotize you with a glance, funky beams of pure power emerging from his eyes into yours, turning you into his helpless slave and twisting you to his incomprehensibly evil schemes for world domination. Once the beautiful young girl is released from her enthrallment, she is restored to moral agency and is eligible to kiss the good guy.

That is, we have got to make some fundamental distinctions between art—even beautiful manipulative art made by bad people—and killing. And we have got to stop conceiving of the arts of political systems as mind control, a position that is the ultimate outcome of the notion of art as "propaganda," as sheer means of manipulation. We had better continue to hold people responsible for their actions even when they are subjected to well-designed posters, Wagnerian opera, excellent movies, and poetry set in blackletter. And with regard to an event such as the Holocaust—in which a whole nation or continent was mobilized as a death machine—we need to see that many factors led to the moral disaster. Of course an exclusively economic explanation, for example, or a psychodynamic Oprah explanation in terms of German self-esteem, is also simplistic; the arts are needed to make the thing fully comprehensible. (In principle, I suppose, it could be explained, even if any particular explanation is inadequate in the face of "radical evil.")

"The problem of Riefenstahl" is sometimes represented in the question of whether her films are "mere" propaganda, but even their propaganda effects cannot, obviously, be separated from their aesthetic features. In fact, without some sense of the theory and history of beauty, for example, you can't even explain the propaganda effects of Riefenstahl's films; and if you think Riefenstahl was basically asking herself questions about how the German people could be manipulated, you don't understand her, or her movies, or their effects at all. But that is also why they were better-than-average propaganda and why they still serve as the fundamental images of the Third Reich.

A basic problem in political aesthetics that is raised by the Nazi case is budgets. One reason why *Olympia* is an amazing and beautiful movie is that Riefenstahl had at her disposal resources that are unparalleled in the history of documentary filmmaking. She answered only to Hitler, and got virtually whatever she wanted. She remade the Olympic stadium into a film set. She shot thousands of hours of film on custom-designed stock, had a crew of dozens of cameramen. There are a lot of filmmakers who could deliver a compelling film if you rained money on them like a sky. The architectural projects that Speer actually carried out were extremely ambitious, and the projects that Hitler approved were insanely so. (I say "insanely," but only in the sense that they would have drained the German economy.) They were buildable, and would have entailed massive destruction; eventually Hitler wanted to tear down and rebuild the center of every major German city. Now, if you devote the resources of your people to making really good films while they starve or are converted into forced labor, that is morally monstrous. And of course we don't have to resort to the Nazis: stroll around Versailles, for example, or Red Square, or gape stupefied at the Pantheon or St. Peter's. But the answer to such aesthetic oppressions is itself partly aesthetic; and though we may speculate that the Huns and Visigoths were no fans of Roman imperial architecture, we know for a fact that French republicans thought Versailles was the very acme of excess and decadence and injustice, and that they sought to replace the system of the arts of the monarchy with something on a smaller scale, more rational and dignified. They were superseded by Napoleon.

Unlimited budgets make for aesthetic gigantism, and the relation of extremely ambitious art in this dimension to political power is obvious. Even Riefenstahl's films, much less Speer's architecture, presuppose a totalitarian regime. They were enabled by totalitarianism and the aesthetic sensibilities that dovetailed with it at a certain place and moment to achieve certain sublime aesthetic effects that are completely unavailable to a painter in his little studio.

It would be nice simply to condemn totalitarian regimes on grounds of their bad art, or even on their general concentration on the arts, but of course that will not do. First, totalitarian regimes ought to be condemned fundamentally for their totalitarianism, and there is certainly no one aesthetic style associated with all forms of totalitarianism. A Marxist anti-aesthetic is potentially as useful and as intrinsically connected to the exercise of totalitarian power as is a Wagnerian sublimity, and internationalism with all its aesthetic tropes (roman script, Mies van der Rohe cubes, form as function) may be as good as nationalism with all of its, as an element in a genocide. So again I want to detach Nazism a bit from its aesthetic, and then bind republicanism, for example, to its. Second, we have to get into the specific aesthetic expressions and show their embodiments of the totalitarian system in question; we need to treat each system as actually composed (in part) of aesthetic elements. The arts of totalitarian regimes are a wildly mixed bag of style and quality, but of course so are their politics.

If you want to show people what Nazism actually took itself to be, the very best approach is to screen *Triumph of the Will*. In fact almost every film about Nazism avails itself of Riefenstahl's images, and many books about Nazism use stills from the film; it is a more coherent and compelling—a clearer and purer and more comprehensible—statement of Nazism than is *Mein Kampf,* by a long shot. If it ever functioned as pure manipulation, it is turned now against itself in the sense that one stares in horrified amazement at the images rather than feeling some sort of rapturous pride. Like the Declaration of Independence, *Triumph of the Will* is a crystallization of a political reality and hence a rich and worthy object of interpretation. But it doesn't come with a capitulation machine; now we look to interpret, or even merely to revile, when once they looked in order to experience exaltation. One thing we could say is that political systems would have less history, would be less clear to us and less amenable to plausible interpretation, if they were not always also aesthetic systems, and this depends among other things on the multivalent cognitive and emotional responses such objects typically can arouse.

I suppose that one could contrast the Declaration of Independence and *Triumph of the Will* precisely on the grounds that the one is a text, the other a sequence of images. But first, you're going to go straight into a cognitive/emotional, universal/particular, mind/body dualism. You're congratulating yourself on your (text-oriented) rationality, condemning others for being manipulated by mere manufactured images, which appeal to their animal emotions, their need to belong, for example. But it's worth saying that our experience of the Declaration is at least in part as an image: few Americans can recite it, but many Americans can conjure up the image of a yellowed parchment with calligraphy. Furthermore, of course, though it famously employed no narrator, *Triumph* was focused on a series of speeches by Nazi leaders, and there were plenty of words bouncing around. But there remains a sense that a document must be aimed at a literate, informed citizenry, whereas a mere movie stirs the animal in the ignorant. This is rather silly. The mechanisms by which human beings interpret images are just as sophisticated and complex as those by which they interpret text; practices of image production are just as complex and perhaps as conventional as practices of textual production; and word and image are always coalescing into segments of a single symbol system. Obviously words can be thrown around with the intent to manipulate, and images with the intent to tell the God's honest truth, or vice versa. The Nazis churned out reams of text as well as newsreels and exhibitions of degenerate art, as Jefferson played the violin or redesigned gardens to bring home the idea of republicanism.

So I note that there are aesthetic and anti-aesthetic totalitarianisms, that there are totalitarian and anti-totalitarian artpolitical regimes, and that incredibly stupid and stupendously sublime art has been made at the behest of dictators. What distinguishes totalitarian political aesthetics from other varieties is precisely its mundane totalitarianism. We may on this basis enumerate some commonalities among totalitarian artpolitical systems.

1. Such systems yield gigantic works that remake the environment and occupy a goodly portion of resources.
2. (Roughly entailed by 1), they rest on destruction: the geography must be cleared to occupy the astounding new creations, harbingers of a transformed world.
3. (Roughly entailed by 2), they are ambitious on a world scale, seek to rebuild the world from scratch, flatten it and start again.
4. They consist in part of symbolic and actual security arrangements: every totalitarianism tries to shield its leaders behind impregnable walls.
5. They are enforced at the expense of rival or idiosyncratic expressions. That is, the repressive political/military machinery is brought to bear in mundane actions of censorship and repression, including iconoclasm of the arts of previous and external regimes.

6. More generally, totalitarian regimes establish and enforce official art-political standards and interpretive schemes rather than just embodying or emphasizing them.

7. Specific totalitarian regimes use specific aesthetic effects: the visage of the dictator, or Riefenstahl's cult of the body and the collective body. We can't understand the specific totalitarian system without understanding its aesthetics. But no specific aesthetic system is identical to totalitarianism in general.

Gigantism and Time

We are not going to escape, nor should we, the political uses of film, architecture, music, clothing (from uniforms to ripped T-shirts), body movement (from goose steps to thrash dance), and the rest. What we should resist, if we are anti-totalitarians (which I hope we are), is official arts, official repressions of the arts, official destruction of the arts. And we should resist really, really big art.

And yet if what characterizes the Nazi projects is their gigantism—if that in part constitutes their totalitarian content—we might point out that corporate capitalism has at times come up with similarly unlimited funding procedures. Movies that clock in at $150 million out-Riefenstahl Riefenstahl, and put their imagery no less at the service of corporate capitalism (to take a minor example, through product placement) than Riefenstahl put hers at the service of the party. The closeness of corporate capitalism to the state in the United States actually makes the sources and effects of our monumental architecture—for example, the World Trade Center—obscure or chaotic, a Babel. But it jacks up the gigantism to extreme levels, pierces the sky. That it then serves as a symbol of the squishy totalitarianism of the West—and that people fly planes into it in a typical art-critical/political act—cannot be puzzling.

The space created by a building is not only a useful emptiness carved out against the weather but also, at least in imagination, a caesura in time: a release from, a pause within its passage; a room in time. Certainly one function of the Pyramids or the Great Wall is as an imaginary hedge against temporality: these structures long outlasted their originators, and one way or another they were meant to fend off death. The Pyramids were sepulchers, intended to guarantee eternal endurance; the Great Wall was meant to fend off the barbarians—a human manifestation of chaos, a human natural disaster. Speer's architecture was to make the thousand-year Reich seem inevitable, and some of it is still there. The gleaming corporate towers that dominate city skylines today serve a similar function: they signal that whatever may happen to the corporation's stock or to its factories or to its employees, the corporation itself endures, transcends the temporal, gleams permanently in steel and glass.

Related to this, or entailed by it, these structures signal a transcendence of the human. As expressions of the weird ontology of institutions, the Pyramids and the skyscraper are consciously built on a scale that dwarfs the body. The members of the board of directors die, but the corporation lives on. Pharaohs and emperors croak, but the dynasty endures. We are still trying to figure out how human bodies could have actually given rise to the Pyramids, and this was meant to be a mystery; it is key to understanding what the Pyramids were trying to accomplish that we cannot understand how human bodies could create them, or that it is difficult to envision the actual building process. One thing is for sure: the building process involved breaking bodies or straining bodies to their utmost capacity. The attempt to disembed oneself from fini-tude always only shows that one is embedded in it utterly. And that makes the ruin or the smoking rubble absorbing or lends it a penumbra of the tragic: not simply the failure of all human creations at overcoming the temporal, but the perverse heroism, the hubris that conceives an annihilating transcendence and makes it the center of political or economic culture—the "sublime object of ideology"—and the subsequent annihilation of that very illusion.

Take the attacks on the World Trade Center in 1993 and 2001. If the Great Wall represents the civilization of the Middle Kingdom, its superiority to the barbarian, its culture, literacy, permanence, and glory, the World Trade Center represented our rationality. Trade itself as it was embodied in the Center is a rational concept encapsulating the administration of the world for human purposes. The World Trade Center was a massive expression of the conquest of time and space: jutting up into the sky and penetrating it dualithically, up into a different weather—shining, simplified, intensely human even as it sought transcendence of the organic. The space it defined is apparently detached from its context, more or less perfectly climate-controlled: even in a blizzard it was exactly 72 degrees within the huge artificial environment. It articulated lower Manhattan at pedestrian level as an arid valley of winds. The perfect aesthetic critique of the Trade Center was mounted by Philippe Petit in his criminal wire walk between the towers: beautiful, ephemeral, political.[3]

The World Trade Center, hence, was not merely a technological overcom-ing of the world, or the illusion of a technological overcoming of the world; it

---

3. Consult the wonderful documentary *Man on Wire,* directed by James Marsh (2008).

was a symbol of that overcoming, a monument to it, an expression of power and pride on a vast scale. The forces that collapsed it come in our imagination out of the chaos, out of an Islamic fundamentalism stuck in an anachronistic temporality and a pure irrational terrorism. For the Westerner such forces might as well be tornadoes or wild animals. The Islamic fundamentalists' attack on the World Trade Center is a sudden conflagration of temporalities: antiquity invading modernity, the safety and control of the gigantic structure suddenly compromised by the absonant force of another era, the international scratchings of cavemen.

The work of time is continual as well as instantaneous, and the World Trade Center, like the Reich chancellery, needed, in order to maintain the illusion of a transcendence of time, to accomplish the constant work of presence, the maintenance that continually returns it "in its original state" to the present. The work of the political/economic/religious monument's maintenance staff is instrumental; it is meant to maintain the building in the sense that it allows the building to emerge more or less pristine into the endless series of futures imagined by the dictator/CEO/pope. But this work of maintenance can be accomplished only in the present. Thus monumental architecture, which is always among other things a problematic, an implicitly totalitarian political statement, whether ancient or modern, exists in a fantastic relation to time that is constantly under attack. The gleaming skyscraper belies or disguises the constant work of maintenance—cleaning, rebuilding, shoring up—that both allows the building to resist temporality and demonstrates that it is always perfectly embedded in temporality, bathed in it, saturated by it in every aspect. The machines that make this environment must be continually tended; energy and money must be continually expended in their maintenance. The minute that labor is withdrawn, the monument will begin to disintegrate, and the disintegration to which it is already subject will become apparent.

When this work is abandoned, things fall apart. And the disintegration is nostalgic and is aesthetic. It is a kind of real-life vanitas; it functions in the imagination as a confrontation and affirmation of human limits—of disease, death, decomposition. This is particularly poignant in the ruin of the political monument: the Coliseum, the Pyramids, the stadium at Nuremberg. And in general, we might say, one function of the aesthetic—of museum practices, for example—is to disguise the time-boundedness of objects. This is one reason why art becomes an essential expression of the state: it makes a claim to dominate the future.

To return to the matter at hand, we should of course not simply equate democratic capitalism with Nazism, or international modernism with Nazi architecture: that would aestheticize politics in a crazily dangerous, and also confused, way. It is important that the architecture and film and costume of the Nazis is imposed by directly totalitarian means, whereas the arts of modernism often conceived themselves as incompatible with, or at any rate irrelevant to, political force. Mies wasn't coming at your family with a goon squad. It is a powerful attack on the films of Riefenstahl that they were made in support of a genocidal regime. We cannot say the same of the films of Cocteau, for example, though Cocteau yielded to no one in his admiration for Riefenstahl, whom he called "the genius of film" (Trimborn, p. 105). But as Cocteau knew, Riefenstahl's films were no less stylistically distinctive and aesthetically distinguished than his own, and any understanding of their effects must also grapple with their aesthetic quality. At any rate, even if we think of the capitalist skyscraper as totalitarian art, it is not Nazi art. It seeks to breach time and transcend the human body in a way common to many totalitarian expressions; but there are many totalitarianisms, and the differences between the gleaming glass box and Speer's Berlin are as significant as the similarities. Even the transparency of glass is important. If the commonalities alert us to the totalitarian tendencies of our own cultures, the differences must show us that the categories are fluid. But in each case we also have to take the aesthetic objects as central to our interpretation of the political realities.

The question of totalitarian aesthetics in the modern era is connected specifically with the growth of eighteenth- and nineteenth-century nationalism, particularly German nationalism. Indeed, as we will see, the idea of aesthetics, and of political aesthetics in particular, emerged in the same context as modern nationalism and romanticism. This has in some way discredited or even precluded the whole inquiry. The connection of the folk arts to national identities—itself something carefully built by figures such as Herder, and then taken up by early academic anthropology and folklore studies—is by itself an amazingly rich theme. The connection to anti-Semitism and genocide, which comes through Wagner and many others, is hardly the whole of the legacy, even if it is morally overwhelming. For example, one need only think of the role of academic folklore in preserving African American musics, or the success of Gladys Reichard in understanding the arts of the Navajo as the center of their culture. The whole idea of folk arts, or even of distinctive cultures and subcultures—at any rate, the actual strategies, basically aesthetic, for differentiating and characterizing such cultures and subcultures—which we owe to this legacy, is problematic. It should be subjected to a rigorous, perhaps postmodern critique; it has been used, massively, to naturalize power relations. Nevertheless, the data provided by such work, or even the art that it has made available, from the music of the Carter family to the preservation of the Lakota sun dance, has deeply enriched the world.

Reifying a culture no doubt always performs exclusions, and always comes saturated with value judgments, in particular about the authenticity of certain sorts of expression, that need constant critical vigilance. But if the construction of German folk culture leads by a long path to the Holocaust, the construction of African American folk culture, or gay culture, or women's arts, or Yoruba aesthetics made genuine contributions to survival and decency, with no genocidal implications. Josef Chytry, in *The Aesthetic State,* ties the idea of beauty as an organizing political idea to the development of German nationalism but also traces its origins in democratic Athens, its revival by the third Earl of Shaftesbury (a Whig and classical republican), and the critique of nationalism in Marx and Nietzsche. It is understandable why people would interpret Nazism as discrediting everything it touched, including the centrality of aesthetics to politics. But that the Nazis aestheticized politics does not at all show that the very idea of an aesthetic politics is wrong. It is, in my view, unavoidable, and as I hope to suggest, anarchist and democratic politics are just as aestheticized as Nazism. Indeed even nationalism, with all its problematic appurtenances, can be a liberating as well as a destructive force. This serves as an illustration of what I take to be a general point: that as closely intertwined or inextricable as aesthetic and political values are in each actual case, they are nonidentical and are complexly related; that every aesthetic value can be applied in a variety of political contexts, with varied sources and effects.

CHAPTER 2

Artphilosophical Themes

Spheres of Value

We are now, I think, armed with a set of examples and issues, developed from concrete situations. We have seen political ideas formulated essentially as aesthetic ideas, a political movement embodied in aesthetic objects. It is worthwhile, however, to try to get some kind of grasp on the theoretical relationships involved in a general way: to move from artpolitical history to artpolitical philosophy.

The idea of political aesthetics would be indefensible if, on the one hand, the aesthetic sphere of value were not intrinsically tied to or if, on the other hand, it were identical to the political, the ethical, and the epistemic spheres. If aesthetic values (such as beauty) were not connected to justice, goodness, or truth, then the aesthetic description and assessment of political systems would be precious, useless, and annoying. That a government or its buildings are pretty, for example, would be an idiotic thing to focus on while it makes war or inflicts suffering on innocent people, or for that matter while it helps people live decent lives. It is in the exploration of such connections that the methodology of political aesthetics will take shape. If I could put this both precisely and vaguely, and as I have formulated the matter already: the values are orthogonal, but each real thing is a place where they intersect. There is both a question about beauty and a question about justice at each actual political node—system, event, figure, poster, building. Neither matter can be separated from the other at that node, though the values are not identical.

In my view, each sphere of value is inextricable from the others; each dimension of value infests, compromises, and supplements the others, in every case. To put it slightly more precisely, in my view the aesthetic is inherent in and necessary to the ethical, the political, and the epistemic, without exhausting those spheres of value. The values are in juxtaposition but, even if for that reason alone, in relation. But I think the relation is somewhat more tight: no fundamental political, ethical, and epistemic value can be fully delineated—in no case can its content as a concept and a norm be fully characterized—without recourse to aesthetic categories. But that is not only more than I could hope to show in this context; it is more than is needed to get political aesthetics as an area of inquiry going. What is needed, rather, is the concession that some aesthetic features of an object, person, institution can be relevant to a full-fledged ethical, political, or epistemic characterization of it, or to take it the other way around, that a moral, political, or epistemic description of (for example) an institution is not complete without an appeal to characteristically aesthetic values. This is of course also a plea to take the aesthetic dimensions of experience far more seriously than has often been the case. Again, I personally believe the connections to be far tighter than that; I think that at their base, for example, aesthetic descriptions always have moral content, and moral descriptions always have aesthetic content: that it is a necessary condition for something to be good, just, or true that it display certain properties best characterized aesthetically. I also believe, however, that none of these dimensions is reducible to, or is nothing but, aesthetics. The distinctions are important, but it's the connections that need emphasizing here, as they are too rarely appreciated, and can be exploited toward new forms of political understanding.

I think that the whole of this book provides evidence for these connections. We have already seen them in application: I have tried to show, for example, the centrality of architecture and film to the content of Nazism, and the centrality of the aesthetics of purity to the Holocaust. I have tried to show that the use of images and objects in Nazism was far more than propaganda or an ancillary expression, but was the very body of the ideology. I have tried to show the centrality of aesthetics to nationalisms, both repressive and (see chapter 4) liberatory. I have suggested the centrality of the body to a fascist conception of beauty, and of the fascist conception of beauty to fascism, while also pointing out that the aesthetic and the political values exceed each other.

Obviously aesthetics can be used as a kind of clothing or ornamentation for political positions; aesthetics is the arena in which political propaganda is constructed. It is used this way quite consciously by all political regimes and has given rise to many styles: Roman mega-classicism or French rococo, let's say, or Confucian robes and flute music, or socialist realism. Aesthetics can conceal the monstrous accumulation of power and its horrendous applications under a glamorous or rhetorically persuasive surface. In this dimension, aesthetics represents the "ideological" aspect of political systems, the need of all such systems to conceal themselves. Yet political aesthetics is also employed in the resistance to ideology, or in the formulation and presentation of alternative ideologies; resistance movements, revolutions, temporary autonomous zones have their iconographies and type styles. The affective dimensions of politics are important no matter what your position, and a politics or political system that does not satisfy people emotionally or at least arouse or mobilize them in some way is unlikely to prosper or endure. But political aesthetics as I understand it is not a study of persuasive strategies; it is the study of the design of political systems as central to an understanding of our political arrangements and of resistance to them. And I quite generally want to throw into doubt the distinction between the affective or persuasive features of a political system and its claims to truth and moral legitimacy.

Aesthetic and Epistemic

In the introduction we have already seen Kant compromise, in a profound way, the aesthetic and epistemic spheres. For Kant argues that the aesthetic attributes of a thing are potentially part of the very concept or identity of that thing, of its essence, we might say. Kant himself draws just such a conclusion, in an exemplary way conflating the cognitive or conceptual content of a sign and its aesthetic properties:

> If, now, we attach to a concept a representation of the imagination belonging to its presentation [for example, attach to a moral maxim a dramatic poem], but inducing solely on its own account such a wealth of thought as would never admit of comprehension in a definite concept, and, as a consequence, giving aesthetically an unbounded expansion to the concept itself, then the imagination here displays a creative activity. (Kant 1, sec. 49)

This is a rather extraordinary formulation. Kant does not say that the aesthetic representation ornaments or even elaborates the concept; he says that the representation gives "an unbounded expansion to the concept itself." It's hard to know exactly what he means, but given basic conditions on the identity of concepts, one would think that the concept has mutated into another, which includes aesthetic materials in its very content, though it may still also include some discursively defined conclusion, moral, truth. This is a familiar theme in eighteenth-century aesthetics. Lessing, for example, says that the suffering of the Laocoön can be understood in one way in sculpture, in quite another in poetry: that they are not the same suffering; that the suffering is understood in virtue of its particular aesthetic embodiment. This would immediately compromise the distinction between the form and content of the linguistic sign, and it would indicate as well that in understanding a political ideology through its design, we explore the very content of the basic concepts of politics: democracy, say, or freedom, or liberation, or nation. "Poetry and rhetoric," Kant continues,

> also derive the soul that animates their works wholly from the aesthetic attributes of the objects—attributes which go hand in hand with the logical, and give the imagination an impetus to bring more thought into play in the matter, though in an undeveloped manner, than allows of being brought within the embrace of a concept, or, therefore, of being definitely formulated in language. (Kant 1, sec. 49)

As an example of an "aesthetic attribute," Kant adduces "Jupiter's eagle, with the lightning in his claws" (Kant 1, sec. 49). That is, the eagle, functioning qua aesthetic representation, is an attribute, in Kant's sense, of Jupiter. The connection of Jupiter to the eagle (or for that matter of the United States to the eagle) is part of the concept of Jupiter, part of its cognitive content. One understands more about the concept of Jupiter or of the United States by understanding that this is one of his or its aesthetic attributes, which requires more than a discursive description. As we will see, it is this refusal to distinguish between the content of a political system and its aesthetic aspects that forms the methodological ground of political aesthetics.

To know the thing comprehensively, to be acquainted with what it is, one must be acquainted with its aesthetic aspects; one must experience it aesthetically. This would, among other things, ground various true and false statements about the thing (a political system, let us say) in its aesthetic formulations. The detachment of aesthetic from epistemic value would lead to the conclusion that an aesthetic treatment of politics would be essentially emotive and irrational. That's about the last thing we need: pleasing symmetries and massively ineffective or destructive policies. But the aesthetic dimensions of rationality are essential to it, a characteristic assertion of the German idealist tradition at which I've been working, but also of the strictest statement of empiricist scientific method.

If the universe displays aesthetic features, then aesthetic methods or standards are potentially epistemic, by which I mean among other things that they produce material that is true or false in the ordinary sense. Exemplary demonstrations or applications of this are found in Shaftesbury—often considered the founding figure of aesthetics—and also in Plato and Plotinus, but also in Bacon and Locke. Indeed empiricism, under whose auspices the scientific method was systematized, depends fundamentally on the notion of picturing, and all truth on its account originates in "sense impressions" conceived as internal (usually pictorial) representations of the external world. Assessments of truth are, on this view, assessments of the realism of representations, and both empiricist philosophy and scientific method arise with the development of realism in the arts. And all these developments arise with modern liberal or democratic political theory. There is a direct connection between Locke's epistemology and his politics, and both are also foundationally aesthetic.

Without aesthetic sensitivity we cannot describe the world in a full-fledged or fully responsible way. For example, if the universe is comprehensible, and if comprehensibility is in part an aesthetic standard of simplicity, clarity, or accurate representation, then all the judgments that depend on rationality— in particular, all scientific judgments—are infected with aesthetic values, or underpinned by them, or justified in part with reference to them. Aesthetic standards operate, as it were, among the truth conditions of any proposition. If the structure or design or ordering of the universe displays aesthetic features, or takes an aesthetic order, then aesthetics might be built in to every accurate description of the world. This would also be true if human perception or reasoning depended conceptually on aesthetic values. These are extremely vague and speculative declarations, though I think the development of case studies has and will put meat on these bones. You cannot understand Nazism or Black Nationalism—you cannot know the truth about them—without emerging from the purely conceptual or descriptive to the aesthetic realm (in fact these realms are not fully distinct in any case), to aesthetic sources and effects. But what I want to emphasize is that the aesthetic rejection or valorization of a political system need not be, is not, separate from its truth claims, as that all men are created equal, or that production is the species-being of man. What it means for such claims to be true, as they emerge within traditions of political discourse, is affected by the aesthetics of the system or the epistemic order in which the claim is made, in its relation to the aesthetic order of the world.

Of course the *epistemic* standard by which a proposition such as "all men are created equal" could be evaluated (for truth value) are extremely obscure and controversial. Notoriously, it is going to be awfully hard to support such a claim scientifically; or perhaps the idea that science could bear on a question like that is merely confused: we're not going to be able to reduce or boil down human beings in order to isolate their equal bits of humanity. Well, what sorts of considerations do bear on such a claim? In part, I think, aesthetic considerations, and the assertion brings a satisfying and cognitively significant simplicity and symmetry to our moral and political deliberations, as we see concretely in political systems that claim to be true. That all men are created equal introduces or detects a moral and political universe of a certain shape; it sorts the world morally and politically in a manner that has both simplicity and broad scope. It clarifies moral and political decision making by making each one $= 1$. And from the standpoint of a certain aesthetic, a clear moral field of universal scope is highly desirable; indeed that is most clearly true of the liberal and Enlightenment figures who kept writing sentences like "We hold these truths to be self-evident &c." (I note in passing that the question of whether or not "all men are created equal" is true—its epistemic value— is obviously also connected conceptually to its moral and political value. It's a good political principle only if it's true, I should think. Only if it is true does applying it yield the right political result.) The clarity and universality of the equality of man are classical and neoclassical, a theme to which we will return.

In addition, of course, implicitly or explicitly, a political system or ideology deploys an aesthetics that could in part be expressed as a series of propositions, which would have the same status as any other propositions: they would be true or false, and be deployed within a set of epistemic criteria or practices for evaluating truth value. For example, the assertion of the Nazis that classicism of a certain kind (gigantic or sublime classicism) is superior in one way or another to modernism—in terms of pure visual form, or in terms of symbolizing or creating a united citizenry—can be evaluated in the way that any art-critical claim can be evaluated, or in the way any political claim can be evaluated: they are what I am calling "artpolitical" claims, and they import whole epistemic methodologies born out of art history, political science, and political philosophy. Or perhaps consider the claim that Albert Speer's designs for the Nazi state are genuinely classical, that they responsibly represent the values of the Greeks. Indeed, now we might have to adjudicate as between republicanism's and fascism's claims to the classical. Such debates are a matter in part of producing reasons, examples, analogies: in short, justifications. They can be argued about, even if they (like claims in many other areas) are hard to punch out or pin down once and for all.

That is, in part a political aesthetics is a series of propositions, true or false, and hence subject to epistemic evaluation. And in part the aesthetics of a

political aesthetics is always also an epistemology: the idea of a classical architecture can be extended to—or perhaps it emerges from—a technique or a
standard by which assertions in a system are evaluated for truth. A classical
architecture is highly unified, comparatively simple, a clear coordination of
disparate and integral elements. These are aesthetic criteria, but they are also
epistemic criteria, and there could be and there are baroque or mannerist or
surrealist epistemic practices that systematically favor multitudinous, bewildering, or arbitrary explanations, or that forgo the activity of explanation
altogether: mystic epistemologies and their mystic architectures, bristling with
arbitrary juxtapositions, constructing teeming, various, and barely coherent
environments. Here we might point to the artpolitical and inseparably the
epistemic procedures of the medieval church, or of the dadaists.

I am concerned, in other words, to defend the idea of a political aesthetics
from the charge that it would ignore or devalue the claims to truth of a political ideology. Quite the reverse: political aesthetics yields a richer set of criteria
by which to evaluate the truth claims of political ideologies, constitutions,
and systems, as well as a richer account of exactly what those claims are. This
is precisely what we should expect if, as again Kant argues, the aesthetic aura
of a concept informs, expands, fills out, or supplements that concept. That
is, for Kant, the aesthetic features of a concept ("unity" for instance) are part
of that concept: full understanding of any thing implicates the aesthetic. Of
course, I am also not asserting that epistemology reduces to aesthetics, and
that the only criteria for evaluating the truth claims of a political ideology
are aesthetic, though I think that the extent to which aesthetic criteria are
inherent in other criteria—for example, social-scientific criteria—are too
little appreciated. Within a given epistemic practice there may be procedures
for fixing truth values that are not primarily aesthetic. But even in such cases
the aesthetic is, as it were, there for the taking, and in an attempt fully to
characterize an assertion and its place within a nexus of assertions, aesthetic
categories are ultimately required.

One way in which aesthetics operates within political epistemology is in
fixing belief or commitment where other epistemic standards are themselves
ambiguous, in conflict, or at stake. If someone believes that an extremely
complicated governmental system is preferable to a simple one, and justifies
this on the grounds that the universe or human psychology is incomprehensible or arbitrary or infinitely profuse (or, more realistically, on the grounds
that the political system is traditional), there is, I think, nothing to be said
by way of sheer empirical refutation. If someone rejects, let's say, the social
sciences or rational decision theory as providing standards for evaluating the
success or failure of political systems and deploys a fundamentally different

set of epistemic values—faith or submission on the one hand, or on the other hand sheer defiance or destruction—the epistemic situation is a standoff. No one can offer reasons to prefer one criterion to the other, because the criteria concern the nature of reasons or the reasons the nature of criteria. These are not academic examples; they are absolutely typical in revolutionary circumstances and in many arguments that put political systems at stake (though not in all such arguments). Of course sometimes the accusation would be that a system fails by the values it professes; that would be a dispute internal to a set of epistemic (and moral and aesthetic) standards.

As an example, I think of the Yippies of the 1960s, led by Abbie Hoffman and Jerry Rubin. They responded, among other things, to the brutal (apparent) rationality of the American state by emphasizing the whimsical, by acts of theater that interrupted the flow of statistics. They stuck flowers in rifles, nominated a pig for president, appeared in court naked or in Santa Claus suits, centered their resistance on identities created and circulated by rock music: "Woodstock Nation." "We become communist-racist-acid-headed freaks, holding flowers in one hand and bombs in the other. . . . So what the hell are we doing, you ask? We are dynamiting brain cells. We are putting people through changes. The key to the puzzle lies in theater. We are theater in the streets: total and committed" (Hoffman, p. 17). Such street theater is a lively American and world tradition: we might think of Bread and Puppet Theater, for instance. An emblem of Woodstock Nation might be Jimi Hendrix's performance of "The Star-Spangled Banner": throwing down a virtually arbitrary and breathtakingly beautiful deconstruction and destruction of the national anthem, or making an anthem for a new nation by improvisation. That was a political act, and if we now ask whether it decreased the poverty rate or brought us closer to some political goal as articulated within the social sciences, the only proper response is that that's the wrong question; that's not what Hendrix's "Star-Spangled Banner" was *for*. It was a psychedelic interruption of the rationality (or pseudo-rationality) by which the American state organized and justified itself. Obviously if one evaluated the Yippies by the same standards of effectiveness that one used to evaluate policies of the Johnson administration, one would have missed the point entirely.

But even the standards by which the Johnson administration might have evaluated the success of its antipoverty effort or its war in Vietnam have foundationally aesthetic aspects, as I have been arguing. If we ask what it is to view the social quantitatively or scientifically, or why we want to, we cannot give a full account without recourse to aesthetic categories. To think about the political as a set of ends and of policies as means to those ends is to impose a certain comprehensible order on the social world; it is to order or arrange it by certain principles, and inscribed within this order is the rejection of previous and external epistemic aesthetics: the mysteries of faith, the power of tradition embodied in scripture or literature. The social-scientific/economic worldview and a technological policy orientation yield the satisfaction of a certain sort of comprehension, unity, wholeness, even in a particular kind of acknowledgment of multiplicity. We might see the satisfactions available in these different ways, for example, in the differences between Plato and Aristotle (who establishes the social sciences with his instrumentalism, his ordering of actions to ends), their accounts of human action, but also in their modes of literary composition: their prose styles.

This would also be the case in cross-cultural and cross-temporal comparisons of widely divergent political systems, where often, it seems to me, we use aesthetic standards in order to achieve an epistemic evaluation. One might say that one resorts to irrational standards, but I am saying that rationality itself cannot be understood except in part as an aesthetic. The question about whether one's procedure for evaluation is rational is itself in part an aesthetic question: Is it the simplest explanation available? the clearest? Does its contemplation yield satisfaction, set your mind at rest? Obviously some art deploys rationality as an aesthetic standard—clarity, simplicity, system— whereas other art consciously celebrates irrationality, or attacks rationality, or appears beyond or before rationality.

Ockham's razor, the systematic preference for the simple explanation, absolutely fundamental to the epistemic procedures of modernity, is, I think, an aesthetic epistemic standard. That has been questioned famously by Karl Popper, among others. Popper says that a simpler explanation is more easily falsifiable and hence preferable from the point of view of scientific process. A more general formulation might be that the simple explanation is not more likely to be true but is more directly testable; the criterion is internal to scientific practice. But offhand I do not see why this should be the case. If we have two theories that have the same observational entailments, one of which is far simpler than the other, each theory would be falsified by the failure of those entailments without regard to its internal complexity. Indeed, one might think that a very complex theory in certain circumstances or with regard to certain disciplines might in fact have more empirical entailments, and thus be more easily falsifiable. Likewise, a simpler theory might have fewer cognitive costs; it is easier to believe in the sense that it requires fewer neurons. But though sometimes for some purposes we are concerned with preserving as much computing power as possible, at other times for other purposes we would like to see our cognition dominated by a particular theory or discipline to the greatest possible extent; we want to learn everything.

Or we might make the razor rest on "purely pragmatic" grounds: it has proved itself the best means to our ends, or it is the quickest way to the truth, the straight line between the point where we are and the point we want to reach. But pragmatism as an epistemology itself embodies aesthetic criteria, as Peirce and Dewey, for example, knew perfectly well, and rounding off a problem, finding the solution by the most direct or effective method, orders experiences in wholes and is driven by the need for rest or satisfaction. This is not to say, however, that Ockham's razor, or for that matter the pragmatic theory of truth, is only an aesthetic system; it is to say that we cannot fully understand them or experience their power without recourse to aesthetic categories.

Quine famously describes his own commitment to razor ontology by saying that he has "a taste for desert landscapes" (Quine, p. 4). Now, it is certainly not right to say that for Quine ontological economy is merely a matter of arbitrary aesthetic preference: the thing constitutes an entire worldview and a history of science, for example, and connects its postulates to the world by a thousand routes. Surely the basic driver is epistemic in the sense that lurking beyond all such strategies must be the belief that the simplest explanation is likeliest to be true. This is a picture of the universe, what in the old days we might have called a cosmology. The simplest explanation is (perhaps) the most quickly stated and the most quickly absorbed, and these are in certain contexts, of course, key standards for the quality of theories. Razor ontology must capture and reflect myriad experiences, theories, a picture of the historical unfolding of knowledge, and so on. Quine makes it clear, however, that the aesthetic aspect is also fundamental. Ockham's razor is a standard for the usefulness of a theory. Perhaps it is a standard for the truth of a theory. But it is also a standard for the beauty of a theory. And I should think that these questions ought not to be isolated from one another: for the idea that the simplest theory is most likely to be true is a statement that the universe itself displays a beautiful order. Again we might mention Shaftesbury, on whose view the truth and beauty of the world are always connected. Or we might mention Einstein, for example, or for that matter Newton, who were constantly connecting their theories to a notion of a beautiful universe. In 1957 Richard Feynman wrote: "There was a moment when I knew how nature worked. [The theory] had elegance and beauty. The goddamn thing was gleaming."[1] That is, to repeat, if the universe displays aesthetic qualities such

---

1. Quoted in Arthur I. Miller, "Science: A Thing of Beauty," Newscientist.com, https://notes.utk.edu/Bio/greenberg.nsf/f5b2cbf2a827c0198525624b00057d30/0ba704cb7f69f3618525711e003a6fa1?OpenDocument.

as order, coherence, simplicity in variety, and so forth, then it really is the case
that the most beautiful theory—on a particular conception of beauty (essentially a classical conception)—is most likely to be true. And if not, not.

Ockham's razor, formulated at the outset of the classical revival, crystallizes
one particular conception of beauty in theories or ontologies, but of course
there could be a completely different aesthetics of ontology. One might even
begin with the negation of the razor: multiply entities unto the limit of
the possible and beyond. Consider, for example, the ontology of a Mei-
nong, or of certain strands of Hinduism, enumerating entities to the limits
of conceivability. Many thinkers have urged lush or mystical ontologies, and
many have urged an absurdist or surrealist politics (I might mention Gabriele
d'Annunzio). The choice between razor and anti-razor ontologies should
ultimately rest on what sorts of things there actually are. But what drives the
formulation of the ontology in the first place is an aesthetic response to the
universe, or an aesthetic yearning in the face of the universe. Or the way I'd
prefer to say it is that the question of what there actually is and the aesthetic
questions are not actually fully detachable from one another. Ockham's razor
might appear simply to be a standard for generating or evaluating theories,
but it can be that only if it is also a sense of how the universe is ordered:
simplicity within multiplicity, a classical aesthetic as applied to everything.
The razor is engaged at one end with the aesthetic and at the other with
the epistemic, but ultimately it binds these in the most intimate relation:
(1) Beauty is simplicity within multiplicity—one reason why the simplest
explanation might be regarded as the most "satisfying." (2) The universe is
(by this standard) beautiful. (3) Hence the simplest explanation of the multifarious phenomena is most likely to be true. To repeat, this is only one possible aesthetic of epistemology; there could be epistemic standards, even, that
sought to de-aestheticize science or other knowledge-producing disciplines.
But it seems to me that you are not going to be able to understand any of
these approaches fully—even an explicitly anti-aesthetic approach—without
engaging the aesthetic dimensions.

We might also consider theories of truth as themselves related to modes
of aesthetic description and assessment. This theme is potentially extremely
rich, but I might point out to begin with that the correspondence theory
of truth is related to, if not identical to, mimetic accounts of representation,
which I explore later in this chapter. It is often said that the question of
truth for linguistic or quasi-linguistic items such as sentences or propositions is disjoint from the question of accuracy in pictorial representation.
It is asserted, for example, that pictures cannot be true or false. Yet language
itself has been treated—famously by Wittgenstein in the *Tractatus,* but also by

many others—by analogy to pictures. And indeed a realistic or informative picture is often enough termed "true." I think such locutions ought to be taken seriously, even if paying off on an account of truth in picturing is an extremely difficult matter. Truth, of course, is an extremely difficult matter in any case. In fact, theories of truth face an intractable problem of circularity insofar as they are themselves to be evaluated for their truth. A pragmatic theory of truth according to which, say, "truth is what works in the way of belief" (James) could turn out to be pragmatically useful, and hence true on its own account; that would not show it to be true. But one possible mode of evaluating theories of truth, or even getting a handle on their content, would be as aesthetic systems, which would only be to shift to an irrelevant dimension of evaluation if aesthetic considerations did not in turn bear on truth, which is the question at issue.

Coherence theories of truth often explicitly appeal to aesthetic categories: the way a set of beliefs or propositions or theories "hangs together" sounds initially like an aesthetic assessment. Certainly various styles of art—for example, classicism—are praised for their coherence while others are attacked as incoherent. Notoriously, sheer logical consistency is not enough to establish coherence in a system sufficient to enable us to evaluate propositions in that system for truth. There can of course be logically consistent sets of claims that are all true; there can be consistent sets of claims all of which are false; and there can be consistent sets of claims some of which are true and some of which are false. But the way a coherent set of propositions is supposed to hang together is much more elaborate than this—perhaps to be formulated in terms of explanatory relations or networks—and I suggest that some sort of classical aesthetic lies at the heart of the coherence theory of truth. It may be, however, that the criteria of consistency can be set out without essential appeal to aesthetic categories, in terms of the inferential connections among propositions or beliefs, for example. At any rate, I just want to mark my sense that aesthetic matters such as accuracy and composition bear on conceptions of truth at a fundamental level, and thus my view that it is premature to detach truth—as it is wrong to detach knowledge—from aesthetic matters.

Aesthetic and Ethical

A potentially devastating objection to the program of political aesthetics is that "aestheticizing" politics ignores or attenuates or deletes its moral dimensions. This is at the heart of Benjamin's or Sontag's attack on aesthetics in politics as totalitarian in itself, which I regard as a fundamental challenge to the whole mode of inquiry in which I am engaged. Aesthetics in the Kantian and modernist tradition refers to the mere way things appear—the "arrangement of lines and colors" (Clive Bell)—or sheer form. And if form itself did not ramify through every aspect of culture and experience, economics and politics, identity and truth, if form did not convey or deflect meanings, this would certainly tend to show that the other values trump aesthetic value. People who worry about being happy over the mere look of things would do well to think about transforming the way they are, or helping people in need, or aiding in a social transcendence from an unacceptable situation. Let them eat art. A nice-looking famine—a famine with a gorgeous view, for instance—isn't any better than a really ugly one. Aesthetics is a luxury—important, perhaps, but a desire to be satisfied when through just means we achieve some sort of leisure. Aesthetic disinterest or distance as understood in modernism specifically requires the aesthetic experiencer to ignore moral implications, or to perform a separation of aesthetic from ethical value. (Whether this requirement can be fulfilled, or whether it is even coherent, is another question.) The works of Riefenstahl beautifully illustrate the possible moral disaster that is under way when we perform this abstraction on politically significant material: we gaze rapt upon the monumental scale and symmetry of it all, as millions die in the gas chambers. Or the aesthetic attracts us to a set of political figures and policies that might otherwise repulse us or arouse our indignation or even resistance.

The relation of the aesthetic and ethical spheres of value in Kant's *Critique of Judgment* is highly complex, and in some ways the radical detachment of these spheres in formalist aesthetics has its origins in that work. But in his early work *Observations on the Feeling of the Beautiful and Sublime,* Kant connects them with a nice directness.

> True virtue can be grafted only upon principles such that the more general they are, the more sublime and noble it becomes. These principles are not speculative rules, but the consciousness of a feeling that lives in every human breast and extends itself much further than over the particular grounds of compassion and complaisance. I believe I sum it all up when I say that it is the *feeling of the beauty and the dignity of human nature.* The first is a ground of universal affection, the second of universal esteem; and if this feeling had the greatest perfection in some one human heart, this man would of course love and prize even himself, but only so far as he is one of all those over whom his broadened and noble feeling is spread. Only when one subordinates his own inclination to one so expanded can our charitable impulses be used

proportionately and bring about the noble bearing that is the beauty
of virtue. (Kant 2, p. 60)

In some ways this echoes the aesthetic praise of virtue that is traditional in
many cultures and eras. And though it hints at a division of affective and
cognitive ethical dimensions that would characterize Kant's critical phase
(in which he locates the center of the ethical in the cognitive and the center of the aesthetic in the sensuous), it might also be interpreted as before
or beyond this opposition. Kant devotes a long chapter to the aesthetics of
virtue, constantly hinting that ethics could not be understood or practiced
or represented except in some aesthetic terms, as noble, beautiful, splendid,
sublime. Indeed Hannah Arendt, in a series of lectures delivered near the end
of her life, tried to read the *Critique of Judgment* as Kant's treatise on political philosophy, and the kind of subjective universality that Kant attributes
to experiences of beauty as the image of a polis that was based on both the
autonomy and the solidarity of its citizens (Arendt 1).

We will see that a politics of resistance such as Black Nationalism—even
while availing itself of aesthetic materials related to German nationalism—
is no less fundamentally aestheticized than fascism. Nevertheless, regimes
differ at a minimum in whether and to what extent, explicitly or inchoately,
they regard themselves as foundationally aesthetic. You see an anti-aesthetic
politics, for example, at least in some moments of Marx and even to some
extent in the most radical attacks on monarchy in the eighteenth century,
for example, in Robespierre. A figure such as Ben Franklin resorts to a completely flat or plain anti-aesthetic as an egalitarian expression. To eliminate
aesthetic considerations, in an atmosphere in which art might be held to be
the leisure activity of the dominant classes, is to issue a class critique, but
it is centrally a display of moral seriousness. Nevertheless—and here we
enter into a key theme—the rejection of a set of aesthetic values, or even
of aesthetics in its entirety, is itself an aesthetic gesture, and a Marxist attack
on the aesthetics of the bourgeoisie is an aesthetic manifesto: a manifesto
for function, for stripping ornament, an austere or minimalist aesthetics.
This point is not merely precious: the urgent moral rejection of aesthetics accounts for the actual way many things look in eastern Europe, for
example; it shapes the physical environment, intentionally; it is, precisely,
an aesthetic system.

Moral systems are also aesthetic systems. To repeat, the justification of a
claim like "all men are created equal" cannot be internal to a scale of moral
(or for that matter epistemic) value because it rests at the foundation of one
such scale. This is not to say that the shape of the moral world produced by

the truth that all men are created equal is in someone's or everyone's head; the equality of human beings is a real feature of the world if it is anything.

Justice itself, as against the claims of which aesthetic concerns can seem insufficiently serious, is an aesthetic concept, as Elaine Scarry has eloquently argued. Justice is best conceived in a general way in terms of such ideas of balance or complex symmetry. What offends us about an extremely unjust distribution of goods, for example, is its impossibly unbalanced composition. Its arbitrary or irrational quality, according to Scarry, is best captured in aesthetic terms. The injunction to treat like cases alike, for example, is at its heart a design concept, and our offense when people do not receive what they deserve or possess far more than they deserve is a response, as it were, to society as a composition: the imbalance compromises the wholeness or unity or symmetry and requires revolutionary redress. In the *Republic,* justice consists of each person and each class of persons performing the task to which he, she, or it is best suited. Socrates praises this arrangement in utilitarian terms: you'll get a good economy this way, a good army. But he continually defines it in aesthetic terms, as a harmony that reflects the order of reality. Certainly ideas such as virtue or karma, for example, are aesthetic at their core, and a virtuous soul is a beautiful soul. Aristotle's location of the virtues at the mean between extremes is an aesthetic-moral system, a celebration of balance that is reflected in his treatment of almost every kind of subject matter, from physics to biology to poetry. The soul one strives to achieve through the cultivation of the Aristotelian virtues is satisfying to contemplate, centered, symmetrical, reasonable, whole.

Thus, again, political aesthetics does not insist that we cease offering a moral as well as an aesthetic critique or celebration of various political systems; it only insists that we acknowledge the aesthetic dimensions of ethics and politics, and take them seriously as, among other things, pertinent to moral description and evaluation. Indeed none of these dimensions can be extracted from the others. Obviously, epistemic values are connected to moral values and any other values in an absolutely fundamental or foundational way. That is, there cannot be a moral system or principle that does not make a claim to truth, and most ethical systems deal at least in a oblique way—and many in an extremely elaborate way—with moral epistemology: questions about the epistemic status of moral claims; how they could be verified, supported, or refuted; what sort of evidence would count for or against moral claims; the relation of moral claims to empirical evidence, and so on. So to the extent that aesthetic values are fundamental to epistemic evaluations, they are fundamental too to moral evaluations. The abstract principles make a truth claim, and their application to particular cases of course depends on the accurate portrayal of those cases. Moral deliberation is constantly concerned with the truth. But truth is constantly concerned with a comprehensible shape or structure, with a place within a system or nexus or chaos, and with questions of accurate representation.

To reemphasize, I am not saying that all values are identical to aesthetic values and that there are not cases in which the question is primarily moral or epistemic rather than aesthetic. This certainly arises in situations where the aesthetics is fixed or where a system of rationality or principles of justice are widely agreed upon; there a political discussion may broach nothing interestingly or foundationally aesthetic. And were I writing a different book, I might move the other way and try to show the epistemic and moral aspects of aesthetic judgments. What justifies political aesthetics as a line of inquiry, however, is simply that, at the foundation, epistemic and moral claims about political arrangements implicate aesthetic criteria, that the various dimensions of value are distinct only as a matter of convenience within a particular subject matter or debate, for example. But that we can try to wall off aesthetic considerations in a discussion of an election or a regime is one thing; that the dimensions of evaluation which we employ in such contexts can be conceptually distinguished from one another in a principled way is something else. They cannot be.

Art as Politics

The question of whether all art is political picks out a central dilemma in political aesthetics. I think the question is too general as it stands: certainly there is no style that may not reveal political implications, and certainly all art reflects the experience and social resources of its maker, which are partly fixed by political factors. Modes of artistic production, such as handcraft or industrial manufacturing, have political as well as aesthetic entailments. But while no art should be eliminated as a possible datum, I think we should acknowledge that aesthetic objects are often made with no political or economic program in mind, and we should take with some seriousness their demand to be considered as something other than political statements.

The abstract expressionists no doubt had political opinions, but anyone who wanted to show that these were directly presented in their work, or that their work was a kind of agitprop, would be barking up the wrong tree, specifically because they would be ignoring the character and origin of the object in a consciously apolitical or antipolitical practice. An exclusively political or economic reading (a Marxist reading, for example) of abstract expressionism would be an attenuated and unfortunate one. Nevertheless,

abstract expressionism arises in certain very specific social/political/eco-
nomic circumstances, which obviously bear on its character. The very with-
drawal of art from the hurly-burly of political or economic power is itself a
political decision, one that could be made only under a certain specific set of
social circumstances, institutions, economy, and political practices. Refusal to
participate politically, or to use one's art politically, or to allow one's art to be
used politically, is a political decision. And indeed, the disengagement of such
works from the political is one reason why people like Hitler condemned
modernism as kitsch. So the question of whether "all art is political" is an
ambiguous one.

I am definitely not promoting a program for the politicization of the
arts. On the one hand, if you want to paint pictures of George Bush as a
chimpanzee, or mushroom clouds, or Che, I say more power to you. I do
not condemn any art on the sheer grounds that it has political content. But
on the other hand, I am not demanding such content, and if you want to
sing about lost love, or paint monochromes, or throw useful pots without
considering very carefully the political context in which you're working or
the location of your works within that context, I will not carp (probably).
As the art world of the last thirty years or more has shown, the obligation
to push justice forward with every little gesture is boring and of doubtful
efficacy. Certainly, as far as the program of political aesthetics is concerned,
there is no reason not to condemn art that is didactic, hectoring, repetitive, or
a sheer expression of ideology. Political aesthetics suggests that the political
is one important dimension of understanding in the arts (as it suggests that
the aesthetic is one important dimension of understanding in politics), but
by no means does it suggest that there are no other important dimensions.
And more importantly—or at least more to the point of this book—political
aesthetics suggests that the arts are a central aspect of all political life, but not
that they are the only aspect of political life. All art has a political context.
But not all art has a political message.

Political Dimensions of Aesthetic Values

Beauty

Asking whether a political system is beautiful might seem...precious.
What we want, we might say, is a political system that works, whatever that
might mean, rather than one that looks good not working, whatever *that*
might mean. Perhaps the French monarchy in the seventeenth and eighteenth centuries was beautiful. That doesn't mean it shouldn't have been

overthrown and its principals publicly executed; and one feature of some segments of the French Revolution was an anti-aesthetic drawn from a critique of the ancien régime. On the other hand, the beauty of political systems, such as it is, serves many possible real functions. Take a High Renaissance, classical, Palladian aesthetic of humanism, clarity, balance, and make a political system by its standards: perhaps you'd get something like the American triune system of checks and balances. That the overall shape of the American political system is clear is—demonstrably, I think—the result of aesthetic attention and understanding; it is quite self-consciously a style, saturated in classicism. But it is also central to making the system comprehensible to the people who operate under it or for that matter those who operate it, and in producing and defining allegiance.

One of the most traditional definitions of "beauty," and one of the most plausible, given how hard a term it is to define, is that beauty is unity in variety. Trying to cash this out will embroil you in a thousand amazing and interminable arguments, but this could be at least a useful way to start to think about the formal elements in painting, for example, or what distinguishes absorbing from irritating drama. Francis Hutcheson wrote, "What we call Beautiful in Objects, to speak in the Mathematical Style, seems to be in a compound Ratio of Uniformity and Variety; so that where the Uniformity of Bodys is equal, the Beauty is as the Variety; and where the Variety is equal, the Beauty is as the Uniformity" (Hutcheson, p. 29). This is obviously not particularly precise or clear, even though it seems more precise and clear than some definitions of this notoriously indefinable term. But it is striking that it represents the coordination problems faced by an artist in a way that might just as well apply to the purposes of political systems: coordination of disparate elements into some sort of unified whole. In this, politics responds to our need to belong, or is an expression of that need, and an inspiring politics places the citizen in the context of a well-arranged whole, or makes the identities of the parts flow from the character of the whole. Indeed Aristotle, considering the question of the proper size of the state, says, "Beauty is realized in number and magnitude, and the state which combines magnitude with good order must necessarily be most beautiful" (Aristotle, 1326a33–35) and hence best.

In this regard one might think of the function of the term "democracy," which is used both in a wide variety of senses and with regard to a wide variety of objects. In John Dewey's philosophy, for example, "democracy" becomes a term for the way a culture conducts its inquiries or generates knowledge: Dewey connects democracy with science, which is, ideally, open to criticism from any quarter, which requires freedom of expression to find truth, or uses freedom to find truth. His educational theories flow directly from what a democracy requires of its citizens, and how democratic institutions treat people (students in this case). Every aspect of Dewey's desired social transformation flows from this ideal: from economic and political policies and institutions to the way paintings ought to be displayed (à la the Barnes Foundation of Philadelphia). So the system is unified in a single concept, more or less. But the concept itself is, in Dewey's hands, supposed to encourage variety in lifestyles and opinions. Dewey's democracy is a pluralistic politics, but that variety is created by the application of a single principle:

> Democracy is belief in the ability of human experience to generate the aims and methods by which further experience will grow in ordered richness. Every other form of moral and social faith rests upon the idea that experience must be subjected at some point or other to some form of external control; to some "authority" alleged to exist outside the processes of experience. Democracy is the faith that the process of experience is more important than any special result attained, so that special results achieved are of ultimate value only as they are used to enrich and order the ongoing process. Since the process of experience is capable of being educative, faith in democracy is all one with faith in experience and education. . . .
>
> Democracy as compared with other ways of life is the sole way of living which believes wholeheartedly in the process of experience as end and as means; as that which is capable of generating the science which is the sole dependable authority for the direction of further experience. (Dewey 2, p.232)

Dewey's characterization of art will connect it directly to democracy, and hence also to education and science:

> Wherever perception has not been blunted and perverted, there is an inevitable tendency to arrange events and objects with reference to the demands of complete and unified experience. Form is a character of every experience that is an experience. Art in its specific sense enacts more deliberately and fully the conditions that effect this unity. Form may then be defined as the operation of forces that carry the experience of an event, object, scene, and situation to its own integral fulfillment. (Dewey 1, p. 137)

It is interesting that Dewey uses the notion of "form" here. For one thing, he is rejecting the idea of form that one finds in such "formalists" as Clive Bell: form for Dewey is the shape of the real world in experience, or the ways the real world is shaped in interaction with an organism. Then the question of political form is also a question of the aesthetic, of the features that unify experiences and persons into coherent wholes. Dewey's philosophy is an extreme application of the identity of politics and art (though there are also some fairly vaguely enunciated differentiations), but it is far from a precious aestheticization of politics; if anything it is a plea to regard art itself as a matter of life and death, freedom and totalitarianism, knowledge and ignorance. In its unified variety, Dewey's is a beautiful democratic politics.

Dewey is not a utopian; he is a meliorist: democracy is preferable as a system that develops openly over time. But we could think of utopias as political visions of beauty. This would be a profitable angle from which to understand Plato's *Republic,* for instance, with its nested tripartite divisions of individual soul, polis, and universe. It's an amazing achievement, a beautiful design. That is of course not to say that it's true, and indeed its beauty might be a seriously problematic aspect of it, because it attracts adherents, as it attracted the interlocutors in the *Republic,* to what is, in the final analysis, a totalitarian vision. One might say it is too beautiful to be true, or rather that its particular variety of beauty—temporally frozen, for one thing—is incompatible with truth (ironically, since that is exactly what Plato takes as the mark of truth). Beauty is always, among other things, seduction, and in deploying its aesthetic, a vision of beauty can be seductive epistemically, ethically, politically. And many people have actually been seduced by beauty into doing evil. This is surely one way to understand the arts in fascism. But it does not mean that beauty is dispensable in politics. We have never seen a politics that dispenses with it entirely, and we would not want to; it would ignore, in its basic configuration, a primary source of allegiance, satisfaction, and understanding.

Of course there are many approaches to the idea of beauty, but even the most subjective or affective have political ramifications. I myself have defined beauty, vaguely enough, as "the object of longing" (Sartwell 3), and here again we might think of the utopian tradition as the attempt to make a beautiful political system, a politics that is a worthy object of longing. Politics traffics in transformation. It is always promising to satisfy one's longings, whether for autonomy or belonging, for cash or power or security or identity. And though I have tended to emphasize the "scientific" aesthetic standards—simplicity, scope, and clarity, for example—there are beautiful things that do not display these qualities, and even systems for understanding beauty that deploy the opposite standards. For certain purposes in certain cultures a state might be hyper-baroque, romantic, Byzantine, mannerist, and so on, and it has been a real attack on liberal republicanism that its state and nation are not sufficiently rich, strange, and mysterious. The rich, strange, mysterious, bewilderingly complex, teeming, or incomprehensible: these too are objects of longing. Indeed one might suspect that these two basic aesthetic standards oscillate systematically, that it is quite possible to feel oppressed by too much clarity as well as by too much mystery, and when you find yourself in one situation or the other, to strike out in the opposite direction.

I suppose that if there's anything sweet or touching about human transactions of power, it is the longing that creeps into them, the moments that are not pure cynicism, or are impure cynicism, the moments of a yearning for pure justice that we see in utopians of all stripes; the itty-bitty objects of ideology, like train sets. This is a vision of beauty always as much as it is an ethical stake or commitment, poignantly expressed by Christian "perfectionists" of the early American republic such as John Humphrey Noyes or the Shakers: we are all already redeemed; transcendence is immanence, Grünewald's tortured and transcendent Christs simultaneously.

Be this as it may, we might point out that the modern bureaucratic state is not a beautiful thing, and that it's not trying to be. Its ugliness, we might say, is an aesthetic sign of its usefulness and its frugality, though of course it is wildly useless and infinitely expensive. If the modern bureaucratic state builds housing projects or schools, they will be pointedly ugly as a way of emphasizing their pure utilitarian purpose, and this is one reason why they will be defaced and eventually imploded. The bleakness of the modern landscape of the state is the product of a scientistic era of extreme gigantic pervasive pseudo-rationality in which the social sciences provide the occasions or the rhetoric of policies; the ugliness is a measure of seriousness and usefulness, and a mark of the fact that the planning has taken place on a gigantic scale. The built environment does not grow up like a forest a little at a time every which way. It is conceived as a whole and then executed systematically.

This, we might say, is a mark of the expansion of longing: it is human longing inflated to a terrific scale, enabled by technology. Or we might say that it is the essence of technology, a transformation of the universe to accord more closely with human desire: "planning." The style is encapsulated in communist architecture, but is no less pervasive as a conception in western Europe and North America. It is a pointed rejection of beauty as a standard in the built environment and hence is itself an aesthetic. And it expresses at its heart an overwhelming desire; it is longing on a gigantic scale for a wholly transformed and humanized world. At its heart, therefore, it is beauty or the desire for beauty, and it is of course a bit sad that in a longing to transform the world we make things of extreme ugliness. The modern mega-school, prison, hospital, housing project are poignant in their ugliness, all too human in their suspension of human scale and individual expression.

The same is true of the modern state as a whole in its spreadsheet distribution of functions, its gigantism and the extreme refinement of roles that this gigantism requires. That a state could be constituted suddenly, in an intentional design, was an innovation that depended especially on the situation of distant colonies in relation to the motherland, in the case of the United States. And though most of the founders of the American republic envisioned a fairly small state, gigantism was implicit in the conception: one made of the state an intentional design, and hence began to regard the whole human surround as a craft object, arranged persons no less than bricks. Human beings cease to be nature and come to be culture, and we admire a society—if indeed we can really admire any society—in the way we admire a sculpture, not in the way we admire a mountain. This removes from ourselves our mystery to ourselves, or perhaps simply represses it, making it all the more mysterious. The desire to design societies as a whole has many dimensions—epistemic, as rationality; ethical, as making distributive justice a possibility; but definitely aesthetic as well. And though the modern bureaucratic state makes ugly things, we might say that it does so in a vision of beauty, in an attempt to simplify the world and ourselves and make it and ourselves comprehensible and useful.

In turning both the human and built environments to account, in making them the subjects of explicit design, we try to expunge many beauties—all the beauties, indeed, bound up with the mysteries of our traditions, all the beauties emerging unexpectedly from millions of decisions. Compare, for example, Paris to the Pentagon. But of course we institute other beauties, and even the modernist rectangular edifice can call out our love and longing, precisely in its intimidation or trans-human scale. Nobody explicitly purports to find bureaucracy beautiful, but people can love it and want it nevertheless; its beauty is concealed in its own commitment to ugliness, or is hidden within the ugliness, or even actually is its ugliness.

In the 1890s George Santayana defined beauty as "objectified pleasure." The idea was that beauty is a quality like "red." We regard redness as a quality of objects, but really it is a contribution of our consciousness. A different sort of perceptual apparatus would perceive different colors, or no colors at all. We consistently regard qualities of our experience as qualities of the objects that cause them. So, for example, we think of a melody as sad. Santayana thought beauty was like that: it is our pleasure, a subjective state, taken in some material presented to our senses, and attributed to the object itself as an intrinsic quality and an emanation. This is an interesting view, as it crystallizes an entire line of thought about beauty that you see in one form or another in the British empiricists and Scottish common sense philosophers, in Kant and Burke and Schopenhauer, that connects beauty to pleasure, or finds in pleasure of a certain kind the cause and purpose of beauty.

Santayana's *Sense of Beauty* was perhaps the last major treatment of beauty in the tradition. Beauty, which used to gad about with truth and goodness and justice in the pantheon of ultimate values, got kicked downstairs to the department of hairstyling. We might try to figure out how something so exalted could come in for such ignominious treatment in philosophy, but above all in art of the twentieth century.

My idea is that the connection of beauty to pleasure is one factor in the deep suspicion that beauty has aroused in art since the early twentieth century. What I think really lies at the center of the situation is what we might call the politics of pleasure, and it seems to me that the rejection of beauty in art and elsewhere is essentially a result of the connection of beauty to the politics of the right, from the traditions of the Catholic Church, to the European aristocracy, to the rise of the capitalist ownership class, to fascism and the Third Reich. The association of beauty with right-wing politics associates it also with all the depredations inflicted on humanity by Catholicism, monarchism, nationalism, capitalism, and fascism. Concepts, even supernal concepts such as beauty, have histories. And beauty has come to be associated with the massively complex, historical political Right, as, we might say, justice has come to be with the Left: the Left and Right are fighting over Italy, let's say, but also over the Realm of the Forms, Beauty as against Justice.

One node of the opposition to beauty is the Protestant Reformation. The most elaborate and beautiful building in every major European city is the cathedral, often encrusted with ornament: stained glass, for instance. When Luther called the Catholic Church "the whore of Babylon," he was referring especially to the cosmetic arts of prostitutes in connection with the ornaments of the church, in particular in the High Renaissance: at once a squandering of wealth and a sign of worldliness, an idolatry or worship of things. So the Reformation was accompanied by a wave of iconoclasm, and a Protestant church is notably plainer and more austere than a Catholic church. The Protestant denominations actually rejected beauty as vanity, but of course the very plainness, simplicity, and austerity of Protestant architecture has its own beauty (consider the Shakers).

We get a secular analogue to this in the French Revolution. And I would say our sense of what "beauty" means in the arts is still to some extent frozen in time as what the French revolutionaries rejected: the rococo. Now, there are many sorts of beauties: conflicted beauties, painful beauties, simple beauties, and so on. But rococo beauty is dedicated to sheer decadent visual pleasure, hyper-elaborated, frivolous in the extreme. It's in the painting, but it's also in the architecture, the landscapes, the outfits. In other words, the French monarchy was characterized by a particular variety of beauty, one devoted to pleasure, delighting in frivolity, in short, hedonist. And what is perhaps more important, extremely expensive: just dressing Marie Antoinette and her ladies, as is notorious, had the effect of throwing the French budget into deficit. We explicitly take the bread from your mouths so that we can have amazing drapes. The origin of the modern Left lies in the thought and events leading to and then emerging from the French Revolution: the avatar is Rousseau. And the initial response was classical in both politics and the arts. Rousseau himself argued for the simple satisfaction of needs, for dignity and simplicity of furnishings and clothing, for a republican citizenry. And the French Revolution was, of course, a neoclassical revolution, a wave of revulsion directed at the rococo in every respect as not merely a symbol of corruption but its very body.

But the French Revolution proceeded from a neoclassical cleanup of imagery and architecture to an iconoclastic outburst: the critique was extended to the very idea of the aesthetic, or perhaps of pleasure at all. One way we might put this: being in a state of pleasure could be conceived to be unjust in a case where others are in pain. Certainly, for example, it is unjust to create one's own pleasures through the pain of others, a kind of societal sadism. So, for example, working peasants to death to make a nice topiary garden seems wrong. But this burden becomes somewhat more generalized: it's wrong to take pleasure, or at least to pursue pleasure, where other people are suffering. Of course, whatever time and energy you are spending on your little pleasures could be turned to some productive account: helping people or overthrowing the exploitative system. The pursuit of mere pleasure in a world of suffering is frivolous, stupid, and wrong.

These doctrines harden into ideology under the aegis of Marxism. To begin with, the arts themselves are understood as superstructure, concealing or revealing, but epiphenomenal to, the fundamental relations of production. Early Marx finds beauty in the slightly idyllic medieval economy of craft guilds; there's a little romantic hangover. And early Marx is capable of identifying the ugliness of industrial capitalism as one of its drawbacks. But as Marxism picks up steam, the whole question of beauty comes to seem frivolous, otiose; and folks like Lenin or Stalin or Mao weren't trying to devise new conceptions of beauty but, at least in ideology, rejecting it entirely. Here one should consult Stalinist architecture of the sort one can still see in eastern

Europe. Beauty, associated at the beginnings of the modern Left with royalism, comes by the end of the modern Left to be associated with capitalism. Nor is this a crazy idea; if you go to, say, the National Gallery in Washington, D.C., or the Metropolitan in New York, you'll keep running into names like Mellon, Carnegie, Rockefeller: breaking strikes and bodies, and collecting pretty pictures to demonstrate their exaltation and their wealth.

The political conniptions of art since the French Revolution have been spectacular. Let me mention a few high points. One excellent leftist move, after neoclassicism itself had been discredited by, among other things, its appropriation by Napoleon, was realism of the sort championed by Courbet. Courbet was a friend of the great anarchist Proudhon, whom he painted, and he participated in the iconoclastic rearrangement of Paris in the 1871 Commune, pulling down the Vendôme column and its statue of Napoleon. But Courbet's work itself was polemical and political: it displayed the condition of the peasantry and workers, and had as its purpose the remaking of their condition. And it proudly, pointedly eschewed beauty, though it is very important to note that Courbet's paintings are often beautiful nevertheless. Courbet could only have emerged before the domination of Marxism in the world Left was complete.

In 1914 a suffragist named Mary Richardson slashed Velázquez's *Rokeby Venus*. She said she didn't like the way men gawked at it. And in the connection of beauty to pleasure, we have to see that the idea of beauty is fundamentally erotic. Indeed, the nude body is the great subject of both Greek and Renaissance art. The pleasures of beauty, describe them as chastely as we like, are at their heart sexual pleasures. But as the *Venus* case shows, sexuality is highly politically problematic; depicting it is at once decadent, trivial, and profoundly oppressive. Pornography is central to patriarchy, and it's not crazy to think of the *Rokeby Venus* as soft-core porn for the well-heeled.

Art is expensive, patronage is cash, and even appreciating the results of all this requires leisure. But even for the aristocratic or capitalist arts patron, beauty conceived in terms of pleasure is a problem. When a Mellon or Rockefeller devotes himself to the arts, he wants to signify, first, his transcendence of commerce. So there has to be value in it that money can't buy, even though, of course, money buys it. And second, patronage of the arts displays one's high-mindedness; it cannot merely be a matter of pleasure, else it's just more sybaritic decadence. But one thing that every reactionary regime of beauty—from the church to the French monarchy to the Third Reich—has in common is amazing funding, itself a measure of the exploitation or extortion that it wields. That is, beauty in each case is associated with wealth, and wealth with exploitation. That is, again, beauty is regarded as being pitted, in the Realm of the Forms, against justice: the more beauty, the less justice.

So I would say that if art gives us beauty, and beauty is to be understood in terms of pleasure, then no one wants to take it seriously, and all of us in our hearts think it ought to be repressed. And at the best of times, pleasure cloys and one reaches surfeit. So Rubens, for example, or Renoir, is too beautiful by half. Idiotically hedonistic, we might say. Or the Pre-Raphaelites: reactionaries at least within art. Now, one constituency of all this is artists themselves. They don't want to regard themselves as craftspeople, having emerged in romanticism as little gods. They're not making useful objects but transforming the world. And somehow their art has to be rendered compatible with their political commitments, and with the very fact that they have any political commitments; it has to be something with the seriousness of justice, or else it's just more high-toned decorating. And as Arthur Danto argues, the rejection of beauty in the arts was a rejection of the society that valued it.

> The concept of beauty became abruptly politicized by the avant-garde around 1915....It became that in part as an attack on the position under which art and beauty were internally linked, as were beauty and goodness. And the "abuse" of beauty became a device for dissociating the artists from the society they held in contempt...It is Dada to which I refer in the project of disconnecting beauty from art as an expression of moral revulsion against a society for whom beauty was a cherished value, and which cherished art itself because of beauty. (Danto 1, p. 48)

Danto proceeds to quote Max Ernst: "To us, Dada was above all a moral reaction. Our rage aimed at total subversion. A horrible futile war had robbed us of five years of our existence. We had experienced the collapse into ridicule and shame of everything represented to us as just, true, and beautiful. My works of that period were not meant to attract, but to make people scream" (Danto 1, p. 48).

The renunciation of beauty in modern art is a claim that what the artist does can at least be compatible with justice, or with radical politics: that art is not mere self-indulgence or decadence or the making of high-class consumer goods or status objects. And it is also one node of the claim that what the artist does is of the utmost importance (though the dadaists among others played with this status ironically): the romantic notion of the artist since, perhaps, Beethoven, as someone remaking the world rather than, say, merely reflecting it, or for that matter decorating or ornamenting it. For the sake of their self-esteem and in order to take themselves seriously, once beauty is associated with pleasure and decadence, not to speak of oppression, artists can no longer regard beauty as what motivates them.

The association of beauty with right-wing politics, and right-wing politics with pleasure, really embodies a very dark moment in the history of our species insofar as right-wing politics has been implicated in genocide, war, and dictatorial oppression. That Riefenstahl's images are pleasurable no one doubts. But insofar as one finds them so, one begins to doubt not only the construction of beauty in art but also the potential destructiveness of one's own pleasures. In fact, that Riefenstahl never doubted the legitimacy of the pleasure she herself took in beauty, that she dismissed every attempt to connect this experience to the moral or political sphere, itself constituted her evil.

Nevertheless, we cannot, it seems to me, jettison beauty; what we need to do is try to enrich the concept and detach it from pleasure, to see it in its widest ramifications and expressions. I think we still need beauty, and that beauty is more or less than politics. I'm a universalist about beauty in this sense: I think the experience of beauty expresses a set of basic human capacities and dilemmas, something that all people seek. To repeat, I've defined beauty as "the object of longing," and though people long for different things in different ways for different reasons, we all long. Beauty is unsatisfied or unsatisfiable desire—impossible aspiration, we might say—and is inherent in the experience of loss. We are always in the process of losing everything we have and everything we are. Loss and longing are a condition of an erotic or desiring life in time, a fundamental condition and dimension of human experience of the world.

Thus there are political uses of beauty; there are political interpretations of beauty; but beauty is ineradicable and exceeds the political. First of all, every rejection of beauty on religious, political, or economic grounds itself constitutes a variety of beauty or deploys a counter-beauty. This is completely obvious with regard to Protestantism, and the idea of perfect craft as a form of worship, labor as prayer, that we find in the Shakers, for example, yields objects as perfectly beautiful as the Sistine ceiling, but with a precisely opposite beauty. The idea of beauty as function which we see even in modernist architecture, for example, is a basically Protestant aesthetic, ethics, and politics. Even the yearning for justice, which we have just seen contrasted with aestheticism, is a yearning for beauty; justice is at its very heart aesthetic, and tries to show or make a universe of balance, harmony, symmetry, as I and many others have argued.

If beauty was discredited by its association with the oppressive Right, then perhaps anti-aesthetics has been discredited by the totalitarian Left. Stalin and Mao, of course, never stopped producing imagery, architecture, music.

But their rejection of aestheticism just led to bad art and architecture: funny socialist realist posters but also bleak industrial or urban landscapes stretching as far as the eye can see. So the association of beauty with the Right, and with luxury goods or obscene displays of wealth, is tendentious. And so also is the rejection of aesthetics by the Left, which is only the result of a particular Marxism, and which is itself an aesthetic position. There are many other beauties: beauty is deployed on behalf of every and any political agenda or none at all. Let's think about the music of Bob Marley, for instance. Beautiful. But not fascist, hyper-capitalist, or church-sponsored.

I'm not one of these people who think pleasure will save us. That's an understandable response, for one thing, to the brutal anti-aesthetics of the totalitarian Left. For example, Foucault toward the end of his life suggested again and again that pleasure was a subversive force. Indeed the forces arrayed against pleasure have been formidable. First of all, the whole communist-type Left. The Protestant churches. The work ethic. A world crying aloud for justice, and so on. Even the aestheticization of politics in fascism is highly problematic with regard to pleasure, because Riefenstahl's films or Albert Speer's architecture *turns pleasure to account,* or associates it with labor and ultimately with genocide. In a way Riefenstahl's films, beautiful as they are, are too serious to be pleasurable.

But hedonism is not revolutionary, and if everyone just drank, danced, had sex, and looked at Pre-Raphaelite paintings all the time, we wouldn't last very long. I think we need pleasure, but I think we need the moment of turning away from pleasure. If beauty is a pleasure, it has betrayed us into the vice that lies at the dark heart of pleasure, seduced us, made us evil. I think, though, that the problem really lies in the identification of beauty with pleasure. Beauty can be pleasurable, and certain beauties are pleasurable in the proper sense: pleasant. Fun, but trivial. But other beauties are more interesting, or maybe they take us via a pleasurable surface to depths of all kinds—moral, metaphysical, epistemic, existential. Even Riefenstahl's films show this structure: the seductive surface and the terrifying annihilating abyss.

Plato, in the *Symposium,* argued that love and sexuality are responses to beauty, that beauty calls out love. But then he argued that love of pretty people (boys) calls us to something deeper (so to speak), that we learn love of knowledge and, possibly, of God by loving the particular beautiful body. This is the thought that shapes Neoplatonism as an artistic movement. It's the thought you see, for example, embodied in a Raphael Madonna. Beauty calls to us to long, and we long through the beautiful thing or person to . . . whatever we long for: enlightenment, death, an erasure or expansion of consciousness, merger, true belonging, God, everything. This is why the beautiful surface can be turned to political account; itself apparently innocent, it calls out to whatever is in us, longing, innocent and not.

This is one reason why beauty is not pleasure: it brings us through pleasure to the human condition, or works on us through our pleasures to transform us. This is what makes it potentially evil. But of course it's also what makes us potentially good. Beauty is not trivial, or not necessarily trivial. It always has a seductive power, or carries with it the potential of a loss or intensification of the self. Kant and a thousand other romantic philosophers were right that beauty is beyond good and evil, but only in the sense that it can be turned to either use or beyond such uses. Beauty has the power both to free and to manipulate us. One is right, that is, to associate beauty with power, with danger, and with evil, in a thousand ways. There is a reason why the Disney evil queen is the fairest and the nastiest of all: she has a power that is preternatural; we are potentially her slaves, for her beauty's sake. Her beauty disguises, we might say, the corruption within and broadcasts that corruption as a contagion. Beauty in this sense is surface, a disguise. But the surface is anything but superficial, and all the many possible relations of surface and depth are called into play in beauty. The beautiful soul shines forth in the face, or is found underneath the ugliness. Beauty, we might say, is semiotic in every possible way: a sign of goodness or of evil, a semiotics of surface to surface or depth to depth, surface against depth, depth against surface; always a sign, fraught with moral or epistemic significance, a route to God or the devil, but always transporting us, taking us somewhere we aren't—yet.

What I want to say is that, first, the experience of beauty is inherent in our condition. Despite where the political critique goes, there's no rejecting it; the most we can do, or really should want to do, is to rearticulate it, reappropriate it, and reconceive it. This is constantly in process: beauty, as much as Europe, for example, has been a battleground. The impulse to close down on beauty, to take it, define it, use it, is the totalitarian impulse, whether of the Catholic Church, the monarchy, or the Reich, but also the communist dictatorship. The attempt to destroy or devalue beauty is simply an attempt to truncate or simplify human experience, itself an aesthetic impulse, spinning off beauties as fast as it can. What we need is not to embrace or resist all beauties but to let beauty go, accept it and see what happens. There could, after all, be a liberatory pursuit of beauty: untheorized, antiprogrammatic. Marley's music might be a good model: beauty emerging from some funky cult, and a revolutionary movement, made in collaborations of all kinds but subject to open creative decision making. Not meaningless frippery, the music turned to account. But supremely pleasurable for all that too, and dedicated to sex, love, and skank, but also to a vision of universal human liberation.

Sublimity

The rise of aesthetics and aesthetic political theory in the eighteenth century corresponds with a revival of the ancient concept of sublimity, which gets more than cursory treatments in Kant, Burke, and many others. Let's briefly contrast sublimity to beauty. Whereas beautiful objects are usually circum-scribed—as, for example, an individual human body, a flower, a painting, a fugue—the sublime is an effect we might term global or environmental, and also amorphous, without clear boundaries. Whereas the beautiful is an object of contemplation and distance, the sublime envelops or embeds us, and threatens us with dissolution into itself. Longinus' most famous example is Aetna, and the eighteenth-century figures tended to grab the storm at sea. In general, the eighteenth century treats the object of beauty as a product of mind; but the sublime object is a threat to mind, though this could also be treated as a dissolution following on expansion, and the sublime treated as an aspect or dimension of consciousness at its limit. Yet the experience of sublimity nevertheless requires an aesthetic distance, and in this case is a dem-onstration that we can achieve disinterestedness even, precisely, in the face of cataclysm or catastrophe. This would be a kind of stoic aesthetics: it asserts that although we may not be in charge of whether we are swept overboard to a watery grave, we are in charge of whether it really bothers us; indeed the sublime suggests that even one's own death could be an aesthetic object, though not (without all the dressings of theatrical tragedy) a beautiful object. Beautiful things are characterized by unity in variety, proportion, harmony, and so on; sublime things tear these features apart. Indeed we might think of the sublime as an attempt to account philosophically for aesthetic experi-ences that could not be encompassed in the rather staid or safe conceptions of beauty current in the eighteenth century. Kant writes:

> Might is that which is superior to great hindrances. It is called domin-ion if it is superior to the resistance of that which itself possesses might. Nature considered in an aesthetical judgment as might that has no dominion over us, is dynamically sublime.
>
> If nature is to be judged by us as dynamically sublime, it must be represented as exciting fear (although it is not true conversely that every object which excites fear is regarded in our aesthetical judgment as sublime). For in aesthetical judgments (without the aid of concepts) superiority to hindrances can only be judged according to the great-ness of the resistance. Now that which we are driven to resist is an evil, and, if we do not find our faculties a match for it, is an object of fear. Hence nature can be regarded by the aesthetical judgment as might,

and consequently as dynamically sublime, only so far as it is considered an object of fear. But we can regard an object as fearful, without being afraid of it; viz. if we judge of it in such a way that we merely think a case in which we would wish to resist it, and yet in which all resistance would be altogether vain. (Kant 2, pp. 99–100)

What I want to point up in such remarks, extremely typical of the eighteenth-century discourse on sublimity, is not any particular argument that Kant makes about purposiveness, nature, or God, but the infestation of the account by political categories from the outset: here, dominion and resistance. As in many accounts of sublimity of the period, the basic examples are huge natural phenomena observed under certain conditions, the gigantic architecture of St. Peter's and the Pyramids, certain passages of poetry (such as the fall of angels in Milton's *Paradise Lost*), and God: objects in relation to which the human body seems puny. Whatever any of its thinkers thought about the source of the sublime, it is obvious that it can be annexed as a political category or strategy, that to the extent that it can be achieved in artifacts or collective action, it can intimidate, overwhelm, make one seek a place of safety, that it can express sovereignty or dominion, that it can call out the impulse to resistance or at a certain pitch make resistance seem obviously futile. The history of totalitarianism—up until Kant writes but especially thereafter—is a history of the sublimization of human power relations, the projection of dominion in gigantic effects, or the imitation of nature and nature's God by the political authorities. There is something pitiable in such efforts, and Hitler or Stalin does not really stack up very well to volcanoes or interplanetary space as an object of the judgment of taste. Yet many of the effects are, literally, sublime, if such thinkers are right about the nature of sublimity. The sublimity of totalitarianism is not a joke, and in its medieval or romantic overwhelming of reason or excess to our capacities of understanding, its mystery and destructiveness, it is opposed to the beautiful, the classical, and the rational.

Above all, sublimity is connected to power of certain kinds. John Baillie, in his excellent *Essay on the Sublime* of 1747, writes:

It's not every power which is the ambition of a hero, nor every power which carries the idea of the sublime. A Caligula commanding armies to fill their helmets with cockle-shells, is a power mean and contemptible, although ever so absolute; but suppose an Alexander laying level towns, depopulating countries, and ravaging the whole world, how does the sublime rise, nay although mankind be the sacrifice to his ambition!...Thus our idea of power is more or less sublime, as the power is more or less extended. The absolute power of a master over his slaves, is a power nothing grand; yet the same authority in a prince is sublime.—But why? from his sway extending to multitudes, and from nations bowing to his commands. But it is in the almighty that this sublime is completed, who with a nod can shatter to pieces the foundation of a universe, as with a word he called it into being. (Ashfield and de Bolla, p. 93)

Baillie even suggests that the extermination of the human race by a conqueror would be sublime...provided that the conqueror was of the right kind. The reversion to God's omnipotence is conventional, but here is perhaps indirectly criticized by a comparison to human absolutism. Nevertheless, mere power, even absolute power, is not, for Baillie, sublime; it becomes so by the scope and nature of its objects and effects. Sublime power, even if ferocious, even if evil, yields a sensation, we might say, of exaltation, a basically religious experience. Here is an extremely dangerous thought, which explicitly aestheticizes effects up to and including genocide, or the destruction of the world. This is not to say that Baillie and other thinkers did not also retain resources for a moral condemnation of absolute political power, but only that they also allowed themselves to feel its compelling aesthetic quality.

The political aesthetics of a Shaftesbury or a Schiller seem friendly and mellow in that they focus on beauty as a feature of the state and of the individual: free play of the faculties, spontaneous ordering of harmonies. But like the medieval church, the state in the nineteenth century, or following Napoleon (to whom Baillie might, of course, if he had been writing sixty years later, have compared Alexander), becomes capable of ever more sublime effects, extreme disruptions, destructions, re-articulations of the physical environment, threats to the whole population, an ever-intensifying dominion or sovereignty. The manmade disaster comes in the nineteenth century, and certainly by the twentieth, to rival the natural disaster, which is a model of the sublime. The natural disaster is, for the eighteenth century, for example, a way the world is remade, in comparison to which human intervention is puny. But in the nineteenth century, human beings become capable of sudden irrational pervasive transformations of the environment; human power becomes sublime. The Roman emperors promoted themselves to godhead. Hitler and Stalin didn't have to resort to such a merely symbolic act; they actually were gods in the sense that they could suddenly remake the countryside. If a volcano is sublime, so are high explosives, so are nuclear weapons, so is a dam that floods a region. The dictator sets himself up aesthetically in rivalry with nature. The eighteenth century could probably not quite foresee industrial sublimity, whole landscapes shrouded in steel and smoke. Technology became sublime, and industrial design became totalitarian, fully, only in the early twentieth century.

One way to read the development of romantic totalitarianism is to trace its shift from the beautiful to the sublime. Speer's work shows the structure very well. He made buildings more or less in perfect (classical) proportions. But he made them on an insanely gigantic scale that in itself entailed thorough transformations of whole environments. That is, through the techniques of beauty he created a sublime effect, an effect of overwhelming, crushing power. And he did that in full consciousness.

The beautiful comports, beautifully and rationally, with the rational in the Greeks. That's one way of stating the meaning of the classical. But in the politics of totalitarian sublimity, the human is exposed as itself an irrational nature and an unfolding natural disaster, no more rationally constrained than a supernova. This is one way that aestheticians and politicians flirt with the dark side: the sublime is one route through which evil enters the world. But even here we might point to the varied uses of power, antirationalism, and so on; and if Wagner gives us the totalitarian sublime as the very center of his work (even as a kind of liberation!), Thoreau and Kierkegaard, for example, allow the sublime to throw us into relation with the natural, or with ourselves, in a fundamentally decent way, or at least in a way strongly opposed to all totalitarianism. Where Speer makes the political sublime, Kierkegaard and Thoreau insist on the sublimity that contains or constrains the human, on the divine and the natural. From such standpoints, sublime standpoints, we might say, a critique of institutions or the "attack on Christendom" is possible, or necessitated.

The British treatments of the eighteenth century repeatedly hint at aspects of the sublime that are in excess of, or evade, or even underlie the aestheticization of sheer force. Indeed Baillie himself points to the sublimity of universal benevolence, or a sublime love that has as its object humanity or the world: God's good or non-scary sublimity, we might say, but also a human ethical sublimity. Addison, who would have been a fundamental source for Baillie, writes in *The Spectator* of 1712:

> The mind of man naturally hates every thing that looks like restraint upon it, and is apt to fancy itself under a sort of confinement, when the sight is pent up in a narrow compass, and shortened on every side by the neighborhood of walls or mountains. On the contrary, a spacious horizon is an image of liberty, where the eye has room to range abroad, to expatiate at large on the immensity of its views, and to lose

itself amidst the variety of objects that offer themselves to observation. Such wide and undetermined prospects are as pleasing to the fancy, as the speculations of eternity or infinitude are to the understanding. (Ashfield and de Bolla, p. 62)

By a nice reversal or deconstruction, Addison takes the sublime as an image not of power but of freedom, as scope, openness, a context of autonomy. One way to conceive an anti-totalitarian sublime would be in terms of the city, not as an object created by grand-scale planning and subsequent obliteration and reconstruction, but as an infinitely varied environment appearing through millions of uncoordinated decisions, a human nature. In fact even resistance in the face of oppression has its sublimity, as Joseph Priestley argued: "The *contempt* of power, wealth, and grandeur, is more sublime than the *possession* of them" (Ashfield and de Bolla, p. 122).

Here, as I hope we are seeing, is a theme typical of aesthetics in relation to politics. Aesthetic qualities are central for understanding political categories, infest them fundamentally. But the aesthetic always seems to cut both ways: it is always ambivalent or ambiguous in its political applications. The aesthetic is not exhausted by or thoroughly annexed by the political; they are orthogonal even as they are always correlated. No more than beauty can sublimity be exhausted by a particular political system or strategy, and for the political system to try to absorb or deploy it or dominate it is always to set in motion meanings in excess of its own purposes. Perhaps these meanings are contradictions to itself that display the weaknesses at which the coherence of the system and the system itself collapses. But in any case, though there is no politics without aesthetics, there is also no politics that can thoroughly dominate or domesticate aesthetics. Here is one possibility, we might say, of resistance.

When Burke discussed the sublime in 1756, he centralized several features that are both natural and artpolitical: the experience of terror; the obscurity of the cause; power; vastness; privation (vacuity, darkness, solitude, silence); infinity—blackness, night, amorphousness, uncontrollability, being faced with a power you cannot fully grasp or comprehend. He points this out immediately as a tyrannical strategy: "Those despotic governments, which are founded on the passions of men, and principally upon the passion of fear, keep their chief as much as may be from the public eye" (Burke, p. 60). And again: "The power which arises from institution in kings and commanders, has the same connection with terror. Sovereigns are frequently addressed with the title of *dread majesty*" (Burke, p. 57). Burke's famous attack on the French Revolution was partly an aesthetic attack on precisely these grounds: the Revolution laid claim to the classical but was embroiled in terror, kept insisting on its rationality but availed itself of the fear and obscurity of the sublime.

By the time we reach the Nazis, Riefenstahl is developing new film stock to shoot night scenes, and black is the color of power: a preternatural, indeterminate power, terror, irrationality, and obscurity. Burke (and Kant) appreciated the sublime as a source of the most intense possible aesthetic experience—for example, he quotes passages from Milton that famously evoked the sublime as among the greatest achievements of English poetry—but he knew it to be a threat to the classical artpolitical order he (and Milton) ultimately prized more. He enumerates some images of the sublime from Milton: "a tower, an archangel, the sun rising through mists, or in an eclipse, the ruin of monarchs, and the revolutions of kingdoms" (Burke, p. 53). This same contradiction, which lies at the heart of romanticism, with its simultaneous political agenda (often progressive) and privileging of irrationality and overwhelming aesthetic effects, is the center of fascist aesthetics and the actual exercise of totalitarian power even in leftism. It is worth noting again, however, the ambi-valence of the sublime: the king's power is sublime, but the kingdom's dissolution is also sublime.

In Burke, as for Baillie and many others, the most sublime thing is God, in whom all the aspects he enumerates appear in full force. Indeed we might say that this conception of God is at the center of the Protestant objection to Catholicism and of the association of Protestantism with classicism and republicanism in the eighteenth century. God is absolutely sublime. But the cathedral, aiming at sublime effects, is the creation of people and the sublime presentation of a human power hierarchy; it is idolatrous and comical, a human attempt to reproduce or image the absolute sublimity of deity. The repetition of the Pyramids and St. Peter's as examples of the sublime in architecture by Protestants such as Kant and Burke is not coincidental; they would have regarded both as the work of idolaters and political oppressors. Classical clarity, proportion, and humility, by contrast, are, though beautiful, human and humanist. They do not swathe human power in the mumbo-jumbo of the sublime. In the face of the totalitarian sublime, we ought continuously to demystify or show the mediocrity, the all-too-human center of the vast artificial and theatrical effects, the need or desperation that drives the dictator to a pretense of godhead.

That is, the sublimity of God can be used to show the tinsel of human political power, even the power of the church itself. The sublime broaches the absolute: omnipotence, annihilation, infinity, a mystical experience in which Protestantism has its origins. Ultimately it is the experience of the absolute, seen through finite effects. The dictator can imitate these effects, but always insufficiently, parodically. And that insufficiency itself is a fulcrum of a moral critique of totalitarianism as monstrous hubris: the comically finite little man scraping together tax dollars for his simulated apotheosis into infinity. The sublime, as in Kierkegaard, suggests the point of view of the actual infinite: the attempt to reproduce its effect in a military maneuver or urban planning strategy is always destined for bathos.

Representation

The centrality of the concept of representation to the political is a demonstration that the latter is always connected to the aesthetic. For centuries, representation was taken in the Western tradition to be the central function of the arts. Plato condemned most poetry and painting, and Aristotle defended them, on the basis of the idea that they were mimetic. But in neither Plato nor Aristotle should mimesis be thought of merely as "imitation"; it has the sense of manifesting or revealing something that it is not here, now, in the work, of standing in for something or marking it in consciousness. The idea of mimesis, we might say, is voodoo semiotics.

The ontological status of the state is a bit of a mystery to political philosophy, but I have argued elsewhere for something like this: a state is the reification or abstract representation of a government (Sartwell 1, chap. 2). And a government is a set of people, objects, procedures that exercise coercive power over a given geographical territory. Martin van Creveld writes:

> The state, then, is an *abstract* entity which can neither be seen, nor heard, nor touched. This entity is not identical with either the rulers or the ruled.... This is as much to say that the state ... is a corporation, just as universities, trade unions, and churches *inter alia* are.... Above all, it is a corporation in the sense that it possesses a legal *persona* of its own, which means that it has rights and duties and may engage in various activities *as if* it were a real, flesh-and-blood, living individual. The points where the state differs from other corporations are, first, the fact that it authorizes them all but is itself authorized (recognized) solely by others of its kind; secondly, that certain functions (known collectively as the attributes of sovereignty) are reserved for it alone; and, thirdly, that it exercises those functions over a certain territory inside which its jurisdiction is both exclusive and all-embracing. (van Creveld, p. 1)

That is, we might think of the state as a representation of a government (nation, people), a personification and reification of a highly diffuse, varied, and scattered object into a name and symbol, or into an agent.

But whatever else may be contained in a state, what the state is made of is in part a perfectly mundane set of physical objects, such as buildings, computers, uniforms, paper, and so on. The physical composition of a state is an aesthetically relevant feature, or a barrage of aesthetically relevant features, of it; so might its form be in some very abstract or supervenient sense, as in a balance of power between agencies or branches. If the state is a coercive power, then we might think of it, provisionally, as a certain sort of artisan, as this might be described in terms of "mastery." A great craftsman or artist is a skillful or masterly handler of materials, and this helps explain why the final result is pleasing, valuable, and useful. We could look upon the state—that imaginary or at least representational persona—or its most statesmanlike or at any rate the most effective of its leaders, as the artist(s) of peoples and places. This metaphor would have to be deployed with extreme care, as the material in this case includes people, who make a moral claim, and display an extreme recalcitrance to transformation. Nevertheless, the metaphor of the state or leader as artist is as old as political thought. And all or most craft materials display complex recalcitrances. Typically, radical, revolutionary, reactionary, and, in short, very ambitious regimes—and less ambitious regimes to a lesser extent—present themselves as craftsmen or artists of the social, molding or entirely reshaping their contexts. These various programs, of course, always fail, but only by their own astronomical utopian end-of-history standards; they certainly do reshape the material conditions under which people live, that is, their lives. But people are nasty stuff. One thing you've got to say for oil paint or wood: however influential the material is on the product, however recalcitrant it is to transformation, it cannot consciously fight back using weapons, opt out, or emigrate.

At any rate, this idea of the state as something that can remake the social and physical environment—whether as a work of art or theater—is central to the history of the idea of the state, and central to all statist political philosophies. If we think that there's something wrong with the current condition of culture, then we need to constitute a power sufficient to reshape it so that the state is presented as inevitable insofar as the present situation is unsatisfactory. The state as shaper or artist of the social is basically entailed in the context of modernity by a critical posture toward current social conditions; it apparently follows trivially from every program of reform. And in the transformation of these conditions, all the values—goodness, truth, beauty, and so on—are at play all the time, and they are all intertwined.

Several writers, notably Eric Michaud, have discussed the notion of the prince or ruler as artist, the people being his material. As Michaud points out, this certainly sounds like a totalitarian idea, and in illustration he produces a cartoon from the 1930s showing Hitler re-sculpting a clay German people into one great united Übermensch. But we find similar images throughout the literature of political systems. Plato availed himself of this metaphor continuously in the *Republic:* "Our first task then, we take it, is to mold the model of a happy state.... It is as if we were coloring a statue" (Plato 1, 420c). Machiavelli also deployed the metaphor of prince as artist. But in any case, any political system is about the business of shaping the social world, though always with very mixed success. The political organization of the British colonies into states, and then a plan for the coordination of these entities: these are political *arrangements* that affect the lives of everyone involved.

The shape of a society is, of course, not simply determined by the state; indeed even in totalitarian circumstances the ability of the state to remake social life is far more limited than it might like to believe. Myriads of conditions affect the shape of a culture: its technological proficiency; its economic arrangements; its geography; what's going on in other cultures and in what ways they come into contact with one another; each person's proficient or perverse decisions; the weather; epidemiology. Obviously even things that are not, all things considered, intentionally designed can have aesthetic aspects: sunsets or mountain ranges, for example. (In many cases the question of whether something was or was not intentionally designed is extremely complex and obscure: consider, let's say, a modern city.) Whether a state is in this regard more like a painting or more like a sunset is an interesting issue, and it bears very strongly on what aesthetic properties a thing can have. For example, I think that if something is not made intentionally, it lacks directly expressive qualities such as being sad or angry, at least in the same way or sense that an artifact, such as a work of art, can have them. Now, whether a *state* can express anger and sadness is an amusing question. Certainly there are states that seem, from an external point of view, sad, or confused, or vicious; but these terms are not necessarily being used in an aesthetic sense in such attributions, since the state is partly composed of persons who can be directly sad, confused, or vicious in a way that a painting cannot be, though of course some paintings are plenty vicious.

More to the point, insofar as something is made, it is an object of interpretation in a different way. We start calculating the motives for which it was made, and can start reading it semiotically, as a symbol of something. This is the way, for example, Arthur Danto delineates the distinction between works of art and "mere real things"; the aesthetic object is *about* something, has a semiotics.[2] This is somewhat too general, one would think, as any artifact has the capacity to be *about,* and this radically shapes the way we

---

2. This is developed classically in Danto 2, and crisply reformulated in Danto 1.

experience it aesthetically, but also, of course, politically, as in the question "Who is responsible?" Or: who is the author or artist, and why this work/ act rather than another?

Hannah Arendt has attacked this idea of the polis as an art object and its correlate of sovereign power as artist or craftsman, and asserted that a much better image is provided by the performing arts, which unfold over time and result from collaboration. Arendt generalizes this theme to Greek and Renaissance political philosophy quite generally, connecting it to the development of the fundamental conceptions of political philosophy—in particular within the republican tradition—including virtue and freedom.

> Politics has often been defined as an art. This, of course, is not a definition but a metaphor, and the metaphor becomes completely false if one falls into the common error of regarding the state or government as a work of art, as a kind of collective masterpiece. In the sense of creative arts, which bring forth something tangible and reify human thought to such an extent that the produced thing possesses an existence of its own, politics is the exact opposite of an art—which incidentally does not mean that it is a science. Political institutions, no matter how well or badly designed, depend for their existence upon acting men; their conservation is achieved by the same means which brought them into being. Independent existence marks the work of art as a product of making; utter dependence upon further acts to keep it in existence marks the state as a product of action.
>
> The point here is not whether the creative artist is free in the process of creation, but that the creative process is not displayed in public and not destined to appear in the world. Hence the element of freedom, certainly present in the creative arts, remains hidden; it is not the creative process which finally appears and matters in the world, but the work of art itself, the end product of the process. The performing arts, on the contrary, have indeed a strong affinity with politics. Performing artists—dancers, play-actors, musicians, and the like—need an audience to show their virtuosity, just as acting men need the presence of others before whom they can appear; both need a publicly organized space for their "work," and both depend upon others for the performance itself. Such a space of appearances is not to be taken for granted wherever men live together in a community. The Greek polis was once precisely that "form of government" which provided men with a space of appearances where they could act, with a kind of theater where freedom could appear. (Arendt 2, p. 152)

This passage, which I regard as something of a classic in political aesthetics, has resonance throughout the material we have been examining and will examine. Arendt explicitly raises it in relation to Machiavelli's *Prince,* but the connection is already explicit in Aristotle's *Politics:* "The excellence of all citizens cannot possibly be the same, any more than the excellence of the leader of the chorus is the same as that of the performer who stands by his side" (Aristotle, 1277a10–12). That is, if politics is similar to art, it is similar to collaborative or collective performing arts. We might also think of the treatment of the Athenian polis as arising from theater that we associate with Wagner and Nietzsche: "theatrocracy." And it is fundamental to concepts of republic and representation that we find in Hobbes and the founders of the American republic.

That the state ought to be considered a representation is of course potentially a rich dimension of aesthetic inquiry; representation is both a political and an aesthetic category. Also epistemic, of course: a representation can be true or false, adequate or inadequate, accurate or inaccurate. A typical example that raises the question: the Bush administration presented "America" as the bastion of freedom and democracy, the harbor for those values wherever they may be found. Of course, as it framed the data this way, it detained people without trial and abused prisoners. Nevertheless, the idea of America as a bastion of freedom and democracy, problematic throughout its history, is also not simply false. So as the flag billows and so on, we're trying to evaluate the general relation of representation, facing the question of what makes a representation accurate or inaccurate, and we're trying to evaluate the particular representations at hand. The gap between picture and reality is the obsession of political aesthetics since Plato.

Obviously, political regimes generate representational systems or resuscitate old ones, and they use and deflect the representational systems they find current. The function of a flag or device or logo is central, for example: it's about as pure a structure of representation as you can have, exemplary in its elisions: a pure symbol of the people, the nation, the state, the leader. It's not an iconic sign in the sense that it depicts these things, and these vast concepts and territories are fundamentally undepictable anyway, though of course they can be mapped, allegorized, characterized, or stipulated as the content of a particular work or word. Even in the world of obscure representations in which people live, a flag is an amazing mirage, eventually encompassing everything—a culture, language, polity, identity—in a few juxtaposed colors.

To take this a little less literally, the foundation of the state is as a representation, as we have seen; it identifies and to some extent imposes some sort of identity on a people or nation; and the people or nation is itself a nest of representations, manufactured in folklore and folk arts, historiography and mythology. Nor is the representation a mere fiction or invention: it encompasses, depicts, and reveals a thousand real details; it is a way of organizing and displaying (but also concealing) real material. Politics in this sense is in its essence or in virtue of its essence a trafficking in representations, and a rich understanding of the representational practices of the ancient Egyptians, or of the Inca, or for that matter of the Lakota or the Yoruba or the French, would constitute a rich understanding of their political systems.

Representative democracy is a development out of this fundamental insight, a way to try to demystify or make reasonable or systematic the structures of representation on which every political system rests. Representative democracy at once demystifies the symbols of monarchy or theocracy and generates a competing set of symbols in which persons ("representatives") are explicitly invested with representational content. We might think of the practices of democratic representation as an attempt to make rational or "scientific" or even inductive the sort of representational practices that any regime calls upon for legitimation. Or, democracy calls on "the people" to become the artificers of their own symbol systems, and the parliament is not merely a bunch of people; it is a bunch of people who function as pictures or images of the people to the state and of the state to the people.

The idea of people serving as representations of other people is familiar enough that it seems inevitable and perfectly comprehensible; it is worth defamiliarizing it a bit and seeing its complexity. The emperor is the sign of empire, a fact revealed by his adornments and surroundings: an emperor is an extremely dense semiotic system. A "president" looks more or less like anyone else. But there is a real act (an election) by which this person takes on the representational weight of millions and speaks for them and contains them within an individual human body. A president is like a flag in that he or she is a symbol whose intrinsic nature seems massively inadequate to its representational weight. But while a flag is a basically arbitrary form in the sense that it does not visually or in any other way really resemble the nation or the people, a president is a synecdoche of the people, a person who is all the people, and this structure is underwritten precisely by the refusal of pomp, by the quiet suit. An emperor is fundamentally detached or is a wild idealization of the people; a president is supposed to be one of the people, depicting or signifying the people in a synecdochic structure.

The concept of "personal" representation, in law and in political philosophy, or for that matter in the theater, under pressure from or in relation to the Renaissance and the period immediately following in depiction, takes on an abstract or idealized quality. In Hobbes's England the model is precisely (and as Arendt's treatment might lead us to expect) portraying a character on the stage.

> A PERSON is he *whose words or actions are considered, either as his own, or as representing the words or actions of another man, or of any other thing to whom they are attributed, whether Truly or by Fiction.*
>
> When they are considered as his own, then is he called a *Naturall Person:* and when they are considered as representing the words and actions of another, then is he a *Feigned* or *Artificial person.*
>
> The word person is Latin, instead whereof the Greeks have *prosopon,* which signifies the *Face,* as *persona* in latine signifies the *disguise,* or *outward appearance* of a man, counterfeited on the Stage; and sometimes more particularly that part of it which disguiseth the face, as a *Mask* or *Visard:* and from the stage hath been translated to any Representer of speech and action, as well in Tribunalls as Theatres. So that a *Person* is the same that an *Actor* is, both on the stage and in common Conversation; and to *Personate* is to *Act* or *Represent* himselfe, or an other; and he that acteth another is said to beare his Person, or act in his name . . . , and is called in diverse occasions, diversely; as a *Representer,* or *Representative,* a *Lieutenant,* a *Vicar,* an *Attorney,* a *Deputy,* a *Procurator,* an *Actor,* and the like. (Hobbes, pp. 217–18)

The variety of societal roles to which Hobbes attributes this mimetic or representational function is remarkable, and representational relations lie at the very foundation of the "leviathan" metaphor or picture: the state is literally, figuratively a person, an actor and mask that is evidently, by the seventeenth century, within the extension of the term "person." But indeed we can see that, for Hobbes, the idea of one person representing another, or many others, is a central social fact in a number of fields. The representative structure, we notice, derives for Hobbes from republican antiquity in Cicero, and despite Hobbes's enthusiasm for monarchy, it anticipates the rise of representative democracy or emerges in the same context.

The mimetic relation on the stage is, more or less, one-to-one even if filled with puzzles: Olivier as Hamlet. But persons who consist of many persons raise the stakes to much higher levels of abstraction, measured as the disresemblance between depiction or representation and its object. The central terms of modern political philosophy—the people, the nation, the state, and so on—pick out levels or dimensions of representation, or constitute highly abstracted imaginary second-tier ontological entities that are saturated with representational content and, qua their conceptual functions, have no other content. There are layers of representation, each of which rests on another, and a question about the ultimate reality that underlies the representational strata as its foundation is one of great obscurity, or perhaps a matter of conceptual preference. In democracy "the people" serves this function. But surely the use of the phrase is itself highly semiotized; it is repeated until it achieves almost full abstraction. It functions as a singular term, of course, and emphasizes or asserts a unity, variously conceptualized, or disguises the disunity.

In this sense we need a political aesthetics that is a political semiotics, that describes how certain things are charged with representational content or serve in the role of pictures. One might trace the same process of progressive abstraction in, for example, painting: Constable-Turner-Whistler-O'Keeffe-Pollock. Or in money: coinage, paper representation of specie metals, bank notes, electronic transfer. Thinkers such as Peirce or Saussure thought there could be a "science" of signs, whether a priori or a posteriori; the extent to which they could pay off on that has been limited, though rich and useful. But even if signs are a matter for scientific or logical inquiry, they are also the object of aesthetic inquiry, and their character cannot be wholly exposed in their sheer logic, or even in an explication of their uses, but leans on their aesthetics; and the history of aesthetics is to a large extent a grappling with mimesis and with the form of mimetic representations.

Again, the earliest work in aesthetics focuses on the relation of representation, on the opposition, as Danto puts it, between works of art and the mere real things they can represent. In this sense the work of art is always charged by intentions, roped into a set of relations out of which it is constituted. But there are many kinds of art and many symbol systems. There are pictures proper, which resemble and distort what they represent (or so I would argue): perhaps a portrait of the dictator. There are eidetic signs such as flags, which make use of visual cues to convey a representational content far beyond their forms, a swirl of wild ideas and objects. Elaborate sets of conventions surround the circulation of such signs, and they are incomprehensible aside from those conventions. And then there are representations that seem to possess nothing salient in common with what they represent, the representational status of which is a pure stipulation, as when you use little markers to show military positions and so on: this "is" the Fifth Fleet. Obviously all political states use or embody all of these techniques. But they have different purposes and different effects, and as the icon approaches arbitrariness or stipulation, the sign drifts explicitly free of the signified, and thus both evaporates or loses content, and gains scope.

The idea of the political is impossible without the faculty of generalization: no political system ultimately addresses or considers people as individuals but rather addresses persons as types, or examples of the violation of certain rules, for instance, or as functions: perhaps the enforcers of those rules. That is, states must, to address themselves to people at all, treat people as representative—of certain groups, principles, functions, violations, and so on. That is, the state contributes to the abstraction of human beings or to the creation of them as nests of representations, as examples (of poor people, embezzlers, cabinet secretaries). The population or citizenry, as it appears to the state, is a set of representations rather than bodies, even as the state is itself in essence a representation, and appears to these entities continuously in this guise. One way to put this is that politics in the modern context is a trafficking in representations that lends to human bodies various sorts of semiotic significance, or treats people like words or pictures. In the modern political world we have been transformed into semiotically saturated bodies, in amazingly complex ways, and both power and resistance to power make use of this fact fundamentally. The power of violence or wealth is power also to rejigger the semiotic system, both of the wealthy and powerful and of the poor and powerless.

One cannot conceive of the modern bureaucratic state without demography, without the activity of arraying a population into groups comprehended under general terms, as income levels, genders, regions, professions, ages, origins, and so on. The modern state, that is, proceeds by comprehension of populations, which is possible only by a series of representations. This releases the individual to conceal herself within a demographic segment; the individual is not the primary object of scrutiny. But it also allows the state to address her continuously insofar as it addresses the groups under which it arrays her. The representation idealizes, generalizes, and neglects her. She may well, of course, come to represent herself to herself in terms of demographic segments or idealized images, as a black woman, or a lesbian, or a wealthy woman, or an elderly woman. An interesting thing is that the categories multiply with information technologies: the refinement of generalizations creates ever more specific categories until we could ideally make each person a category of one by a process of division, like Carnap dividing the universe in half between each predicate and its negation, making reality an array of facts. So the more thoroughly the universe is understood in terms of generalities, the more it ramifies into an incomprehensibly profuse level of individualities.

Let us retrench. We might consider the various modes and theories of representation, as developed in the history of aesthetics, in relation to political life. They are theories not so much of what representation is but of what it's for.

a. The earliest and most persistent account of representation is that it
is mimesis or "imitation," which is both Plato's definition and the
object of his attack. Dryden gives as good a statement as any: "To
imitate nature well... is the perfection of art.... [T]hat picture, and
that poem, which comes nearest the resemblance of nature is best"
(Dryden, p. 332). The mimetic account of representation persists
from the earliest to some of the most recent accounts.[3]

b. Partly motivated by this attack and beginning in Aristotle (or, just as
clearly, in the actual art of classical Greece), an alternative is developed in which, we might say, to represent something is to raise it
up a level of generality, to expose its essence or to idealize it. This
sense or use of representation dominates the Renaissance and displays
not only its artistic practice and philosophical orientation (Neoplatonic), of course, but also its reading of the Greek artistic, philosophical, and political heritage. Mimesis, we might say, is appropriated and
deflected to a program of idealization and hints at a transcendence—
within human activity, of human activity. Aristotle calls poetry "more
philosophic and of graver import" (Aristotle 1, 1451b) than history
because it generalizes, comprehends, arrays facts comprehensibly, or
sheds light on the world.

c. Finally, we might say, in the late nineteenth century and through the
twentieth, the idea of representation was a reverse mimesis: as Oscar
Wilde said over and over, life imitates art. In the work of Gombrich
in art history and of Heidegger, Nelson Goodman, or even Dewey
in philosophy, the idea is that to represent something is to call it into
existence as a perceptible object. Gadamer writes that "a picture is
not a copy of a copied being, but is in ontological communion with
what is copied.... Word and picture are not mere imitative illustra-
tions, but allow what they represent to be for the first time what it
is" (Gadamer, p. 126). No doubt such a view has its origins in Kant,
according to whom the world itself is a sequence of representations, as
it were a perspective system; we order an incomprehensible universe
through procedures analogous to picturing, the pivot into romantic
modernism. This view takes many forms. At times it lurches into a
pure idealism, wherein reality is the merest artifact of representational
and referential activities. The "linguistic" idealism of a Rorty or
Derrida might be mentioned here. But there are far milder or more

---

3. E.g., Hyman, Schier, Halliwell.

nuanced, and certainly more plausible versions of the view. Gombrich, for example, we might say, makes of perceptible reality a dialogue in which we bring our representational systems to every act of perception. Perception would not be possible without antecedent representational capacities: categories, forms, perspectives, vocabularies of talk and picturing. Yet these capacities are vulnerable to correction from the actual world, and both realistic picturing and perceptual experience as a whole employ what Gombrich terms a rhythm of schema and correction, wherein the world is articulated by a system of expectations, and the system of expectations is vulnerable to the world.

We might call these "regimes" of representation insofar as they establish (in a conceptual sense) and track actual art practices and institutions. Let's term (a), (b), and (c) the "mimetic," the "eidetic," and the "articulatory" regimes respectively, and add that a fourth option is pure stipulation. It is worth thinking about whether these accounts or uses of representation have analogues in the political realm, or whether the treatment of representation in the aesthetic and the political traditions constitute separate histories or even semi-intentionally diverge, as the aesthetic and political spheres are conceived to be subject to entirely different forces, as politics is conceived as moral or purely practical and art as "aesthetic" in the modernist sense: useless and beyond good and evil. One way of putting the question is whether a political system represents an antecedent reality (a nation, or the people, or a land), whether it picks out the essence of such things, or whether it calls them into being.

There are many ways that states function or purport to function as representatives of the people they encompass or subordinate. But in any case "republicanism" in the Madisonian or early French Revolution sense rests the whole of the polity on the relation of representation. That the state represents the people, and that there are concrete measures such as elections to ensure the "accuracy" of this representation, is the foundation of the (alleged) legitimacy of the modern democratic state. Now, the idea that the representation in the polity of the will of the people can be more or less accurate appears to deploy a mimetic concept of representation. Such a concept also imports a series of related ontological underpinnings. The will of the people, and their needs, their character, their beliefs, and so on, are the reality of which the representative institutions are the image. That is, the fundamental political reality is the people in their many aspects, and the function of the representational state is to represent this reality honestly and accurately. Indeed the Athenian direct democracy conceived of itself in exactly this way, and the state and the citizenry merged into identity. Direct democracy is, we might say, the political application of a flat mimetic view of representation.

Madison and his ilk, however, did not resort to direct democracy, precisely because it placed too few layers of filtering or interpretation or... idealization between the motif or subject or object ("the people") and the representation. If the state is a picture of its citizens, we must ask to what extent the citizenry is an appropriate or uplifting subject for representation. We might compare direct democracy to, let's say, Dutch genre painting, a fun and colorful portrayal of the people's everyday life. But of course this is not the most exalted subject matter and is potentially corrupt. Why would an artist, capable of real sublimity, or at least capable of providing a picture of virtually any subject matter, stick to peasants drinking beer or the like? Indeed, I think of Dutch genre as a response to and rejection of the Renaissance, with its inspiring movement of the real world toward a perfection in beauty that is also, pointedly, the rejection of the world it takes up and transforms. This sort of representation constantly thematizes the inadequacy of the world. To the extent that a Jefferson or Washington functions as a representation of the people, it is a supernal representation or an eidetic representation: they supposedly show "the best in us," or what we would believe or be capable of if we were closer to perfect than we are. The idea is "senatorial," a meritocracy of wealth, power, and virtue.

The mimetic and eidetic conceptions of political representation were explicitly a source of the conflict between the proponents and opponents of the American Constitution, and corresponded to the rift between those favoring more or less direct democracy. The anti-federalist "Brutus," writing in the *New York Journal,* said:

> The very term, representative, implies, that the person or body chosen for this purpose, should resemble those who appoint them—a representation of the people of America, if it be a true one, must be like the people. It ought to be so constituted, that a person, who is a stranger to the country, might be able to form a just idea of their character, by knowing that of their representatives. They are the sign—the people are the thing signified. It is absurd to speak of one thing being the representative of another, upon any other principle.[4]

Partly one's response to the issue of political representation is a matter of "taste" and tracks social class: while the lower strata are satisfied with coarse popular entertainments and genre pictures, gentlemen such as John Adams

---

4. "Brutus," "Representation Is Merely Nominal—A Mere Burlesque," *New York Journal,* November 15, 1787, reprinted in Bailyn, 1:320.

have a more refined sensibility forged as a taste in the Renaissance, always a rediscovery of a primordial classical/republican ideal.

In *Federalist* 56, Madison, with characteristic lucidity, says:

> It is a sound and important principle that the representative ought to be acquainted with the interests and circumstances of his constituents. But this principle can extend no farther than to those circumstances and interests, to which the authority and care of the representative relate. An ignorance of a variety of minute and particular objects, which do not lie within the compass of legislation, is consistent with every attribute necessary to a due performance of legislative trust. In determining the extent of information required in the exercise of a particular authority, recourse then must be had to the objects within the purview of that authority.[5]

Here the legislator is considered in the role of the artist, as interpreting, idealizing, simplifying, generalizing (from its minute and particular objects) the will of the people. Or, for that matter, the representative is the scientist in the Newtonian sense: transforming particular observations into comprehensive theories. And there is a traditional response here to a Platonic criticism of mimesis that, for example, an artist who paints a pair of shoes knows less about shoes than a cobbler but purports to convey knowledge about them. It is not necessary or desirable to know everything: the technique of representation is concerned with filtering out irrelevant features. A representation is accurate only relatively to certain purposes.

Fisher Ames, speaking to the Massachusetts Ratifying Convention, January 1788, in favor of the proposed Constitution, observed:

> Much has been said about the people divesting themselves of power, when they delegate it to representatives; and that all representation is to their disadvantage, because it is but an image, a copy, fainter and more imperfect than the original, the people, in whom the light of power is primary and unborrowed, which is only reflected by their delegates.— I cannot agree to either of these opinions.—The representation of the people is something more than the people.[6]

Here the idea of representation reaches Kantian formalism. This is a declaration of the autonomy of the artpolitical sphere, as the fine arts are theorized at this very moment as autonomous. Ames shows what is distinct about the

---

5. James Madison, *Federalist* 56, in Bailyn, 2:208.
6. "Fisher Ames on Biennial Elections and on the Volcano of Democracy" [to the Massachusetts Convention, January 15, 1788], in Bailyn, 1:891.

artpolitical realm: it rests on an aesthetic idea, a conception of representation. But what is transmitted from the object (people) to the work (legislation) is power. Political representation is representation whose object or motif is power, and the representation "wields" power as the picture of a tree "is" a tree. The period of the late eighteenth and early nineteenth centuries is a moment when the representational regime is at stake, in flux; the period is characteristically in a crisis about the concept of representation, in Hume, Rousseau, Kant, Burke, Hegel, Schopenhauer. One moment of this crisis is the debate about the American Constitution, when the concept of representation is thematized perfectly clearly and all available positions are taken up.

We still inhabit these structures. I might adduce the examples of Sarah Palin and Barack Obama in the 2008 election. On the one hand, Palin was supposed to be "just like you," a housewife from a small town who rose through her PTA to the mayoralty, the governorship, and hoped to rise to the vice presidency. The relation was conceived or at least presented as mimetic: even her supposedly limited education and folksy syntax were signifiers of her membership in what she hoped to represent, her synecdochic relation to the people. Obama, on the other hand, was an ideal—kind of like you, only smarter, better-looking, more expert, more educated. And he was multiracial: we are all one in the body of Obama. Here is an ancient motif of eidetic representation: beauty is found in combining the best features of many individuals. The election, that is, raised fundamental issues about the nature and purpose of representation in a democracy, and also displayed all the conceptual difficulties of treating persons as though they were pictures.

With the Renaissance comes a wave of political republicanism. And with the rise of political republicanism in the late eighteenth century comes a renaissance, which is in part a renaissance of the Renaissance, in a nested representational structure that eventually is supposed to reach to the Greeks and Romans. One reason why classicism is congenial to republicanism is that it deploys an eidetic representational regime: it simplifies, clarifies, and exalts its subjects. It is "architectonic" in its architecture and in its political arrangements: it is a design culture. It is comprehensive, which makes the simplicity a necessity: it conceives the political constitution as something to be conceived fully and then implemented. We do not simply leave the political arrangements to an unfolding tradition or the chaotic contradictory decisions of particular persons and sections of the population; rather, we conceive the political system as a whole, and as a coherent whole, and as an aesthetically satisfying whole, as a rational whole, and as an inspiration to us all to participate: an eidetic vision.

In Ames as in Kant there is a declaration of aesthetic autonomy. In the arts, this mood of the high culture was reflected in the modern museum and the discipline of art history as a Hegelian historical narrative. We might trace the metaphysical foundation again to Kant's Copernican revolution, as seen in Schopenhauer and many others: the universe as a form or matrix of sensibility, the phases of "transcendental idealism." All reality is conceived in terms of the forms and conditions of representation. This "modernist" orientation, we may say, flows into the postmodern doctrine that the sign is/creates/constitutes reality or that life imitates art. In a Baudrillardian way we might trace the phases of the sign: it reflects what is real; it takes it up and transforms it autopoetically, idealizes or abstracts it; it supersedes it; the real reflects it; everything dissolves into pure syntax.

F. R. Ankersmit, in a squarely postmodern vein (though calling to his aid Machiavelli and Tocqueville, and saying much the same thing as Fisher Ames), writes:

> Political power has its origin neither in the people represented nor in the representative, but in the representation process itself. Political power is a quasi-natural phenomenon that comes into being in the relation between the representative and the person represented and cannot be claimed by either one of the two parties.... Not photographic precision, but a new style of painting is what is called for in this circumstance.... [W]hen asking himself or herself how best to represent the represented, the representative should ask what political style will best suit the electorate. And this question really requires a *creative* answer on the part of the representative, in the sense that there exists nothing in the electorate itself that is quietly waiting to be copied; neither does the landscape itself suggest the style in which it shall be depicted by the artist. (Ankersmit, pp. 53–54)

The relation of representation here does not obtain between "the people" and a person but inheres in the political *system* qua person itself, in the Hobbesian sense. The political system, as it were, represents itself, as in the idea of abstraction in the criticism of Clement Greenberg: the work achieves inherence in its own medium.

Ankersmit concludes that our problem today is precisely that the political system does not take on this role, that it seeks to efface itself or to represent itself as the mere figure of the people or an imitation of it. Again we might call to mind various postmodern conceptions of signs without origins or originals, as in Lyotard or Baudrillard. Indeed, the very size of the state or multinational institutions forces one to conceive of political representation in articulatory rather than mimetic terms: in a many-as-one representation, the degree of abstraction is proportional to the number and diversity of the many. But I think that any of these aesthetic systems is vulnerable to a totalitarian reading. The legislator who wields great power while purporting merely to reflect the will of the people is the demagogue of antidemocratic polemic. The elite and well educated who know what's best are secretive and have various economic stakes in the outcome. The modern regime that thinks it can create reality through deploying a system of signs could be either happily multicultural or a regime of total censorship.

CHAPTER 3

Dead Kennedys and Black Flags

Artpolitics of Punk

Perhaps the most direct way to detach the idea of political aesthetics from totalitarianism is, again, to demonstrate that it can profitably approach anti-totalitarian political systems. Here I want to show that anti-politics is as aesthetic as politics, that political aesthetics is as applicable to anarchism as to fascism. If the state is always an aesthetic object, so is its destruction or rejection. If the Prince is an artist, so is liberation that repudiates all princes. Indeed, perhaps no political tendency other than fascism has been as aestheticized as anarchism, and the relation of anarchism to the avant-garde arts of the nineteenth and twentieth centuries is extremely rich. Emma Goldman's main concerns were anarchism, feminism, and the aesthetics of radical drama. The declaration of the freedom of imagination, so central to modernism in the arts, has intersected throughout with a critique of political constraints. But the idea of freedom in anarchism is not merely the destruction of existing powers and institutions; it constitutes a positive anarchic aesthetic, a vision of liberation embodied in aesthetic events and objects. One example of such a construction is found in the artpolitics of punk.

I've characterized political aesthetics as being concerned with the aesthetic features of political systems, not the political features of aesthetic systems. But one should expect this distinction to collapse in some cases. If political systems are always also aesthetic systems, certainly also some aesthetic systems are political systems. This strikes me as being especially true of "resistant" artpolitical systems, and it is often easier or for that matter more enjoyable— or in any event safer—to make music or images than to take up arms and overthrow the existing arrangements. In modernity the political space seems virtually monopolized by the state and by the competition to control the state and allocate its resources. And in modernity as well, the arts themselves are colonized by dominant political and economic powers: multinational corporations supply the music and dominate the landscape with imagery and text; the state funds the arts and regulates the media. This symbolic dominance is also a real physical dominance: it is a power exercised over the space in which the political-economic system operates. And while intervening in the political system itself is not an option for most young people or members of other dis- or semi-enfranchised groups, interrupting the flow of imagery, sound, and text is always an option. Partly this is a result of the remarkable cheapness of some reproduction techniques in modernity. At this point practically anyone with a computer can make decently recorded music. One can easily reproduce the screed or flyer with cheap printing and copying technologies, or tag the cityscape inexpensively with a stencil and a can of spray paint.

The gigantism of the contemporary state and corporation make intervention by most groups or individuals seem entirely hopeless. You'd have to negotiate the infinite layers of the authority-bureaucracy even to deliver a message, and when you did, you'd find that message attenuated by its context (at a minimum). And yet the gigantism of these institutions leaves fissures, holes, hiding places, like a big, slow army trying to deal with an insurgency. For young people in particular, the arts provide a mode of individual expression, collective solidarity, and commentary on the situation; zones of evasion are always associated with the arts. The arts—with their absorption in process and communicative capacities—are, unlike political treatises, inherently pleasurable. For reasons that are difficult to articulate fully, music in particular is an almost preternaturally powerful medium; it is difficult for people— particularly a certain type of disaffected teenager—to imagine life without it. Music has driven the rise of each of the youth-oriented subcultures since at latest the 1950s (see Hebdige).

Punk is usually thought of as a musical style. But first, it is a style of all the arts. And second, it is a political movement or coalition or structure of political movements. The politics is sometimes sophisticated, educated, coherent; and punk has produced some remarkable political figures, such as Jello Biafra and Henry Rollins. But the fact that much of it has been made by confused and substance-abusing teenagers helps explain why the politics usually seems almost casual or incoherent. Yet the explicitly political themes are remarkably pervasive, and punk in various parts of the world has led to alternative institutions: not only record labels and club circuits but also squats and cooperative economies. To the extent that the contemporary antiglobalization movement has a single style or identity, it is punk.

A particularly interesting feature of punk politics is that, by the standards of conventional political ideologies, it is incoherent if considered as a single movement. It produced expressions of doctrinaire Marxism (Millions of Dead Cops), fascism (Skrewdriver), and anarchism (Crass). In what follows I take the anarchism to be the dominant strand, for reasons that I will explore. But one thing about all these ideologies: they are marked by their resistance to the power structures of "liberal democracy" and "late capitalism." Initially, I think, the young people who started punk simply wanted to distinguish themselves from the previous generation of musicians and young people (the hippies) and from the power structures (schools, anti-drug campaigns, record labels) in which they were embedded. What united them was sheer opposition, which they often expressed as hatred and nihilism. (Richard Hell: "I belong to the blank generation.") This could be accomplished through any taboo set of symbols: swastikas or black flags, Che or Hitler. As the punk movement matured, it coalesced into some fairly and occasionally thoroughly well thought out oppositional political expressions, central in the lives of the participants, but remarkably central as well to the culture, considering that many people have been barely aware of the whole thing. The punk fringe articulated the shape of the dominant culture, or both punk and dominant cultures (partly) defined themselves by mutual opposition. And the extent to which punk was able to reconfigure the arts as a whole, especially the visual arts, is only slowly coming to be appreciated.

The artpolitics of punk might be considered in terms of Hakim Bey's (Peter Lamborn Wilson's) notion of the TAZ: the Temporary Autonomous Zone (Bey). The basic idea is to carve out a space in which undetected subversive activity is possible, then, as the authorities get wind of it or institute surveillance, to disintegrate, re-coalescing in a different place and configuration later on. Wilson's favored examples include pirate utopias: lawless islands or cities dedicated to criminal activities. But any squat in London, Athens, or Barcelona is also a good example. At the beginning, punk was, with extreme self-consciousness, time-bound, and the people who did it initially had no notion of a decades-long progression. Of course they eventually had to make artistic and political peace with their own maturation, which they did in a hundred different ways, including death. But the apparent permanence of political and economic institutions—their being framed in marble, as it were—was the precise opposite of the ephemerality of punk, as labels, crash pads, clubs, and bands came and went with bewildering speed. The TAZishness of the punk movement helped make it vivid and important for its participants, but by definition insulated the larger culture and its power structures from the scenes of subversion. This allowed punk to survive but also made its actual intervention in the culture a limited affair. Punk demonstrated that resistance was possible even against the gargantuan bureaucratic power structures of the era, but it also demonstrated that this resistance must be veiled, elusive, and disorganized, a lesson even al-Qaeda has absorbed. Punk was not, for the most part, a real revolutionary movement; it was an attempt to find places outside the system or in its interstices.

One way into punk as an artpolitics is through the postmodern anarchist political theory associated with Guy Debord and called Situationism. If anyone invented punk, it was Malcolm McLaren, who by the mid-seventies was spouting Situationist ideology and "styling" aspiring proto–punk rock stars, such as the New York Dolls. Indeed, both the cynical understanding and use of the media and style by McLaren's protégés the Sex Pistols ("the great rock 'n' roll swindle," "Do you ever have the feeling you've been had?") and the anarchist twist to the lyrics can be traced to French Situationism. In some ways punk could be considered Situationist visual and aural expression. Indeed this influence is surprisingly pervasive: one sees references to Situationism and anarchist theory, for example, throughout the run of *Search and Destroy,* a definitive zine on both visual and journalistic grounds, which covered the late-seventies punk scene all over the world with remarkable thoroughness and verve. In fact in the fourth number of *Search and Destroy* (1977) there is a reasonably rich history of anarchism, written by Nico Ordway, as well as articles connecting punk to surrealism and the Beats.

According to the basic Situationist document, Debord's *Society of the Spectacle,* the modern media spectacle is so powerful and so pervasive and so univocal as an expression of late capitalism that it has become our universe; there is no way out or around. Debord's Situationism has an element of extreme alienation and despair; there seems to be no exit from a "reality" that is wholly a glamorous simulation provided under the auspices of gigantic corporations. Punk might be thought of as a complex response to the challenge embodied in this despair. First, the representation of punk, punk's own spectacle, was opposed to the smooth spectacle of capitalism; that is, punk participated in the media spectacle by signifying its opposite: fucked-up, poor, messy, hateful, dangerous, in short, jagged. This was compelling both as a critique of the spectacle and as an element in it; it of course possessed its own perverse glamour. It made use of the media spectacle to infect the youth of the whole world with the spectacle's other.

Here it is worthwhile to recall Debord's basic set of axioms as well as their concrete political effects in youth culture, such as the 1968 insurrection in Paris, and also the sense that 1968 had failed, been co-opted, or that the heritage of it had itself become oppressive or ideological.

> The images detached from every aspect of life fuse in a common stream in which the unity of this life can no longer be reestablished. Reality considered partially unfolds, in its own general unity, as a pseudo-world apart, an object of mere contemplation. The specialization of images of the world is completed in the world of the autonomous image, where the liar has lied to himself. . . . The spectacle is not a collection of images, but a social relation among people, mediated by images. . . . It is a world vision which has become objectified. . . . It is not a supplement to the real world, an additional decoration. It is the heart of the unrealism of the real society. In all its specific forms, as information or propaganda, as advertisement or direct entertainment consumption, the spectacle is the present model of socially dominant life. It is the omnipresent affirmation of the choice already made in production and its corollary consumption. (from the first few sections of Debord)

Punk culture might be looked upon as a rejection of every aspect of the spectacle. It pointedly involved the spectators as participants; there is all the difference in the world between contemplation and slam-dancing. Its governing value was reality: authenticity, a peek into the dark side of the human mind and body. It created extremely intense social relations, at least in part through direct extreme physical contact. Of course, punk also presented itself as a set of tropes: of saturated signs, images, styles. Punk entered into the spectacle, and though it expressed continuous reservations, ultimately it entered the spectacle enthusiastically and with extraordinary skill. It both demonstrated that the spectacle swallows all things and that the spectacle is never as univocal or consistent as Debord renders it as being; if there could be a Situationist strategy of resistance, McLaren's would be it. The spectacle, we might say, yearns for its own destruction, like the Dead Boys. Or it feeds on its own critique and needs it and uses it, even as it can be wielded as a weapon against itself.

Punk had an extreme facility for the construction of signs. One look at Johnny Rotten's safety pins, his contorted features, his torn-up clothes, one listen to his shattered voice snarling "anarchy," was enough to send Britain into a tizzy of revulsion overnight; it probably took less than five seconds onscreen to think that you'd gotten the whole thing. The arrival of the Pistols was the moment punk emerged from New York City bohemia into world consciousness, and though punk originated in New York, and the New York groups were fundamental musically and visually, the power of the punk signifier was only fully formulated by McLaren and the Pistols in London.

But the punks, in a way different from Debord, or even the students of 1968, were children of the spectacle. If you were eighteen in 1976, you were born in 1958; you'd never known a life without television, or a set of experiences unaffected by it. Other music spectacles originating in 1958 include Madonna, Prince, and Michael Jackson, amazing shape-shifters and geniuses at wielding the spectacle to make art and cash and fame. Punk's fertility of symbols, all of them recognizably punk (for one thing, black and white and red) but also remarkably resonant and various, can be seen in the proliferation of band emblems. The logo was directly absorbed from advertising and above all from political propaganda: punks flew flags or anti-flags and communicated in geometrical arrangements that encapsulated extremely detailed content and in a semi-parodic way tried to create a nation of pissed-off kids.

Punk showed that the spectacle could be deflected from within. The actual changes it wrought are of course a matter of dispute. What is beyond dispute is that punk has both been used ever since as a mere trope and has resisted this use and continued to achieve a jaggedness to it. The clothing styles that came to be associated with punk were developed by McLaren and Vivienne Westwood in their shop SEX in London, influenced by the fetish wear and the proto-punk scene on New York's Lower East Side, including the Dolls and ur-punk Richard Hell, who cultivated a devastated, damaged, demented, and derelict clothing style, whether by intention or default. The Hell look was also adopted by the Ramones, and it has been adopted and adapted by punks ever since. It refers, like the term "punk" itself, to youth culture before the arrival of the hippies, the group above all that punks looked upon as their opposite. The seventies punks were referring to the leather-clad punks of *The Outsiders* or *West Side Story*. Where they didn't emulate 1961 was in coiffure, though the first act of a newly minted punk was often to cut off his hippie locks. In the first flowering of punk in London, the amazing hair came out: the Superglued spikes, the bright orange foot-long Mohawks. The good folk of London must have been horrified, fascinated, and puzzled, all at once, and at a distance.

I take punk roughly by medium, starting with music, and then moving on to visual culture, clothing, body adornment, and so on.

Music History

The basics of punk style can be understood through a characterization in a few words of what it rejects. In the seventies, popular music and graphic design had achieved an emphasis on polish, finishedness, surface, and production values as an aesthetic style and statement. Within music we might call this a mature phase of pop, emphasizing beautiful production without urgency, as in the art rock of Yes and Pink Floyd, the disco of Chic and Donna Summer, the California pop of Fleetwood Mac and the Eagles, or the arena rock of Journey and Styx, excellent exemplars of Debord's spectacle. One way to interpret this is as the hippie movement betraying itself or selling out: from Woodstock to Journey is rather a sad slide into meaningless absence of urgency. Punk music arose as a neoclassical rock, stripping back to the early Stones or before. The early Stones were barely competent musicians, but they slammed through basic blues and rock numbers with tremendous freshness and urgency, as though the world depended on it; it was that effect that punk strove after and that shaped its direction. But the Ramones' music is traditional rock 'n' roll with an ironic twist, or an undertone of fucked-upness: full of references to surf, doo-wop, girl groups, garage rock, as well as British Invasion material, but also psycho-surgery, glue-sniffing, and failure.

Punk as a music uses rough edges or amateurism self-consciously as an artpolitical stance, a global critique of power relations. This has been relative to time frame, so that what sounded extreme in 1977 (Ramones or Pistols) seemed by the mid-eighties to be positively urbane. It is articulated and deployed as against the dominant aesthetic systems of the moment, which have in common their shimmer, surface, craft, glamour. These are properties of dominant and expensive aesthetic systems in modernity: the televisual images of Ronald Reagan or the recordings of the last *American Idol* winner, each of which gives rise very specifically to a series of punk responses. The posture of negation, that is, yields a coherent, persisting aesthetic, if not exactly a perfectly coherent sound, for example, and positions punk as a continually rebellious form, as the very emblem and acme of aesthetic revolt. It would be useful, for example, to contrast the aesthetics of the Sex Pistols to that of *Triumph of the Will:* they are exquisitely poised opposite each other.

The professionalism or corporatism of pop music in the mid-seventies imposed a gulf between producers and consumers. It was difficult and expensive to produce a hit record. A feature of punks that is annoying, amusing, and delightful is that they started out going the Stones or the Kingsmen (the garage band responsible for "Louie Louie") one better by declaring that they couldn't play their instruments. Oddly enough, even the early Ramones albums, or live recordings of ur-punkers Johnny Thunders or the Dead Boys, or the early records of the Sex Pistols and Stiff Little Fingers, are reasonably well played, even as the vocalists reach for tuneless lout: Joey "singing" "Now I Wanna Sniff Some Glue." Both Joey Ramone and Johnny Rotten turned out to be excellent rock singers as they went on, and of course the musicians improved; playing a hundred gigs a year for five years will have that effect. At any rate, punk was designed to mobilize young people, to obscure the lines between performer and audience, for one thing by drawing the highly adorned crowd into participating in the show. But it's notorious that, in Austin and Los Angeles, for example, people created bands, put up posters, and only then learned instruments (future Go-Go's singer Belinda Carlisle was listed as a drummer for the Germs, for example). This has radically egalitarian consequences, and makes the homemadeness and jaggedness of the recordings and performances a critique of existing institutions, political, economic, and musical.

Dead Kennedys leader Jello Biafra, in an interview conducted in 1996 concerning the era around 1980, made the participatory relation fundamental:

> Nobody saw the point in even having a cover band. It was as though rock had finally been made into a spectator sport in which multinationals called the shots....Music was for older professionals who'd been "paying their dues" (god I hate that term) since the Beatles. And in Colorado [where Biafra grew up] people just wanted to hear Eagles and Firefall clones. It was very depressing....Punk broke down the barrier between performer and audience to the point where Coliseum rock was long-forgotten. Who needs rock idols when you could get so close you could see the sweat dripping from the guitar strings![1]

Almost everyone who has participated in punk or written about it has emphasized this openness, the first meaning of DIY: do it yourself: never be a mere listener or consumer.

The most explicitly political of the early punk bands, and the fundamental inspiration in the history of punk as a directly political expression, was the British group the Clash, who emerged in London roughly contemporaneously with the Sex Pistols. They sang about racial and class tensions in Britain, and as they injected new content, they brought new form. As they matured, their music was formed fundamentally on top of Jamaican ska,

---

1. From the reprint of the punk zine *Search and Destroy* by RE/Search (San Francisco, 1996), unpaginated.

rock steady, and reggae. Jamaican music (which I examine in some detail in the chapter on Black Nationalism) was a part of punk/skinhead origins in the U.K., and other early punk bands such as the Ruts immediately saw the connections too. The Clash played these styles pretty well, and to a world familiar with Bob Marley and a London with a large Jamaican community that knew every signifier involved, the Clash connected their punk to a world movement for liberation of the third from the first world. The coding is not merely linguistic; the reggae throb of "Guns of Brixton" is itself saturated with significance. Even to play that beat is to try to express some solidarity across racial among other lines.

But the Clash started articulating a variety of political stances and thematizing themselves and punk as social critics and criticism. This from "Know Your Rights," a theme itself echoing Bob Marley and Peter Tosh:

> You have the right not to be killed
> Murder is a crime!
> Unless it was done by a
> Policeman or aristocrats.

This points to the anarchist conclusion that the agents of the state always necessarily exempt themselves from the strictures they enforce. A second verse is relevant to the "dole culture" in which punk emerged.

> You have the right to food money
> Providing of course you
> Don't mind a little
> Investigation, humiliation.

A third emphasizes the dissident status of the Clash's discourse.

> You have the right to free
> Speech as long as you're not
> Dumb enough to actually try it.

Building on the Clash tradition (and often attacking the Clash for having sold out), a complex of alternative/punk/squatter cooperatives/bands opened for business in the U.K. in the late 1970s and took to calling themselves "anarcho-punks" or "peace punks." From this movement emerges the red circle-A symbol that is now one of the world's most recognizable graffiti. Perhaps the best known of these was the atheist-anarchist-pacifist-vegetarian band-nation Crass. They performed and recorded their own vision of anarchy, which was notably intense, or perhaps extremely obnoxious. For example, seventeen snarled repetitions of the phrase "Screaming babies" are followed by "Shaved women collaborators / Shaved women are they traitors?" and so on. One might also mention Conflict, Flux of Pink Indians, Poison Girls, Icons of Filth, Zounds, and Subhumans, all parts of U.K. anarcho-punk of the late seventies and early eighties. They distributed their music for free via cassette, encouraging duplication; now these same people and those who emulate them distribute their music free over the Internet. Several of these bands started making really pretty brutal noise for the era (late seventies), and could be termed early hardcore bands. As befits punks, the British anarchists more or less entered into a competition to take the most extreme political stances: they were militant vegans, PETA or Earth First terrorists, total pacifists, or hyper-violent revolutionaries. Eventually the movement devoured itself in a kind of ascetic rage. The demands of moral purity it imposed were eventually impossible to satisfy, and people gave up in disgust or just went on to the next phase: back to school or to work.

American hardcore punk originates in D.C. and in Los Angeles, with the Bad Brains and Germs, among others, around 1980. Where the first wave of punk was neoclassic rock based on a blues scale, hardcore drifted toward extreme speed, lurching, stomping drums, and sheer screaming or bellowing. Where the first wave of punk sounds pretty friendly in retrospect, hardcore will never emerge retroactively as melodic pop music no matter what hell popular music may next unleash. But hardcore is directly connected with earlier punk music by, among other things, an emotional stance, which emphasizes sheer rage and hence negation, an impulse that ultimately wants to expunge the world, a hypertrophically creative, temporally compressed nihilism. Of course, rage is potentially a political emotion with political and economic causes and effects, even if it is also a personal psychological state, stance, or disorder. The rage is directed above all at authority—police, parents, presidents—and whatever else punk is, it is antiauthoritarian. Indeed more recent bands have names such as Against All Authority and Rise Against. Punk is negation as affirmation, or an affirmation of negation; it takes the stance of creative destruction or destruction as an artistic act. And above all, this destruction is aimed at power and institutions, from the school to the corporation to the state.

Perhaps the most politically interesting scene arose in Washington, D.C. If I may be allowed an autobiographical moment: The kids who composed Minor Threat and the other D.C. hardcore bands (The Faith, Void, and Government Issue, for example) were by and large from the neighborhood I grew up in: upper Northwest Washington. But they were a couple of years younger than I was. My generation was still tail-end hippies, and I, like my neighborhood, listened to a lot of Grateful Dead and Jefferson Starship. We smoked dope all day and worked ineffectually toward the revolution. Many kids ended up drugs-and-alcohol casualties; I myself have lost three brothers to causes relating to addiction. Ian MacKaye of Minor Threat entered a radical revolt. "I don't drink, don't smoke, don't fuck," he bellowed, "at least I can fucking think," and in that lyric he founded perhaps the only spontaneous ascetic youth movement in the history of the planet: straight edge, which eventually led to communities of sober anti-sexist vegans infesting many urban areas. And the D.C. punks tried to take command of their own art and their own destiny. MacKaye and associates documented the scene with Dischord Records, selling music at cost; the point was to make rock 'n' roll music without any input from corporate entities.

It's hard to express how deeply permeated by politics Washington, D.C., is. No matter what your parents do or what enclave you inhabit, growing up in (white) D.C. is being steeped like a teabag in politics, and it can be a radicalizing experience. I'm still expecting the revolutionary vanguard to emerge from Wheaton, ravening hordes of revolutionary high school students descending on the White House. Jay Robbins of the harDCore band Government Issue says, "My dad sells cars, so at first it gave me pause, 'Oh the ambassador's kid's onstage screaming' but that makes the famous DC Punk Rock conscience more interesting in a way—like already being aware of the World Bank because your dad works there" (quoted in Blush, p. 137).

The music of MacKaye and Co. took an activist twist quickly and became among other things a fund-raising wing of the non-state social service system that existed in D.C. in the eighties, including such punk-charity groups as Positive Force. And they quickly came to see the male-dominated scene they had created, with its glorification of violence and slight fascist overtones, as deeply problematic. When harDCore arrived at Guy Picciotto's band Rites of Spring by the mid-eighties, it had exchanged pure aggro for "emo": the bands added melodies, and the lyrics became confessional. MacKaye's project Fugazi arose almost as an explicit answer to the culture of Minor Threat and the L.A. hardcore bands: Fugazi pointedly changed speeds repeatedly in a single song, making the violent dancing far more difficult. And though Fugazi's lyrics were rarely explicitly political, they operated within an alternative economy that they created themselves; they never charged over $7 for a ticket, amazing considering how popular they became. MacKaye's label Dischord was never sold to a major corporation, despite many offers. MacKaye tried to make the production and distribution of records an anarcho-punk thing: cooperative, informal, proceeding by handmade promotion, and doing good for people. Fugazi the band was regarded as fundamental by a generation of "alternative" groups of the nineties such as Nirvana, and the Dischord model was a factor in Kurt Cobain's self-loathing for his own work for major labels and MTV.

By the time harDCore's Henry Rollins is spitting lyrics for Black Flag in Los Angeles, the anarchist symbolism is explicit (the black flag is the flag of anarchy and a brand of roach spray). Ian MacKaye visited Britain in 1983 and was converted to vegetarianism by the anarcho-punk band Crass as he refined his anarchist impulses. The New York City band Reagan Youth was thought of as "American peace punk" and displayed perhaps more skill in the manipulation of symbols than in music: they deployed classic images of Nazi officers and Klan members with burning crosses with the sort of sarcasm embodied in their name. The Dead Kennedys out of San Francisco and Millions of Dead Cops were quickly conveying anticapitalist and antifascist slogans, as in "John Wayne was a Nazi." Both Rollins and Dead Kennedys front man Jello Biafra have had second careers as political lecturers/poets. Indeed "Jello Biafra," combining a famine and a quivering confection, is a perfect punk name, as for that matter is "Dead Kennedys": these are specifically political transgressions. Biafra ran for mayor of San Francisco on a platform that called for all businessmen to wear clown suits on Fridays. A series of Bay and other area bands took up political punk in the nineties. We might think especially of Rancid, which also made use of the Jamaican material through the influence of the Clash. Anti-Flag out of Pittsburgh enjoyed tremendous popularity with anti–Bush, antiwar, antiglobalization post-punk. Subhumans from Vancouver (there was another anarcho-punk band by that name in London) was actually cross-pollinated with a Canadian anarchist revolutionary front known as Direct Action; the bass player was convicted in a series of bombings in 1983 as one of the Squamish 5.

The Clash, Billy Bragg, even the Dead Kennedys take up a tradition of protest music, instantiated in the States by Joe Hill, Woody Guthrie, and Bob Dylan, all of whom had also availed themselves of a style of intentional roughness to convey urgency and sincerity and to bring the music closer to the audience. This is certainly the approach of, for example, the seminal nineties anarcho-punk/metal/hip hop band Rage Against the Machine, which came out of your CD player attacking technology on behalf of anarcho-primitivism. Even as they sold tens of thousands of records and appeared on MTV, they were constantly jagged to those contexts, and finally disintegrated in an enactment of mass-mediated misbehavior. Now, probably the audiences of Rage Against the Machine and Pete Seeger hardly overlapped; neither audience would have recognized the other as responding for similar reasons to a similar set of ideas. But they did. Of course, protest songs are a bit . . . feeble as a genuine means to transform injustice. More profound was the community formation partly created around the music as protest.

Indeed, music has a peculiar power to create solidarity (which is also to say, to shape social exclusions). The tribes of youth culture who have crisscrossed the globe in the era of mass media might be defined economically, through political slogans or texts, or through body-shaping and adornment. But they understood their own solidarity above all in terms of music, from greasers to hippies to punks and with dozens of permutations of each (again, see Hebdige). The role of Woodstock or the Grateful Dead in crystallizing hippie subculture and its politics and conveying it, reproducing it everywhere, cannot be overstated. The clothing styles of each wave of disaffected youth are disseminated primarily by musicians: the leather jacket, the lumberjack shirt, bellbottoms, or safety pins. And one might think of the ways music, understood to create social solidarity, has been put to use by regimes and political systems: the function of Wagner in the rise and dissemination of Nazism, for example, or the response of people to hearing their national anthem. Or consider the uses of music within consumer capitalism—its ubiquitous use to articulate and control store environments or to market products. The political history of music is still being written, but we are soaked in it all the time.

In punk, however, the focus on music specifically limited the effects of the revolt, which was detoured from insurrection to art. Punk was never an effective revolutionary front; it was a transformative and transforming social identity, highly ambiguous except for a generalized signifying of opposition. Real punks withdrew from rather than attacked the culture they rejected and created local zones of solidarity and autonomy.

Attempts to create solidarity in punk include the two-tone and two-sex bands of the late seventies in the U.K. The Specials, Madness, and the English Beat were ska bands that not only were multiracial but made black and white their basic visual symbol. They played ska—a Jamaican style from the sixties—and featured artists from London's Jamaican community: they were "postcolonial." They consciously formed a bulwark against the rise of the right-wing, National Front, anti-immigrant skinhead punk movement, and they also made excellent records, though not only excellent records. Crass and many of the anarcho-punk bands featured women in various roles, which could still be a bit surprising in 1979. But punk had from the first featured a fair smattering of women, as in Poly Styrene and Lora Logic of X-Ray Specs, not to speak of Patti Smith. Many of the biggest female rock stars who emerged in the eighties were essentially punks: Chrissie Hynde of the Pretenders (a rock journalist who ran with the Pistols); Joan Jett (who produced what may be the first hardcore album, *GI* by the Germs); and of course Debbie Harry. Some of later punk and post-punk's most excellent bands have been composed of women and have produced strident feminist documents: L7, Hole, Bikini Kill, Sleater-Kinney. By contrast, hardcore punk, especially early on, was notorious for its sexism, often forming an alternative to playing on the high school football team. The jocks of Southern California, for example, were notorious for treating dancing as a full-contact sport. Black Flag bassist Kira Roessler quit in disgust at the band's absolutely explicit misogyny.

It is worth worrying about the use of fascist or Nazi symbolism in punk music and about explicitly white supremacist and anti-Semitic punk music of the kind issued by labels such as Die Hard and Victory. When punks defined themselves as the opposite of hippies, they took on a right-wing politics by default, and many of the fundamental hardcore bands had moments that could be construed as right—or white—wing. D.C. was Chocolate City; MacKaye talked about being a "white minority," a song later appropriated by European white supremacists. In "Guilty of Being White," Black Flag made fun of leftist guilt about racism. Seminal New York hardcore bands such as Agnostic Front and Cro-Mags flirted more enduringly with anti-p.c. themes. The early L.A. hardcore band Fear featured hilarious and appalling racism and sexism—"the trouble today with women: the mouth don't stop"—and a back-to-back "F" symbol that was a kind of fuck-you swastika, along with American/German eagles and so on. Skinheads in Britain in the late seventies became associated with the anti-immigrant quasi-fascism of the National Front—ironic given the subculture's use of black Jamaican music as the source of its beat. At latest since the hardcore era (1980–1984) there has been a world underground of racist or anti-immigrant punk music (already in 1983 the Dead Kennedys could sing "Nazi Punks Fuck Off"), distributed hand to hand, inbox to inbox in the old-fashioned DIY manner. Such bands have garnered predictable, occasional attention, and are sometimes prosecuted under anti-Nazi laws in Germany and Austria. Here is a lyric from the band Ethnic Cleansing, and though it is obviously repugnant, we also should begin to wonder about its possible parodic quality:

> You know hardcore has gone to shit
> When niggers and faggots are in the pit
> *Maximum Rock'n'Roll* [a punk magazine] supports this crap
> Says sucking dick is where it's at.
>
> I beg to differ, I disagree
> Punk's for straights, people like me
> Green Day's got AIDS and they piss from cunts
> Cock-sucking Kikes who call themselves "punk."[2]

---

2. See http://www.nazipunk.8k.com/ethniccleansing.html.

Were I to try to give a serious reading of such material, it would go like this: On the one hand, it is parodic in the sense that it is not produced without an intentionality and distance that give it the whiff of irony; it is specifically constructed or tailored as a provocation or an anthology of offenses, of forbidden words. On the other hand, the views expressed are not without effects, and one would be rash to say that the person who wrote this is not a potentially violent homophobe. The racism and the anti-racism of punk are spectacular; they are a matter of hyperbolic signs that reflect ambiguous or multiple intentions.

The audience for that lyric is probably ultimately left-wing anarcho-punks, as the reference to the leftist punk periodical *Maximum RocknRoll* shows. Punk enacts a schism from the get-go or fragments into a million bits in a happier or less deadly recapitulation of what happens within the defeated liberation front in a third world country. First the Right broke with the Left over the swastika and the hammer and sickle, then each side started splintering, with leftist anarcho-punk especially notorious for schism. This half-self-conscious tribalism comes from reading *Lord of the Flies* in middle school and leads to various audible and visual cues of belonging and exclusion.

Without excusing the fascism of some punks (or of anyone else), I point out that one feature of punk is that it always avails itself of the most extreme possible symbolism. Early on, in the Pistols and their comrades, the point was simply the transgression, not the content, and putting swastikas on the queen's eyes was almost nothing but a provocation. Anarchism and fascism, whether we consider them related (through Georges Sorel, let's say, or even Mussolini) or at opposite ends of the spectrum, have a similar preternatural ability to freak decent people out, a potency as word or symbol virtually unmatched in our vernaculars. They almost cannot be heard, which is why to use them has the flavor of raving meaninglessly. The Dead Boys tossed around the word "Schweinhund," but probably didn't really care whether they were anarchists or fascists as long as they weren't Democrats or Republicans. The fascists in particular, too, as we have seen in spades, had a vivid symbolic repertoire of Iron Crosses and swastikas and lightning symbols, adapted by right punk as instant, infinitely reproducible (Xeroxable, stencilable) signs of transgression that everyone could read in shock. The punks availed themselves of the symbolism before they thought through the politics. And when they did, they split into camps, Right and Left punks, anarchist and fascist punks. In Britain the Right railed against immigrants; in the United States they tossed around supposed Klan affiliations. A few of the musicians or hangers-on who casually adopted the swastika on their torn-up leather jackets (in fact an early version of the Clash was called London SS) eventually set up shop in secret revolutionary enclaves, Falangist squats (Clash: "Spanish bombs, they killed Garcia Lorca"), and militia camps; one rightist group adopted the name Rock Against Communism, as though this was 1930s Germany, but with electric guitars. Fascism and anarchism have in common a global attack on the established order, which both regard as diseased and inauthentic. Punk— the musical style—expresses this critique perfectly, even as it avails itself of musical signifiers that were long in construction, such as Jamaican elements or militaristic drums. These elements function in immediate political expression, argument as beat.

Nevertheless, one might argue that the aesthetics of punk are more suited to an anarchist than a fascist use, and indeed Nazi and racist punk is a fairly small subgenre. Far more frequently the politics are libertarian/leftist in my experience; the ratio might be 90-10 with local variations. First of all, punk design and punk music are often what we would merely call anarchic, using the term not primarily in a political but in an aesthetic sense. That is, the material presented is apparently disorganized, purposefully disordered, undisciplined, arbitrary, not rule-bound. Punk proceeds by collage and by at least the signs of improvisation. It is notoriously undisciplined, even where it becomes a convention or a fashion. That punk is antiauthoritarian is compatible with its being fascist in a situation wherein the power that it is responding to is not itself fascist but, say, social democratic. It is hard to imagine the sorts of skinhead punks attracted to the Right merging into a Hitler youth or a disciplined corps of soldiers or workers. Certainly right-wing punk never produced a Führer. But it not at all hard to imagine punks living without a state; many have tried to do so even in the midst of state power. In the course of researching this chapter, I was a bit stunned by the pervasiveness and seriousness of the anarchism in punk: it's everywhere from Vancouver to Sydney, from magazines to album covers to lyrics to interviews. As you examine the politics of all the seminal bands, from the Pistols and Clash to Black Flag and D.O.A., from Dead Kennedys to Minor Threat, from Bad Religion to Anti-Flag, it's hard not to see the thing as a whole as an anarchist movement.

Punk Visual Culture

Virtually all the punk bands, however, produced some of the signs of fascism in part because of the vagueness and ambiguity of such signs ("black" for instance). Indeed nonlexical signs can be particularly replete or can sustain multiple interpretations. The idea of "black" is a decent generalization of this: in reproduction it indicates obsolete technology (black and white television, photography, printing, and copying), but it symbolizes negation, the void (Voidoids), nihilism (Nihilistics), and also Nazi uniforms and fascist Blackshirt thugs. Then again, it signifies Marlon Brando on a motorcycle. Or race treason. Or anarchy. And the people wielding black as a sign may specifically intend all of these references simultaneously, as did, say, the Misfits, who pillaged pop culture (Marilyn and horror movies), and also created a skull logo that has infiltrated the whole culture. They latched onto extruded or illicit codes and symbol systems in order to express a generalized disillusionment. Even the leftist bands, such as the Dead Kennedys and Crass, communicated by logos wherein you could see the "A" or the swastika as may be. A comparable idea is the use of bondage wear, which in turn has fascist overtones, albeit with irony. But the leathers and piercings convey sexual as well as musical underground cultures which employed Nazi symbols, as neat a confirmation of human depravity as could readily be imagined.

The icons are eclectic, and communicate by a rich visual language of biker chicks, beatniks, surrealism and dada, comic books, traditional tattooing, slumming and slums, heroin chic. Punk is now an instantly recognizable language of both form and content: the scumbled-up chaotic black and white snapshot of a gig, bodies stopped in furious motion, singer in mid-snarl; the faux-naïve incompetent black and white flyer collage; the chains and leather and victory spikes and boots; the squat or crash pad with spray-painted walls; the fucked-up and jaded but somehow sweet and optimistic eyes of self-consciously squandered youth. Punk is as much a visual as a musical style. One function of this is to confront people with punk's subversive identities, since in most cases most people could ignore and avoid the music. But punk transformed fashion and the urban environment and people's relationships to it. Punk's romanticism of filth and slums lent a series of different meanings to the nasty part of town, starting with the Bowery in New York City. In addition, punk plastered these environments with its graphics, which transformed even mainstream visual arts and design to a remarkable degree.

From the first, the graphic arts were central both to the internal communication among punks and to their presentation to others. Flyers were the basic ways to publicize shows, and record covers and coats of arms became iconic of the bands. From the start, punk generated graphic artists who were comparable to its musicians, and some of them turned out to be important visual artists by any measure. Jamie Reid's cover art for the Sex Pistols immediately became iconic. Reid combined homemade, screwed-up design with Warholesque pop colors and almost pushbutton use of transgressive symbolism. The type appeared to have been collaged out of letters from magazines or newspapers, at once a postmodern reuse of the spectacle and an implied threat: the cover of *Never Mind the Bollocks, Here's the Sex Pistols* looks like a ransom note and hence appears to have been made by criminals. Type styles varied, but all were purposefully unprofessional or unprinted-looking, as in childish or angry scrawls (X-Ray Specs, Dead Boys) or stenciled letters, which quickly became the fallback position, and anticipated the explosion of urban stencil art that followed. The types were iconic, but so were the icons, and Reid, for one, tossed around Union Jacks and defaced the image of the queen and the British pound with a Jasper Johnsesque, Duchampian insouciance that managed to be both highly offensive and highly amusing.

Steve Blush gives a lucid description of the punk image.

> The scene's creative types corrupted words and images lifted from books and magazines, or drew outrageous, offensive pictures. No subject was sacred or taboo. At that point in history a large supply of deteriorating Vietnam-era mags offered plenty of war photos, which when mixed with porno, celebrities, mushroom clouds and cut-out type made for arresting presentations. President Reagan's photo loomed as an iconographic metaphor for repression. Angry political themes merged with B-movie imagery. Abortions, assassinations, atrocities, auto wrecks—it was all there, degraded by countless generations of xeroxing. (Blush, p. 288)

Perhaps the most potent visual sensibility in punk belonged to Raymond Pettibon, who has since gone on to become a major figure in biennials and museums. It was Pettibon who named his brother Greg Ginn's band Black Flag and designed the simple, clear, and utterly punk four bars logo that began to cover Los Angeles in 1979. Pettibon also drafted the definitive punk flyers for Black Flag and other L.A. hardcore artists, and where he did not actually do the work, his imitators showed considerable ingenuity. Pretty soon everything looked like it was a Pettibon: sloppy as hell, dramatic, clear as day, a complex interchange of icon and text, phantasmagoric. Somehow Pettibon drew perfection out of a celebration of amateurish mistakes. He achieved a perfect craft of unskilledness: you really couldn't tell whether it was made by someone with an MFA or a complete visual ignoramus. The black and white flyers appear to be collages; text is crooked or runs off the edge, and Pettibon draws on rich veins of popular imagery. His later works confirm his sophisticated reading of American films, American tattoos, American sports, American comic books and other graphic and hand-lettering styles, American race, American sex, American religion, American vice, American political history.

As the early punks belonged to a generation soaked in television, Pettibon lived in an art world that by his generation took appropriation completely for granted. He was a child when Warhol and Lichtenstein were pulling images from movies and comic books. (Winston Smith, who designed the Dead Kennedys' logo and album art, used a similar but more complex technique/iconography of "montage," a kind of anthology of American popular imagery in ironic juxtapositions.) From the early flyers, Pettibon is giving us half-recognized masks—devils, nuns, strange ambiguous scenes of violence and perversity that emerged from American noir novels: Stop me before I kill again. Pettibon's album covers for Black Flag boiled the full-to-overflowing flyers down to a few icons: the Black Flag bars, hedge clippers, killer clowns. It was analogous to the punk musical aesthetic of boiling music back down to a few ragged but intensely meaningful chords that was found as clearly on the Black Flag records as anywhere.

As means of mechanical reproduction become obsolete, the images they produce regain their aura as originals, albeit to an attenuated extent. One might consider this process with regard to music in relation to the vinyl LP and the CD. The hisses, pops, and skips of an LP now connote authenticity, and there are many punks who still prefer vinyl versions even of new music. Pettibon's mediums were cheap as dirt: Xeroxed flyers, rudimentary silk-screened T-shirts, and stripped-down album covers, disseminable to a fair mass, yet cheap and real and gritty and dirty. There are, of course, perfectly practical reasons for the use of these: among other things, they are inexpensive. Their cheapness is itself an artifact of their maturity as technologies. And whether Pettibon took up the copy machine as the perfect medium for his unique sensibility or adopted it from necessity is in a way neither here nor there; medium matched craft. Even the mere cheapness of the product was itself a protest against the expensive design culture of the era and a badge of self-sufficiency. The same aesthetic focuses on torn clothes or thrift shop items, recycling both by need and by preference, both tearing up and replacing the commercial products and hence their design.

The graphic style of punk influenced many of the artists of the period who have fallen out of life into MOMA retrospectives and so forth. Or the influence was mutual, especially since the artists and punks coincided on New York's Lower East Side. Indeed a sharp 2007 exhibition at the Barbican managed to fold an extraordinary group of visual artists into a wide punkish framework, from Gilbert & George to Gordon Matta-Clark and Cindy Sherman. Certainly we don't have to speculate on the relation of Nan Goldin or Robert Mapplethorpe to this scene; they were residents. Their work, of course, not only emerges from the same milieu but also deploys the same values, down to Mapplethorpe's preference for black and white. But Mapplethorpe himself made paradigmatic punk images, as in his portraits of

Patti Smith, including the cover of Smith's classic *Horses*. (Eventually Mapplethorpe achieved a mature craftsmanly style of beautiful images that was an interesting refinement of and rejection of punk.)

An extremely rich intersection of visual languages is found in the work of Keith Haring and Jean-Michel Basquiat, who participated in both punk and hip hop (graffiti) circles and fused them into globally different visual languages. At first glance, Basquiat's images seem punkier: hand-scrawled lettering, childishly drawn recycled imagery. But Haring's work shows more of the simplicity and incisiveness or quest for essence of the best punk graphics. The color is boiled down and the image reduced to an iconic outline, instantly comprehensible at a distance. To be honest, however, I think both Basquiat and Haring were more or less arbitrarily promoted to art star or master. I prefer the informal and occasional work of punk graphic artists on walls to the punk canvas designed for collectors or hanging in a museum. The former are not less mannered or more improvisational, but they are often more urgent and more fun, and they have a function: promoting a show, for example. Function is extremely underrated in Western fine arts, still a disqualification, but also still a pretext to focus your activities in a coherent way. To be fair to both Basquiat and Haring, neither was in control of the reception of his works, and both had worked on the streets.

The best punk visual art has often taken the form of stickers and stencils. Indeed the stencil—quick, cheap, semi-mechanical—is a primary visual art of our moment. It is certainly the way a left/anarchist/antiglobalization/squatter/vegan/punkfan community communicates with itself and others in a purely visual dimension or through urban installations. The stencil always takes on an emblematic quality because of the way the medium itself, when it is successful at all, must strip an image to its essentials; it speaks with a concision bordering on instantaneity. It has the same effect with letters, though in this case the initial forms are more restricted and so the process of reduction is less dramatic. The stencil itself took on the status of a meta-icon: many, many punk albums have been released with the band's name in pseudo-stencil. The medium itself—again a rough or obsolete or quasi-technology—is romanticized, and certainly by the time images of stencils themselves are in circulation, the stencil is radiating an aura of authenticity. Its ontological status is somewhere between sheer handwriting (for example, in hip hop graffiti of the same era) and mass media. Like a print, for example, it is mechanically reproducible but also shows the intimate involvement of the hand, both to produce the template and to produce the work/object or specific token. Prints vary from state to state along a thousand dimensions; stencils can be painted in different colors, with more or less diffusion along the edge, with or without drips, and so on. Then again, stencils have often been used to express official prohibitions, including in schools, and once again the symbolism is at least double.

The stencil has in turn reverberated into fine art, and the great political punk street artist Banksy has infiltrated the museum in every sense. First, he actually went into museums and surreptitiously planted his own paintings, complete with explanatory cards; eventually the museums came to him, wanting to buy. His stencil on the Israel-Palestine "barrier" of a girl in silhouette holding a bunch of balloons, floating over the wall, is a very pure inspiration. Banksy's body of work is the visual correlate of a Crass show: it touches on animal rights, police brutality, consumer capitalism, war, loathing for authority, and it begins to exploit the stencil as a medium in fundamentally new ways. Banksy, that is, is not merely subversive; he is a superb craftsman of the stencil, and the technique gives the idea credibility, makes you take it seriously, as excellent prose style makes an argument plausible. The work of stencil and sticker artists such as Banksy and Shepard Fairey can also be made or at least disseminated by people other than themselves and have a tendency suddenly to reproduce all over the world. Fairey's "Obey" image of Andre the Giant, arbitrarily cut out of mass media, proliferated "virally" everywhere in the early 1990s, and Fairey's posters for the Obama campaign both helped define the ideology of the candidate and completed Fairey's co-optation. Anyone with the skill can reproduce a Banksy or Fairey image: it is unowned as soon as it is installed in the street. Or Banksy or Fairey could just mail you a stencil or sticker and send you out bombing. Banksy's practice, like Haring's, originates in a fusion of punk and hip hop graphic forms (which come from the same city at the same moment), but now passed through a thirty-year history of image making. The iconography he can call upon—including Haring's—is extremely elaborate and refined.

Banksy intervenes materially in the city: his work is neither more art than politics nor more politics than art. It is beyond didactic in the sense that it is not made in order to teach lessons any more or any less than it is designed to be beautiful. The politics is the occasion or excuse for the visible intervention and the experiences it supports as much as the reverse.

Artpolitical Body/Artpolitical Environment

An important aesthetic dimension of punk is the practice of body transformation. Every social identity, every profession, every economic era, every war produces its own body styles. The unadorned body can be turned into an aesthetic object, with exercise or eating regimens or taboos transforming the body into the sign of certain sorts of disciplines. This idea is central to the art of Leni Riefenstahl, for example. Every culture and many subcultures practice direct intentional intervention in the body, as in piercing, scarring, tattooing, and of course if hair is part of the body, coiffure. This was certainly true of the youth cultures out of which punk emerged or which it defined itself in opposition to: no feature of the fifties punk was more conspicuous than his greased hair, and hippies were just "longhairs." The first thing a punk did in the late seventies was, again, to cut his hair, and probably the hardest punks were skinheads, whose pates embodied an explicit repudiation of the hippie era (L7: "This ain't the summer of love"). Especially in London, the streets outside punk venues became festivals of extreme hair. Hairstyles, I suppose, fall somewhere between clothing styles and body modifications, being more permanent than the former and less than the latter, more intimately bound to the body than the former and less so than the latter. But of course all of these are similar in that they present the body in public within various semiotic systems. Punk fashion eventually extended from mere clothing to gestalt transformations of the flesh.

The punks began a youth fad for tattooing and piercing which has hardly faded in the interim, and which has penetrated other subcultures, for example hip hop. Often the tattoos were fundamentally traditional, especially darkside quasi-satanic motifs like grim reapers and skulls, though these had heavy metal connotations (punk and metal of course intersect in myriad ways). Many punks, however, were decorated with the names and symbols of their favorite bands, or generic representations of the Mohawked head or skull. Later, as explicitly "tribal" and abstract tattooing became fashionable, the material shifted. Punks began placing tattoos in places where they could not be readily concealed: up the neck or even on the face, on the back of the hands, and so on. This expressed a very clear message: you were committed for life; you were planning never to work in the banking industry.

The music is essentially an internecine communication: most people can avoid it; the people who listen are the people who seek it out. But body adornment, like the flyer, is both an internal and an external mode of communication; it enacts its dissidence in public space, expresses a detailed critique of the dominant culture. Sometimes there are slogans literally plastered on, but whether there are or not, the extreme punk body displays a contempt for polite standards and a rejection specifically of the ways the dominant society perpetuates itself by obtaining and shaping the bodies of its youth. The appearance of people is of course a constant political or power negotiation and a constant interchange among cultures and subcultures. Clothing and body styles, including movement styles, express disgust with or indifference to or acquiescence to or enthusiastic participation in power structures. And they express these things in the most personal way: the actual identification of you the body with a set of values or rejection of it, enacted continually even while you sleep, having transformed your personality, that is, your person. The moral panic accompanying punk in the U.K. had as much to do with the appearance of the punk bodies as anything; no one was pausing to give a critical assessment of the chord structures. Punk body style is a public performance of repudiation.

We might sum up the artpolitics of punk as the festival—the whole thing, more than all its parts and identical to them—the aesthetic-social-political unification in the live performance at CBGB's or the Masque. The point of each feature of punk arts—the flyers and posters, the clothing and body alteration, the music and dance—is that it is incorporated into a total aesthetic environment, a context of ecstatic release. This release is itself political: it is a measure of one's rejection of mainstream art and politics. It is above all an exercise in solidarity, and there can be few experiences of human unity as intense as a mosh pit.

By the time peace punk got politically serious, it created these contexts with extreme care, even as the contexts themselves persisted as celebrations of chaos. Penny Rimbaud, one of the spirits behind Crass, said this about the live shows that Crass played in halls and squats all around the U.K.:

> It was orchestrated; it was very, very rehearsed; it was like a Nuremberg rally, and the closer we could get to that sort of undeniable visual and emotional perfection, the better. That's what we were looking for; we wanted to produce a backdrop that was absolutely unbreakable... because we wanted to smash through the banality. We were like a torpedo going straight at all this stupid music business, media crap, and we were strong enough to blow straight through it. And we didn't sit around making conditions on the other side either; we created a breach in their wall, and fuckin' thousands of kids ran through it! (quoted in Glasper, p. 17)

Of course, solidarity is dangerous and equivocal. People in solidarity are by and large released from self-examination. And solidarity is also exclusion: the punks not only attacked "society" or the values of their parents, schools, neighborhoods; they also attacked one another, and the vegans hated the mere vegetarians, the Nazis the mere fascists. Punk, by inducing intense feelings of belonging, introduced a kind of tribalism to suburbia that was the opposite of its apparent values: the nuclear family, the lonely commute, the polite social interactions. Indeed the nastiest and most destructive punk (Circle Jerks, for example) came out of Orange County, California, perhaps at that time the world's largest or at any rate most suburban suburb. Partly, of course, punk was about exposing the strange moments and recalcitrant facts concealed by good suburban landscaping. In the words of Joey Ramone in "We're a Happy Family," "Daddy likes men." Some of the hardcore runaways saw the under-side of American suburbia at extreme firsthand: Dee Dee Ramone, Darby Crash, and Black Randy, among many others, were "hustlers" before or dur-ing their musical careers, and no doubt the clientele was largely composed of men from the suburbs. In some ways, in fact, punk attacked suburban values in part by aping them in exaggerated fashion. The promiscuity and substance abuse that might infest any golf club became something to wallow in or to declare to be positive values, even as at the golf club they were politely con-cealed in the service of their continuation.

Art and Anarchy

In the chapter on Nazism I quoted Hellmut Lehmann-Haupt:

> Art that is the expression of individual search, of experiment, of intui-tive play, art that penetrates the surface of the visual world, that is pro-phetic, sensitive, apprehensive, art that challenges the individual, that demands concentration, effort, art that heightens perception, sharpens the eye, nourishes thought—that art cannot be tolerated by the dictator. (Lehmann-Haupt, pp. xviii–xix)

This is, we might say, a squarely modernist conception of art as the sphere of untrammeled individual expression and social transformation. Thinkers of that period could associate art with freedom in a very direct way and hence conclude that the arts of totalitarianism were mere contradictions, or in the favored term "kitsch," not properly art at all: as art, debased or empty. And it is worth exploring the connection of art and political freedom at a bit more length.

Alan Antliff, in his book *Anarchist Modernism,* shows the intimate connec-tion of the advent of American avant-garde modernism (centered in lower Manhattan) with the anarchist political movement of the early twentieth century. He argues that "anarchism was *the* formative force lending coher-ence and direction to modernism in the United States between 1908 and 1920" (Antliff 1, p. 1). Antliff makes this claim remarkably plausible, but I think that a better formulation is that modernism in art of that period and anarchist politics were mutually influential, that the artists were united by the political philosophy than the political thinkers by the art. The figures that Antliff makes direct precursors of this synthesis—Oscar Wilde and Leo Tolstoy—were both anarchist political theorists/heroes and, of course, major literary figures. But as Antliff shows, the most central figures of both the production and presentation of the new art in early-twentieth-century America—the painters, teachers, critics, gallery owners—regarded themselves as anarchists. These would include Alfred Stieglitz (important as a photographer and even more as a mentor and public advocate), Arthur Dove (the first American abstractionist), Robert Henri (important as an artist and even more as a teacher), George Bellows, Maurice Prendergast, John Sloan, William Glackens, Rockwell Kent, Marsden Hartley, Man Ray, and so on: these are in some sense the very central figures of American modernism. Indeed the signal moment in American modernism, the Armory Show of 1913, was described as an anarchist event by both its organizers and its detractors.

Modernism in art was above all conceived to be a rejection of academic art: official art; beautifully crafted art; art that, we might say, above all observed rules or laws of design and facture. The academic art institutions in both France and the United States were intertwined with political and economic power in a thousand ways. Little wonder that the artists spearheading modernism explicitly considered themselves revolutionaries, and little wonder that—whether they came to anarchism through their art or to art through their anarchism—they regarded individual expression and rejection of received forms and trainings as a political matter, and as related to a much wider context of oppression and liberation. In their visionary moments they conceived a utopia in which every person was an artist, and in which art proceeded under no rule of law. That was precisely, for example, Emma Goldman's vision of an anarchist future: every person the artist of her own life, and every person a maker of art; labor transformed into self-expression. Art in this structure of thought is not, say, a liberatory strategy or a propaganda device—though Goldman used it in precisely that way in her magazine *Mother Earth,* for which Man Ray drew some covers in a style somewhere between his own abstract conceptualism and socialist realism—but the essence and end of liberation. When life and art merged, then the world would be free. Specifically of Henri's art classes, Goldman wrote that there was "a spirit of freedom which probably did not exist anywhere else in New York" (quoted in Antliff 1, p. 27). The circle around Henri specifically tried to broaden the access to exhibitions, to get rid of jury systems, or to create spaces where artists could show whatever they pleased in whatever way they pleased. This was the position, too, of Henri's bible, Tolstoy's *What Is Art?*, according to which an old peasant's story was a more authentic work of art than the paintings of all the world's academies combined, or indeed asserted that the latter were not art at all because they were insufficiently sincere, intense, emotional, individual.

Anarchists of the period commonly used art as an image of human liberation and human liberation as a program for art. In an ecstatic vein the great American anarchist writer Voltairine de Cleyre characterized anarchism as follows in 1901:

> To turn cloudward, starward, skyward, and let the dreams rush over one—no longer awed by outside powers of any order—recognizing nothing as superior to oneself—painting, painting endless pictures, creating unheard symphonies that sing dream sounds to you alone, extending sympathies to the dumb brutes as equal brothers, kissing the flowers as one did when a child, letting oneself go free, go free beyond the bounds of what *fear* and *custom* call the "possible,"—this too Anarchism may mean to you, if you dare apply it so. . . . [And] if then you look across at your lowbrowed neighbor, who sweats and smells and curses at his toil,—remember that as you do not know his depth neither do you know his height. He too might dream if the yoke of custom and law and dogma were broken from him. Even now you know not what blind, bound, motionless chrysalis is working there to prepare its winged thing. (de Cleyre, p. 80)

Such a vision of liberation as art and art as liberation can be seen as central to avant-garde art of the first few decades of the twentieth century, to Fauvism, cubism, dadaism, surrealism, and so on.

It is hardly surprising that one expression of the rejection of academic art was precisely roughness of finish: the retention of the trace of the eccentric or individual gesture. Of the Armory Show, the critic and anarchist Hutchins Hapgood wrote that the artists expressed themselves in the "simplest, most intense way" (quoted in Antliff, p. 42). Here we might also consider the influence of "primitive" art (for example, African masks) on the modernism of Picasso or Matisse. This material signified not only directness and simplicity or roughness of execution but also the tribal or pre-state cultures of Africa and, as famously in the case of Gauguin, the South Pacific. The rough technique of, for example, the "Ashcan" school connects early-twentieth-century anarchist modernism to punk design very directly: it is a sign of the immediacy, intensity, urgency, and sincerity of individual expression, as opposed to the strictures of either academic art or corporate pop music that required perfect finish. It is also a democratization of art, and explicitly in both cases tries to make it possible for anyone to participate by removing requirements of training or refined sensibility. In Henri's educational programs, for example, at the anarchist Ferrer Center and Modern School—as in MacKaye's Dischord Records—an attempt is made to identify audience and artists, to bring access to artistic expression to more people: ideally to all people. This corresponds closely to subject matter, and Henri and his students (as well as many others) dedicated themselves to depicting the sorts of people that academic art omitted, such as workers, prostitutes, substance abusers, the poor, the homeless, and the hopeless. This in turn had already been a theme in radical European art at least since Courbet, himself close to the anarchist philosopher Proudhon, whom he painted at least twice. Proudhon returned the favor by writing a book in defense of Courbet's realism. And as Courbet painted Proudhon, Henri painted Emma Goldman. The Ramones depicted the lives of substance abusers and alienated working-class or middle-class teenagers, though often with great irony or hyperbole.

Yet another connection between anarchism and modern art lies at the center of perhaps the most radical art movement of the last few centuries: dada, which overlaps with Stieglitz, the Armory Show, and the anarchist avant-garde I have been examining. Both Marcel Duchamp and Francis Picabia were immersed in the anarchist Max Stirner's anti-essentialist book *The Ego and Its Own* when they produced art that was intended not only as a political intervention but also to destroy the concept of art itself (Antliff 2, chap. 3). Picabia, for example, transformed his work under the influence of Stirner from an almost academic cubism to a series of "portraits" of people as meticulously drawn machines; already in the 1910s he was breaking down distinctions between the handmade and the mechanically produced, the fine and the popular, art and culture, art and political expression. If there could be, in the face of such serious purpose, a political aesthetics of whimsy, if there could be a comedic revolution or a revolutionary comedy, its avatars would be figures such as Duchamp, Picabia, Man Ray, and Jello Biafra. Indeed, we could tell a story connecting anarchism of this stripe to a whole history of twentieth-century art, including such nodes as Tristan Tzara, André Breton, Situationism, Andy Warhol, and from Warhol's Velvet Underground and Debord's McLaren directly into punk music.

Now, I said at the outset that I was concerned here not with the political aspects of art systems but with the artistic aspects of political systems. But again the distinction is in question in any given case. And the anarchist arts have been not only central to art history in surprising ways but also central to extra-state social systems all over the world, from the Paris Commune to the antiglobalization movement. And the liberatory ideas of anarchism have in turn been central to the self-concept of avant-garde artists since the nineteenth century. Among other things, they are central to the sort of art and artists that the Nazis devoted themselves literally to annihilating. That is, art was no more central to the politics that the Nazis espoused than to the politics they suppressed.

Of course, modernism itself generated various academic and hierarchical forms as it became the dominant art style of the twentieth century. We have already seen this transformation in action, for example, in the works of Clement Greenberg, in which modernism becomes as much an arena of connoisseurship as Old Master painting. Indeed Clyfford Still—an anarchist and for my money one the best handful of painters of the twentieth century—explicitly barred Greenberg and others of his ilk from reviewing his work, on the grounds of their academic formalism and rigidity (Antliff 2, p. 117). This is the price, we might say, of aesthetic victory; and again the progress of punk music and design traverses a similar path, and its conventionalization and commercialization are routinely decried by its original practitioners or newly arrived underground artists and participants. Nevertheless, the "gestural" painters whom Greenberg championed—and however Greenberg may have theorized them in relation to the history of painting, in terms of their truth to the medium, use of paint as paint, and so on—deployed what we might well consider a punk aesthetic of extreme roughness, intensity, and populist anti-craft. Pollock himself was less theorist than proto-punk. As well, anarchism as an important political movement in the European and American Left faded in the face of Marxist communism and bolshevism. Emma Goldman was a celebrity in 1913; by the time she died, in 1940, she was largely forgotten, and Greenberg's advocacy of "international socialism" was, by the time he wrote, conventional leftism.

Neither punk nor, for that matter, New York modernism of the early twentieth century transformed the world or created a golden age of anarchy. Even a basic rehearsal of the complexities of the values punks deployed makes it impossible to say what the "success" of punk would have consisted in. By almost any standard, dying by overdose or self-inflicted gunshot wound is not exactly success, but the punks obviously romanticized self-destruction, whether of Sid Vicious, more or less all the members of Battalion of Saints, or Kurt Cobain. But of course here punk is again systematically ambiguous, and I don't expect we'll lose Ian MacKaye to an overdose. And the continued existence of MacKaye's Dischord shows that the changes punk wrought were significant, if limited: small zones of economy and sociality where we evade collusion as best we can.

A portion of each cohort of kids finds punk again and reanimates it with bands. Punk, after all, is older now than rock music was when punk was devised. In each successive appropriation the imagery is adapted according to informal standards of kidly interpretation. The imagery is used at first with little comprehension, eventually maybe with much. Each time the images are adopted, they are transformed, then sold and marketed, then appropriated and transformed again. Still the signs remain, and retain their power to transform people's bodies and their cities. Punk is/was an artpolitical movement based on negation. It takes the shape of what it negates at a given moment, as what it negates takes shape around it. If you don't think that's enough, you grow up and out of your nihilistic phase; you become Fugazi. If you do think it's enough, you proceed into self-destruction. In all phases you transform the material situation; you change what people see and hear all day. As an art style or as political movement, punk is a sheer opposition: immensely valuable and not nearly as dangerous as the positive program to transform everything. That's important: we need punk in that sense now as ever.

CHAPTER 4

Prehistory of Political Aesthetics

It's fair to say that the centralization of aesthetics to the account of politics is not a recent innovation. Confucianism, for example, is largely based on this idea. In the West the aesthetic and the political had to be teased apart and distinguished. And in many versions of classical republicanism and of totalitarianism, the values are represented as connected or identical. We might attribute the conscious merging of distinct dimensions of value, however, to the modern idealist and romantic traditions, and we see versions in Shaftesbury, Schiller, Herder, Hegel, Wagner, and Nietzsche.

Aesthetic and Anti-Aesthetic Political Philosophies

Insofar as the sources of various traditions in Western political thought can be traced to the pre-Socratics and to Plato as presenting the polity in the world in an aesthetic system, and in Eastern thought to the ceremonialism embodied in Confucianism, the political realm has entered into self-consciousness in aesthetic terms. Anaximander says, "Into those things from which existing things have their coming into being, their passing away, too, takes place, according to what must be; for they make reparation to one another for their injustice according to the ordinance of time" (Robinson, p. 34). He then describes a cyclical temporal and political order: the situation is conceived geometrically, ethically, historically, physically, at once. I suggest that the only way to make these orders perspicuous in their overall structure and in their relations to one another would be in aesthetic terms, that the aesthetic view is the one that gives the shape and the flow at the widest scope. The system is connected in aesthetic but not so clearly in other terms to the systems of Heraclitus or Parmenides, who speed up or slow down Anaximanderian cyclic temporal symmetry, or find balance, justice, harmony at different moments. Everyone is soon drawing diagrams.

We owe our understanding of the origins of Western political systems in large measure to Homer and Hesiod, and then to the Hebrew Bible and Herodotus. Much of the knowledge of political systems, that is, is transmitted through poetry, and many of the monuments of political theory survive (in part) because of the aesthetic excellence of the writing, from Augustine to Machiavelli to Jefferson to Hume and Nietzsche. Indeed for Aristotle, it is language that makes human beings political—rather than merely herd or hive or social—animals. Vico connects political to linguistic history and locates the origins of political systems in poetry. This seems relatively plausible from what we know of the foundational documents of ancient civilizations, such as the Upanishads, the Torah, the Gilgamesh epic, the *Iliad,* the Chinese *Book of Songs,* and so on. Such texts served many functions simultaneously or serially: they were histories; expressions of laws and moral principles or authorizations of laws by the will of the gods or by antiquity; foundations of the education of the ruling class; sources of theology; storehouses of language and linguistic exemplars; sources of the visual arts, drama, and many other expressions; unifications of cultures. They shaped and authorized political systems. They are also, of course, fundamental sources for our reconstruction of the cultures from which they emerged, and history—including political history—in many places and many times is a reconstruction out of poetry.

Political theory as a separate branch of human learning and systematic speculation in the West, however, commences so far as we know in the writings connected with Socrates, and in the East with writings connected with Confucius. Here too it is worth noting the literary force, the artistic center, of these texts; and though Plato may have condemned most visual arts and most poetry, he was himself a dramatic poet. The governing metaphor of ruling in Plato is *techne:* craft or art. The first several books of the *Republic* are largely a series of arguments drawn from this analogy, and the *Statesman* is based largely on the parallels between "the art of ruling" and "the art of weaving" (Plato 2, 279b–311c). Plato gives a kind of manifesto for politics as an art or craft, a form of skill and knowledge.

[S]tatesmanship is a form of knowledge. . . . [T]he real criterion in judg-
ing constitutions must not be whether few or many rule, whether rule
is by violence or consent, or whether rulers are poor or rich. . . . [T]he
criterion must be the presence or absence of an art directing the ruling.
(Plato 2, 292c)

Of course we cannot identify Plato's "art" (*techne*)—the *technai,* the disciplines, the crafts, the skills, the professions—with what we in modernity
might call "art." We perhaps mean the fine arts: the stuff you might run into
in museums or concert and performance halls. But first of all I would hold
out for a closer connection than is sometimes allowed between the Platonic
or Greek sense of *techne* and our modern use of the term "art" with regard
in particular to the ways we measure and appreciate works of art. Certainly
"the art of medicine," "the art of weaving," "the art of statesmanship" are
perfectly good locutions in contemporary English and would give no competent speaker much pause. And though in some cases art has been pointedly
separated from skill, much of the hush that falls over the Louvre is in response
the awesome skill of a Leonardo or Hals: the dialogue with and mastery over
materials that are the essence of *techne.*

Once we throw into question the modernist or formalist separation (always
less pronounced in practice than in theory) between skill and aesthetic quality,
we can reconnect to the pervasive philosophy of craft in Plato, Aristotle, and
the Greeks generally. And we can reconnect the idea of aesthetic value with
knowledge. Indeed, as is well known, knowledge for Plato is at the heart of
virtue, the heart of justice, the heart of beauty, the heart, even, of desire. Thus
it is not surprising to see him emphasizing the connection between craft,
knowledge, form, and morality or collapsing them all into one dimension of
value (epistemic), which I think is extremely problematic. Nevertheless, we
may envy the facility with which Plato, using the concepts of his culture—
what can look from here like a failure to make obvious distinctions—shows
that regarding each value as implicating the others sheds light on them all.
Or we may admire in principle the procedure of achieving unity before once
more emerging into diversity, for example, in Aristotle.

The reordering of materials is the exercise of authority in the arts and
crafts, but for Plato of course this authority derives from—or simply is-
knowledge. And it is worth saying that the power of any crafter over her
materials is not like the power of a tyrant over a prisoner but is a dialectical
process that emerges in contact with the materials. Plato is a totalitarian not
in advancing the metaphor of craft or the idea of statesmanship as an example
of craft, but in virtue of the plasticity he attributes to the human person as

the material of political craft. His political arrangements are designed to shape the consciousness of all individuals, but shaping is only one moment in the dialectical process of any craft. The materials of a craft are recalcitrant; they resist certain sorts of transformations, and are suitable for one purpose rather than another. Indeed these recalcitrances are what demand skill; they constitute the phenomenology of materials; working with them and through them is what produces, through craft, excellence and satisfaction. A political philosophy of craft might start with a celebration of the strangeness, perversity, and cussed common wisdom of the human being as material. Even *The Prince* might be adduced as an example of this sort of text: above all it is an elucidation of the nature of persons as the objects of statecraft, and the Machiavellian theme of *virtù* nicely captures and collapses all these themes: skill, goodness, spirit, art, intelligence, courage.

Notice that, first of all, a *techne* is, for Plato, a form of specialized knowledge, and that each *techne* comes with an intrinsic set of governing purposes and related dimensions of value. The form of the Platonic argument in the *Republic* is always an inference from the telos or purpose of a craft to the reasons and ways it is to be pursued. The real purposes of the *techne* of medicine are internal to the activity of medicine, and a person is an excellent doctor in virtue of these, not in virtue of whatever else he may achieve by his activity: wealth, prestige, and so on. One could fail by the external standards and still be an excellent physician. The art of governing also has a telos: the good of the whole polis. Accumulation even of political power is external to this goal in the sense that insofar as one is truly a ruler, one seeks political power (for example the power to censor) not for its own sake but for the good of the polis. Thus the art of governing can be described as epistemic and ethical, but it is also aesthetic or at its heart precisely an art, subject not only to knowledge but also to inspiration.

When Plato then goes on to describe, in what is after all in some sense a work of literature, the education of the guardians and the order of the polis, he does so in a construction of intense classicism, of perfect symmetry in metaphysics, epistemology, politics, ethics, educational theory, and so on. Reality as a whole has three levels: the Forms, the everyday world, and the realm of shadows or illusions or representations. The human soul has three parts: reason, will, and desire. The polis has three classes: rulers, soldiers, and the rest (tradesmen, farmers, and so on). The *Republic* is an extremely aestheticized political theory, which as many commentators have pointed out is ironic or perhaps even bizarre, given that one of Plato's obsessions throughout is the condemnation of poetry and the other representational arts. And here we might meet an objection that we have seen in relation to Nazism: the aesthetic politics of the *Republic* yields totalitarian results. It is precisely the perfection, symmetry, and rigidity of the design which detaches it from reality, and which entails that to be achieved it must be imposed. And the metaphor of craft itself, with its overtones of "mastery," of power over plastic materials, suggests a totalitarian approach, an imposition of form as the essence of statecraft, deriving from the imposition of form as the essence of any craft. In response, I would note that the system of the *Republic* is subject among other things to aesthetic critique: it is too neat to be interesting, too pat to be true to the real chaos of life and the world, too rigid to inspire, too condescending to be constructive. Plato ends the *Statesman* by nailing the idea of statesmanship as a *techne* about as hard as a metaphor can be nailed.

> Now we have reached the appointed end of the weaving of the web of state. It is fashioned by the statesman's weaving; the strands run true, and these strands are the gentle and the brave. Here these strands are woven together into a unified character. For this unity is won where the kingly art draws the life of both types into a true fellowship by mutual concord and by ties of friendship. It is the finest and best of all fabrics. It infolds all who dwell in the city, bond or free, in its firm contexture. Its kingly weaver maintains his control and oversight over it, and it lacks nothing that makes for happiness so far as happiness is obtainable in human community. (Plato 2, 311b–c)

This is about the wielding of political power, and it is as explicitly as possible utopian. But it is just as much about the form or arrangement of communities, of the ways men and women really intersect or create some sort of pattern together. Here "metaphors" drawn from the arts and crafts seem immediately to present themselves. But the relation is more than metaphorical, insofar as statesmanship could be thought of as the art or skill of shaping the polis, quite literally.

Though Aristotle likewise deploys the metaphor/identification of ruling or statesmanship as *techne,* his political philosophy is far less directly concerned with aesthetics. Again, this is ironic in that Aristotle is much more sympathetic to the arts than is Plato, and explicitly resorts to them as central sites of political formation. But if there is a governing metaphor that serves Aristotle where *techne* serves Plato, it is the idea of the polis as an organism, which is in tension with the *techne* idea. For Aristotle, the polis is a natural object, though also subject to conscious intervention. (Of course that too is natural for creatures such as ourselves.) Since man is a political animal, the polis is an expression of our nature, an instinct as it were. Thus he puts the question mainly in terms of the *constitution* of the polis; he thinks of it by analogy to the body.

> Again, the state, as composed of unlikes, may be compared to a living being: as the first elements into which a living being are resolved are soul and body, as soul is made up of rational principle and appetite, the family of husband and wife, property of master and slave, so of all these, as well as other dissimilar elements, the state is composed. (Aristotle 2, 1277a1)

He immediately quotes Euripides, which again seems a double-edged source, given the subtlety of Euripides' art: "No subtle arts for me, but only what the state requires." And in Aristotle's teleological ordering of all political means to the end of the happiness of the polis, we get a very pragmatic, or at least insistently practical, approach to politics. And we get it in conspicuously more workmanlike prose (though the state of Aristotle's literary remains makes an assessment of him as a stylist problematic). The *Politics* is throughout presented as a response to and amendment of the *Republic,* with the disagreement about the art of rulership a constant underlying theme. The *Republic* is beautiful, says Aristotle, but useless for getting us busy in the real political life of Athens: "The discourses of Socrates are never commonplace; they always exhibit grace and originality and thought; but perfection in everything can hardly be expected" (Aristotle 2, 1265a12).

That is, Aristotle not only rejects Plato's totalitarian politics but rejects his political aesthetics as well. He rejects aesthetic ends as proper to or internal to politics. His vision of politics is ethical rather than aesthetic, and the classical beauty of the utopia that Plato presents is itself a problem; it might seduce us away from the practical task of actually making things a little better. Aristotle presents economics, for example, with reference to his account of the virtues: the polis should encourage a large middle class, should steer a middle course. And one begins in the community one actually inhabits. The question is how to introduce incremental reforms while respecting the traditions of the polis.

> For if what was said in the *Ethics* is true, that the happy life is the life according to excellence lived without impediment, and that excellence is a mean, then the life which is in a mean, and in a mean attainable by everyone, must be best. And the same principles of excellence and badness are characteristic of cities and of constitutions; for the constitution is so to speak the life of the city.

> Now in all states there are three elements: one class is very rich, another very poor, and a third is in a mean. It is admitted that moderation and the mean are best, and therefore it will clearly be best to possess the gifts of fortune in moderation; for in that condition of life men are most ready to follow rational principle. (Aristotle 2, 1295a34–1295b26)

Aristotle himself, I think, does not appreciate how very Platonic this architecture is, only it is less insistently prescriptive. But within a classical vocabulary of tripartite distinctions and rational principles, Aristotle tries to frame the issue as ethical rather than aesthetic, and to bow to common sense.

But "constitution" itself is the dominant theme of Aristotle's political theory. He collected constitutions, and to his school we owe the preservation of the "Constitution of Athens." Thus, despite his critique of Plato precisely for the aestheticization of politics, Aristotle insistently evaluates political systems by their arrangement, their structure, and he insistently evaluates these in terms of their poise or balance. Even in his rejection of an aesthetic politics, in his insistence on the practical, Aristotle's politics is unavoidably aesthetic as well: aesthetic composition and evaluation remain at its heart, though perhaps they are not fully acknowledged. And the idea of the mixed constitution follows Aristotle and provides the dominant descriptive vocabulary of political republicanism from the Renaissance to the present: balance, mediation, symmetry, and a coherent whole emerging from disparate elements. Aristotle's politics becomes the political aesthetics of Cicero, Machiavelli, Shaftesbury, Hutcheson, Montesquieu, Adams.

This opposition between Plato and Aristotle about the place of aesthetics in politics constitutes a theme that repeats itself at various moments, places, cultures. We might think of the French monarchy against the Reformation and then against the Revolution or Confucius against Mozi (which I'll get to shortly). Once a politics is articulated by means of its aesthetic, however, once it presents itself self-consciously as an aesthetic system or according to aesthetic principles, attacks on it—even when the objection is precisely aestheticism—also take on an aesthetic weight or gain aesthetic properties. For example, if we reject the curlicues of monarchy, we are deploying an aesthetic of directness, simplicity, sincerity, clarity. The revolution that replaces and burns the curlicues defines itself by what it rejects aesthetically. Aristotle's rejection of Plato's "grace" is a plea for complexity, or even for awkwardness, as a sign of sincerity, moral seriousness, and dedication to the truth. This plea expresses, of course, aesthetic preferences, in part deployed as a critique of Plato's political aesthetics; hence it *is* a political aesthetics. Thus once it is conceived as a central element of politics, aesthetics *cannot* be jettisoned. But it would be quite wrong to think that, historically, politics was governed by considerations of utility and has become more and more precious and aestheticized. On the contrary, politics began aesthetically and has developed a more practical or utilitarian function or rhetoric, even as practicality and utility have revealed themselves as having aesthetic content.

Of all the ancient political philosophies that we know, Confucianism is easily the most explicitly and self-consciously oriented toward aesthetic values. Music serves as a metaphor of the state again and again: "This is what we can know of music: It begins in the sounds of harmony—then, pure, clean, and unbroken, it swells into completion" (Confucius, 3.23). But music is also portrayed as a perfectly practical way of creating political order ("After returning from Wei to Lu, I trued up music" [9.15]) and as a central strategy for self-cultivation ("Be incited by the *Songs,* established by ritual, and perfected by music" [8.8]). It is worth noting that there is also a section on music in the *Republic* that gets down to attributing political and martial effects to different modes and measures: "A change to a new type of music is something to beware of as a hazard of all our fortunes. For the modes of music are never disturbed without unsettling the most fundamental political and social conventions" (Plato, 424d).[1] Thus Plato; but Confucius does precisely the same things, evaluating the musical expressions of different states and their political implications. Indeed Aristotle concludes the *Politics* on the same note.

The basic directive to the individual in Confucianism is, precisely, self-cultivation, which is the necessary condition for making a contribution to the public welfare, and the basic image of self-cultivation is of a craftsman carving jade; he is "as if cut, as if polished, as if carved, as if burnished" (1.15):

> Such a noble-minded man [as Confucius] never wore purple or maroon trim. And in his informal robes, he never wore red or chestnut brown.
>
> In summer heat, he chose thin open-weave robes, worn over something light to set them off.
>
> With black silk, he wore lambskin furs. With undyed silk, he wore deerskin furs. And with yellow silk, he wore fox furs.
>
> His informal furs were long, with the right sleeve cut short so his hand was free. And for sleeping, he always wore robes half as long as he himself was....

---

1. And cf. 2.654b.

> When offering condolences, he never wore lavish lambskin furs or caps
> of black silk. For the new moon, he went to court in his full court
> regalia. And during purification for the sacrifice, he wore bright
> robes of plain linen. (Confucius, 10.6)

And as in Plato and Platonism, Confucius and Confucianism end up with
a perfectly composed and symmetrical universe, an ontology based in aesthetics. Confucius', however, is an aesthetic political/metaphysical system
without irony or a bad conscience. The change of seasons and the procession
of the stars are ritual cycles; the individual, the language, the state, and the
universe are nested in perfect symmetry, and hence correction to any of them
would be correction to all. Rectification of names, self-cultivation, political
leadership, balance of elements in nature—each of these was effected by and
effected the others. The *Zhongyong*: "Those who realize how to cultivate
their persons realize how to bring order to others; those who realize how
to order others properly realize how to bring order to the world, the state,
and the family." And how to "cultivate one's person"? "Fasting, purifying
oneself, putting on one's finest clothes and not making a move that violates
ritual propriety" (Ames and Hall, pp. 102, 103).

Of course, Confucianism was a governing philosophy in China for millennia, and that history shows something fundamental about political aesthetics. To think of Confucian aesthetics in calligraphy, landscape and landscape
painting, music, fashion, or bureaucratic structure merely as a form of political
propaganda would be unutterably impoverished. No doubt it functioned as
an effective ideology and shaped the consciousness of dozens of generations.
But it had that effect precisely because of its profundity, because it was something beautiful and true enough not only to command allegiance but also
within which to shape an identity. It was never merely imposed strategically,
and indeed could not be by its own lights. That in itself partly explains its
effect: its profound sincerity is affecting even if you repudiate the system.

The great Confucian thinker Hsün Tzu says:

> When music is performed in the ancestral temple of the ruler and his
> ministers, and superiors and inferiors listen to it together, there are
> none who are not filled with a spirit of harmonious reverence. When
> it is performed within the household, and father and sons, elder and
> younger brothers listen to it together, there are none who are not filled
> with a spirit of harmonious kinship. And when it is performed in
> the community, and old people and young together listen to it, there
> are none who are not filled with a spirit of harmonious obedience.

Hence music brings about complete unity and induces harmony. It arranges its accouterments to comprise an adornment to moderation; it blends its performance to achieve the completion of form. It is sufficient to lead men in a single Way or to bring order to ten thousand changes. This is the manner in which former kings created their music. And yet Mo Tzu [Mozi] criticizes it. Why? (Hsün Tzu, p. 113)

And a millennium later we have Chou Tun-i, apparently conflating all varieties of value.

Thereupon the sage-kings created music to give expression to the winds coming from the eight directions to appease the feelings of the people. This is why the sound of music is calm and not harmful, and is harmonious without being licentious. As it enters the ear and affects the heart, everyone becomes calm and peaceful. Because of calmness, one's desires will be appeased, and because of harmony, one's impetuousness will disappear. Peace, calmness, and moderation—these are the height of virtue. As the world is transformed and brought to completion, government reaches its perfection.[2]

On the one hand, the Confucians wax ever more rhapsodic about the effects of music until it seems to be mere hyperbole or metaphor. But on the other hand, music does indeed induce unity: think, for example, about a good rock concert. And many subcultures in these days, to repeat, are centered on music, from punk to redneck. Thus the normative culture is characterized by exclusion of certain musical styles as well, as we might easily see in the rejection of hip hop or punk by various persons in positions of cultural authority. Indeed we might easily imagine the response of Plato or Confucius to such styles. And of course we should be worried about the authoritarian uses of music in both Hsün Tzu and Plato: the censorship, the "spirit of harmonious obedience."

The great opponent of the Confucians with regard to the role of the arts in politics is Mozi. He's often called a "utilitarian," and there has rarely been a more straightforwardly practical and fundamentally egalitarian philosopher. People are morally better when they have enough than when they are starving; if you want to improve a nation's morals, make sure its people have food. From this point of view, the courtly architectural, musical, gustatory, visual

---

2. Chou Tun-i, "Penetrating the Book of Changes," in Chan, p. 462.

arts, and costume traditions so valued by Confucians cannot but have been thought a ridiculous and useless expenditure of valuable resources.

> The reason why Mozi condemns music is not because the sounds of the big bell, the sounding drum, the qin and the she and the yu and the sheng are not pleasant, that the carvings and ornaments are not delightful, that the fried and the broiled meats of the grass-fed and the grain-fed animals are not gratifying, or that the high towers, grand arbours, and quiet villas are not comfortable. Although the body knows they are comfortable, the mouth knows they are gratifying, the eyes know they are delightful, and the ears know they are pleasing, yet they are found not to be in accordance with the deeds of the sage-kings of antiquity and not to contribute to the benefits of the people at present. And so Mozi proclaims: To have music is wrong. Now the rulers construct musical instruments as an undertaking of the state....Inevitably heavy taxes have to be collected from the people....The ancient sage-kings had, indeed, collected heavy taxes from the people to build boats and vehicles. But when they were completed, and when the people asked: "What use have we for these?" the answer was: "The boats are to be employed on water and the vehicles on land, so that the gentlemen can rest their feet and the labourers can rest their shoulders and backs." Thus the people contributed their money and dared not grumble about it. (Mozi, bk. 8)

Essentially all the "fine arts" of the Confucian scholar class are condemned here as useless frippery or mindless ornamentation, and as an unnecessary and unconscionable squandering of the nation's wealth. Obviously this is a directly revolutionary text.

But that the Confucians and their ilk had already presented politics as aesthetics entails that Moism, in its conscious rejection of that aesthetics, took on all the trappings of a design style, one familiar to "utilitarian" and many other sorts of designers ever since. The simplest design, the design most efficiently fulfilling the function, is the most dignified, the most appropriate, even, perhaps, the most beautiful design.

> The house shall be built high enough to avoid the damp and moisture; the walls thick enough to keep out the wind and cold; the roof strong enough to stand snow, frost, rain, and dew; and the walls in the palace high enough to observe the propriety of the sexes. These are sufficient, and any expenditure of money and energy that does not bring additional utility shall not be permitted. (Mozi, bk. 1)

Or with regard to clothing:

> The sages made their clothes just to fit their stature and size, and not
> for the purpose of pleasing the senses or to dazzle the common people.
> In that age, durable carts and gentle horses were valued, but neither
> sculpture nor adornments were prized. What is the reason for this? The
> reason lies in the kind of leadership. The people had sufficient means
> of livelihood in their home to meet either drought or flood, dearth or
> famine. Why? Because they understood the needs of self-support and
> paid little attention to external appearance. (Mozi, bk. 1)

This is always the objection to "aestheticism" or a precious or superficial
reading of a political system in terms of its beauty, a retrenchment that we see
repeated in many cultures at many moments: from Art Nouveau to Bauhaus,
Catholic to Protestant, rococo to neoclassical, expressionist to minimalist,
and so on. The objection, that is, is not just directly utilitarian in the sense of
food or maybe cash; the objection is in part directly aesthetic, and the staff of
musicians is not only a concrete theft from the people but also an undigni-
fied and unserious approach to both justice and beauty, which are found in
simplicity, directness, clarity, equality.

Against the ideologies set forth by such thinkers as Confucius and Plato
there has always been a revolutionary response that is partly aesthetic. Often
this is merely spartan, or self-consciously proletarian, as in some segments of
Marxism. But then again there are arts that arise in criticism of things like
the lovely music Confucius produced on the "Chinese lute": something
rougher, bawdier, or with political allusions, something less well made or
more apparently improvisational, something slightly too intense or transgressive. If whatever music Confucius made is lost, so much more lost are the
parodies of it by rowdy Moists. And of course the victorious revolution does
not stop producing objects or structures; it does not stop shaping the environment. And the standards or principles by which it does so are of necessity
aesthetic, no matter how flat their commitment to pure utility, or no matter
how much they purport to reject the aesthetic of the previous ruling class,
or to administer all toward justice. They have to figure out what to censor,
and they have to figure out what to build, and hence they are still inexorably
engaged in the question of aesthetic value.

There are many flavors of aestheticism and anti-aestheticism in political
philosophy. One might contrast Kant, for example, with Schiller. Kant apparently aims at a rather austere (Protestant) ejection of the aesthetic (just fully
explicated as an autonomous realm in Shaftesbury and Baumgarten) from
the ethical and the political, summarized synthetically as the "kingdom of

ends." But the Third Critique attempts many sorts of provisional reconcili-
ations: beauty and art turn out to be similar to the ethical and its political
extensions in a thousand ways; the imaginary universalism of all aesthetic
judgments is the subjective counterpart of the ethical universalism proposed
in the categorical imperative. For just this reason aesthetic phenomena are as
a whole analogous to the ethical. Of course, in works of art one finds ethical
truths symbolized. One gets the feeling that although ethics does not require
aesthetics, *we* require aesthetics in order to live ethically. One way to read
German idealism is as a variety of attempts to move from this rather conces-
sive connection to the ethical to conceiving the aesthetic as the source of
or model for the ethical and the political. Already this is fully developed in
Schiller's dialectic. Hegel, Schopenhauer, and Nietzsche each presents a new
way of adjudicating this relationship of similars, in the latter two cases at any
rate in favor of the aesthetic.

The Aesthetic State and the Discipline of Aesthetics

At the origin of the modern discipline of "aesthetics" or "philosophy of art,"
Anthony Ashley Cooper (the third Earl of Shaftesbury) addressed questions
about beauty and literary composition from the standpoint of an exquisite sensibility, saying that the beautiful object must be appreciated disin-
terestedly, or merely for its intrinsic sensible quality, or "form." He termed
that "taste" and cultivated taste assiduously precisely as a style: that is, he
was self-consciously a "connoisseur." But because taste is a matter of a personal, virtuosic standpoint on everything, because it has no particular subject
matter—because taste is an identity—in Shaftesbury an approach to political
aesthetics is already nascent: a man of sensibility had only to turn his attention
in the direction of politics, which had to some extent formed the context in
which his sensibility could emerge, and consider the political as a question of
taste. Indeed the beauty of political systems is higher or more important than
the beauty of particular objects such as works of art. "The Enjoyment of such a
single Beauty," Shaftesbury writes, "is not [enough] to satisfy [the] aspiring
Soul. It seeks how to combine more Beautys, and by what Coalition of these,
to form a beautiful Society. It views Communitys, Friendships, Relations,
Dutys; and consider by what Harmony of particular Minds the general Harmony is compos'd, and *Commonweal* establish'd" (Shaftesbury, 2:121). Plato
(Shaftesbury's hero) argued much the same in the *Symposium*. It is hardly too
much to say that for Shaftesbury the state exists in order to produce men of
taste: men enabled to achieve the intrinsic end of our species, to know the

world in beauty and truth. But such men in turn exist in order to help create and to hold dear the harmonious state.

Aesthetics is conceived at its outset as having political sources and implications. Shaftesbury evaluates all regimes by their artistic culture. From Italy, in 1712, he writes:

> Every thing co-operates in such a[n ideal] *State,* towards the Improvement of *Art* and *Science.* And for the *designing arts* in particular, such as *Architecture, Painting,* and *Statuary,* they are in a manner linked together. The Taste of one kind brings necessarily that of the others along with it. When the *free* Spirit of a Nation turns itself this way, Judgments are form'd; Criticks arise; the public Eye and Ear improve; a right Taste prevails, and in a manner forces its way. Nothing is so improving, nothing so natural, so *con-genial* to the liberal Arts, as that reigning Liberty and high Spirit of a People, which from the habit of judging in the higher Matters for themselves, makes 'em freely judge of other Subjects, and enter thorowly into the Characters as well of *Men* and *Manners,* as of the *Products* or *Works* of Men, in Art and Science. So much...do we owe to the Excellence of our National Constitution and Legal Monarchy; happily fitted for Us, and which alone cou'd hold together so mighty a People; all sharers...in the government of *themselves.* (Shaftesbury, 3:247)

This makes a number of subtle connections: between taste and freedom, the design of political constitutions and technological advancement, monarch and artist. Shaftesbury is the first and still among the most profound of aestheticians in that he is the first thinker to try to see all of the issues he addressed in aesthetic terms, and then to emphasize the centrality and seriousness of aesthetics in moral, political, and religious life. He looks upon each phenomenon—the character of men or the orbits of the planets—in terms of the principles that order it into a coherent system: the parts that compose it and how they are comprehensibly, rightly, naturally, beautifully ordered; a "post-empiricist" approach to science. In other words, he is not merely a precious aesthete in the late-nineteenth-century sense; there is moral (and religious, and scientific) seriousness in the aesthetics of the state, typical of all the early discourse of aesthetics. Art has, if nothing else, urgency, in Kant, Lessing, Schiller, Herder, Schelling, Schopenhauer, Nietzsche: the gigantic figures of late-eighteenth- and nineteenth-century ("romantic") aesthetics.

Another route to political aesthetics, roughly contemporary with Shaftesbury, is provided by Vico's philosophy of history. Vico's cyclical periodization into "the age of gods," "the age of heroes," and "the era of men" equally concerns the nature and uses of language, as in hieroglyphs and alphabets and literary genres, the use of architecture and images, and the nature of political institutions. As to the three kinds of language constituting the "lexicon" of his "New Science," Vico describes them thus:

(1) The first dates from the age of families when pagan peoples had just embraced civilization. We find that it was a mute or wordless language which used gestures or physical objects bearing a natural relationship to the ideas they wanted to signify.

(2) The second language used heroic emblems—such as similes, comparisons, images, metaphors, and descriptions of nature—as the principal lexicon of its heroic language, which was spoken in the age when heroes ruled.

(3) The third language was the human or civilized language which used vocabulary agreed on by popular convention, and of which the people are the absolute lords. This language is proper to democracies and monarchies, for in those states it is the people who determine the meaning of the laws, which are binding for nobles and plebeians alike. (Vico, pp. 22–23)

The very idea of the philosophy of history, which, complete with the obsession with tripartite distinctions (itself an aesthetic), is imported by Hegel into the main line of Western speculation, implies the unity of aesthetic and political categories, betrayed above all in architectural and literary forms. Indeed the centralization of law connects political and textual questions fundamentally, or gently suggests the relevance of hermeneutics to political history and philosophy. And Vico's treatment of representation, though highly eccentric, is also central: it immediately connects political and aesthetic matters in a profitably confused way. It is hard to assess the direct influence of Vico on the development of German idealism. Nevertheless, the latter's basic conflation of politics and aesthetics, its social constructionism and zeitgeists embodied above all in the arts, are explicit in Vico, whose new or anti-science collapses distinctions or puts them into relation, reunifies the taxonomy of human activities that separates the aesthetic and the political.

One finds observations on government that employ an aesthetic vocabulary throughout our tradition. But as a concerted or systematic strategy for accounting for the political, political aesthetics can be attributed to Friedrich Schiller, with Shaftesbury and Vico the most important precursors. Perhaps the clearest formulations of the program of political aesthetics are found in Schiller's *Letters on the Aesthetic Education of Man,* which gives a liberatory politics in terms of beauty, and accounts for beauty in terms of play. Schiller speaks of the "statesman-artist" and describes the arts as the element that "might pave the way for a transition from the realm of mere force to the rule of law" (Schiller, p. 30). In other words, the aesthetic or the realm of sensibility provides the solution to the basic political dilemma concerning the relation of the force of the state to the autonomy of the individual. Here we might think of a game: bound by rules, but the players acting freely within those rules, in fact enabled to act freely in this context precisely by those rules. Schiller in rough terms describes a political system as a design regime. The people are recalcitrant, even to the statesman-artist.

> In vain you will assail their maxims, in vain condemn their deeds; but you can try your fashioning hand upon their idleness. Drive away lawlessness, frivolity and coarseness from their pleasure, and you will imperceptibly banish them from their actions, and finally from their dispositions. Wherever you find them, surround them with noble, great and ingenious forms, enclose them all round with symbols of excellence, until actuality is overpowered by appearance and Nature by Art. (Schiller, pp. 54–55)

This sort of "aesthetic education" is practiced by all who try to control their corporate or state sector environment with music, posters, color schemes, and so on, though no doubt Schiller would have done better. And we work on the citizenry as art by the use of art, shape them by shaping their world. Schiller even scouts the objection that what is beautiful may be morally repugnant, that to aestheticize politics is to run into the danger of creating a beautiful yet brutal or unjust order. He replies, in the tenth letter, by saying not that this objection is exactly false—Schiller agrees that moral and aesthetic qualities can come apart—but that judgments about beauty are unavoidable, a dimension of value that is always in play, that can never be eradicated. The centrality of aesthetic value "can be inferred simply from the possibility of a nature that is both sensuous and rational; in a word, Beauty must be exhibited as a necessary condition of humanity" (Schiller, p. 60).

The history of which Schiller represents one high point coincides in many respects with romanticism. And as romantic political aesthetics unfolds—and despite its origins in a kind of classical republicanism—it raises our dark question: the accusation that "aestheticizing" politics, or understanding politics in aesthetic terms, has totalitarian implications. It is not difficult to draw the intellectual connections from Schiller all the way to the Third Reich, though of course such retroactive Nazification is profoundly unfair to Schiller and many of the other figures that might be drawn into such an account, such as

Herder. Nevertheless, the aestheticization of politics is indeed characteristic of German nationalism and a style of sublime aesthetic spectacle that is, as a matter of fact, connected to the Holocaust.

"Aesthetics" as a discipline, then, in Germany and England, arises within a new conceptual nexus that includes the "modern" use of the term "art," decisively distinguishing the fine arts from the crafts and professions. One might say that it coincided too with an extreme refinement of connoisseurship that had begun in the Renaissance, a "baroque" connoisseurship and multidisciplinary virtuosity. Indeed the idea of the cultivation of the individual, which Burckhardt so memorably made central to the Renaissance, is brought to an intensified pitch in the eighteenth century. "Taste" is the most characteristic artphilosophical theme of the age, as in Shaftesbury, and even in Hume's demystification in "Of the Standard of Taste." The term "aesthetics" itself in its modern acceptation is owing to Alexander Baumgarten, who defined it provisionally in the middle of the eighteenth century as the "critique of taste."

The way both works of art and the natural world were experienced or appreciated aesthetically—or what that means, the discovery or invention of the aesthetic—is a dominant theme of Shaftesbury, Hume, Kant, Schiller in a way it simply had not been previously. This coincides with a global shift in aesthetic/cultural practices, such as how "works of art" were displayed, or where people took a vacation (someplace scenic). In its origins it is remarkable how bound up this new conceptual terrain is with the political, as several thinkers—for example Josef Chytry and Terry Eagleton—have noted; aesthetics as a discipline was put at stake by the French Revolution and its German aftermath.

Eagleton, in a Marxist vein, connects the rise of aesthetics to the rise of the bourgeoisie, though he does not on those grounds alone condemn aesthetics. On the contrary, in its moment (circa 1789) it is revolutionary (see Eagleton, p. 20). The aesthetic served a transcendent purpose (of whatever sort) for Shaftesbury, for Winckelmann, for Schiller, while politics, of course, concerns worldly affairs. Yet precisely for that reason, all these thinkers found in the aesthetic (or what, following Ranciére, I will call "the distribution of the sensible") the telos of the political, its final cause and its form. Their utopianism, and the utopianism, for example, of a Fourier in the nineteenth century, can be understood as emerging consciously from a comprehensive aesthetic vision. Nor can Hegel or Marx be said to have forsworn this vision entirely, even as they trained upon it some suspicion or self-consciousness, and some chastity or restraint of reason, though in its properly romantic expressions it arrives with an effusion of feeling captured early on by ecstasy about classical antiquity.

Burckhardt, in 1860, famously discussed the Renaissance republics of Italy—especially Florence—under the title "The State as a Work of Art." He connected this idea with the notion of the ruler as artist, and with tyranny. Of course, these aesthetic republics—including the Weimar of Goethe, Herder, and Schiller—were by others lionized for their sublimity and freedom. And the construction of political aesthetics, paradoxically, has been insistently retrospective and even anachronistic with regard to the Italian Renaissance city-states and classical Athens, models of "the aesthetic state" to be reproduced in Weimar or Bayreuth. The application is anachronistic in that it deploys a concept ("the aesthetic") with which Athens and Florence were unacquainted. But that, for example, Leonardo Bruni or Aristotle did not in any principled way distinguish political from aesthetic concerns was precisely what attracted the eighteenth- and nineteenth-century aestheticians to that variety of politics. In Winckelmann, Lessing, and Schiller it takes the form of what is literally a cult of the classical, a political aesthetics of Athens that renders it supernal and connects it vaguely to all sorts of aspirations, erotic, political, transcendental: the Platonism of the *Symposium,* seen by Shelley or Schiller as an eroto-epistemological-political ecstasis, an access of truth, beauty, and justice.

This above-all German aestheticization of politics was discredited by its eventuation in mystical totalitarian political theory. It is an understatement to say that the politics of a Schelling or a Nietzsche was reactionary. But the extent to which the nascent discipline of political aesthetics was discredited as a whole is unfortunate. For example, in Shaftesbury the idea of aesthetics and an aesthetic politics is surely put into the service of some sort of classical republicanism. And indeed it is the arc of the French Revolution and the Napoleonic Wars that turns the whole idea from republican classicism to romantic totalitarianism. Winckelmann and Schiller also, to whatever extent they made their political ideas clear, were classical republicans. The same might be said of Goethe. In England, Shaftesbury's freewheeling liberalism had its effect even on radical advocates of universal freedom such William Godwin, and English romanticism was never permeated by the taint of totalitarianism (though it had hints, for example, in Carlyle and Coleridge), in part because of Godwin's influence.

But in Germany, Herder and Hegel drove a stripe of romanticism that aestheticized the German *Volk* and the German state, and that provided some of the impetus for actual German political consolidation in the nineteenth century. Nietzsche as well has some relation here as both avatar and critic, as does the Bavarian theatrocracy of Wagner, at once a revival of the Athenian tragic polis and a romantic sublimization; in a nutshell, the aesthetic of Riefenstahl

and the Third Reich. And again, we know where this leads: to National Socialism and the aesthetics of purification, the sublimity of genocide.

Chytry's discussion in his magisterial work *The Aesthetic State* is exemplary
here. While acknowledging the historical connections of aesthetics to totalitarianism, he points to its neglected capacities in this regard.

> Surely among the favorite slogans of the political right will be found
> such preeminently aesthetic categories as order, harmony, totality, and
> organism. . . . In other words, regardless of the early humanism of our
> theme, does not the quest for a beautiful totality inevitably favor the
> conservative proclivity for stability and hostility toward disruptive
> innovation? It is certainly undeniable that subsequent German thought
> gives ample historical evidence of the alliance between budding fas-
> cism and poetic gesture. . . . But obsession with these aesthetic catego-
> ries hardly qualifies by itself as a sign of aestheticism, let alone of an
> authentic inquiry into the aesthetic dimension as an aid to further
> the human quest for personal and communal freedom. It leaves out,
> for instance, many equally cogent aesthetic qualities, such as creativity,
> originality, and innovation, that are anathema to the political right.
> (Chytry, pp. 143–44)

Chytry describes perhaps the crux of the reactionary appropriation of aesthetics in politics in Schelling's disillusioned-revolutionary view.

> The *Nachlass* of 1804 also shows a shift by Schelling, the former politi-
> cal anarchist, from an abstract-rational view of the state (a "divine
> realm") to the organic state of political romanticism. The state is no
> longer a mechanism that has banished the "beauty of political life,"
> but a creation that reflects an "ethical totality" under firm laws. It is
> an "art-work" in the sense that it constitutes a work shaped by human
> history on behalf of commonality. (Chytry, p. 139)

But Chytry is right that totalitarian romanticism was only one possible
outcome or reading of politics as aesthetics. What aesthetics took itself to
be in German idealism and romanticism is contingent from the beginning.
The location of the work of art in a transcendent realm—a realm exempted
from time, for example—an eternal ideal, paradoxically created a raw means-
and-ends reading of politics. It made material changes wrought on men and
women unreal in comparison with the supernal ambition to remake the
world into a worthy object of contemplation. In Hegel, as Kierkegaard spent
an immense authorship arguing, the individual has disappeared entirely into
a dialectic, *aufhebung*ed into universal consciousness and the end of world

history. From 1800 or so classical political aesthetics—of the sort displayed, for example, in the elaborate neoclassical emblems that accompanied Shaftesbury's writings—moved into a rococo phase and began to ornament itself in mystical symbols: Wagner's theater of archetypes, a new Homer but... more elaborate and exalted.

Even in Schiller the aesthetic state appears far more humane and liberatory than it became in Schelling, and the disinterested free play of our faculties is conceived as the meaning or goal of political freedom and of political organization. Indeed Schiller turns to the aesthetic, as the first sequence of the *Aesthetic Letters* makes clear, under a political urgency: first of all to fill a lacuna he sees in Rousseau between the savage and the rational—neither of which adequately grounds a state in the moral life of a people. In fact it is clear that in the third letter Schiller makes the aesthetic serve the function that the social contract serves for Rousseau: it is the mode of transition from natural necessity to moral life, "a third character which, related to these other two, might pave the way for a transition from the realm of mere force to the rule of law, and, without impeding the development of the moral character, might serve rather as a sensible pledge of a morality as yet unseen" (Schiller, p. 30). This in turn suggests the whole subsequent development of European romantic nationalism in which the arts serve as the fundamental cohesive force in the state. Later in the *Aesthetic Letters* the aesthetic seems to emerge as the very telos and essence of the polis (thus marking the transition from neoclassical to romantic political aesthetics), rather than a means to achieve the ethical. But in either case, Schiller treats the discovery of the aesthetic as the solution to the question of freedom and constraint in the polis. This conception of political aesthetics is fundamental to nineteenth-century German thought, and is appropriated in one way or another by Hegel, Schopenhauer, Wagner, Nietzsche.

> In the midst of the awful realm of powers, and of the sacred realm of laws, the aesthetic creative impulse is building unawares a third joyous realm of play and of appearance, in which it releases mankind from all the shackles of circumstance and frees him from everything that may be called constraint, whether physical or moral.
>
> If in the *dynamic* state of rights man encounters man as force and restricts his activity, if in the *ethical* state of duties he opposes him with the majesty of law and fetters his will, in the sphere of cultivated society, in the *aesthetic* state, he need appear to him only as shape, confront him only as an object of free play. *To grant freedom by means of freedom* is the fundamental law of this kingdom. (Schiller, p. 137)

The aesthetic state, in other words, is Schiller's relocation of the Kantian "kingdom of ends," with a massive infusion of... feeling. But it is a vision of human beings released from toil and made objective, engaged in play as freedom: ludocracy. This is an inspiring vision indeed (it inspired everyone from Marx to Greenwich Village anarchists). It can be twisted or reappropriated in a totalitarian polity, but you don't have totalitarianism without work; "dictator" is not exactly a playful persona, which is precisely why we replace real dictators in our imagination with Groucho Marx ("Hail, Freedonia!") or Charlie Chaplin.

One (admittedly simplistic) way to organize the history of romanticism and the coinciding development of political aesthetics is suggested (and perhaps driven) by Schiller. Early romantic political aesthetics, emerging out of republicanism, regards the aesthetic as the transition from a natural to a political state; mature romantic political aesthetics regards the aesthetic as the culmination or telos and ultimate ordering principle of the state; late romantic political aesthetics regards the aesthetic as the origin of the political. That last is Nietzsche's position, surely, in *The Birth of Tragedy,* in which he indicates that the Athenian polis emerged from the Dionysian aesthetic festival in its transition to tragedy. And by then we are ready for an aesthetic metaphysics as well: the aesthetic as the origin of the universe, as in some sense the reality at the heart of all regimes of value, moral, political, and epistemic. That is not—I cannot emphasize enough—the point of view of this book. Nevertheless, the aesthetic origin of the state is, as we have seen, an important theme, even if obscured by all the difficulties of distinguishing or locating such concepts in ancient cultures. But the earliest systematic political philosophies we know—in Plato and Confucius—certainly mark the centrality of the aesthetic in the emerging world of the political. And if we go much earlier, we go straight to poems and songs, to Heraclitus and Anaximander, or to the Chinese *Book of Songs,* to which Confucius constantly expressed his debt.

Romanticism and the nascent discipline of aesthetics took various totalitarian turns in Germany in the nineteenth century. But in England and America, for example, they simply did not have this shape, though of course the movements cross-pollinated both aesthetically and politically (in Carlyle and Coleridge, for example). Percy Shelley's poetry was put at the service of a lovely aesthetic of liberation. American romanticism—in Thoreau, for example, or Whitman—was anything but totalitarian. Thoreau's romantic aesthetic of wildness and his political anarchism are utterly congruent. And Whitman's political vision is as aesthetic and as nationalist as anyone's; indeed Whitman's poetics and politics are perfectly integral to each other, and he

gives an Americana version of Schiller's aesthetic republic of free experienc-
ers, connoisseurs of the sensuous.

> I hear America singing, the varied carols I hear,
> Those of mechanics, each one singing his as it should be blithe and
>   strong,
> The carpenter singing his as he measures his plank or beam,
> The mason singing his as he makes ready for work, or leaves off work,
> The boatman singing what belongs to him in his boat, the deck-hand
>   singing on the steamboat deck, . . .
> The delicious singing of the mother, or of the young wife at work, or
>   of the girl sewing or washing,
> Each singing what belongs to him or her and to none else,
> The day what belongs to the day—at night the party of young fellows,
>   robust, friendly,
> Singing with open mouths their strong melodious songs.[3]

The nationalism and aestheticism are as democratic in Whitman as they are
proto-fascist in Wagner.

At any rate, many a line of inquiry has origins that don't bear inspection;
anthropology, for example, had to transcend the racialist theories from which
it arose, because it had a legitimate, if problematic, object of inquiry. That
the idea of political aesthetics emerges in romanticism is a mixed bag, and
though it has formulated a motivation and an expressive and ordering mode
for totalitarian regimes, that does not entail that it has no legitimate object of
study, or that it is a study of totalitarian systems, the political theory of totalitarianism. There is much in it, even, that exceeds or attacks the atmosphere
of connoisseurship in which it originated. Many of the disciplines of which
there remain practitioners originate in the neoclassical and romantic movements, which coincide with the rise of the social sciences, for instance. The
marking off of the terrain in aesthetic terms that you get in Schiller plays its
role, or finds its way, into Comte's or Spencer's conceptions of the social as
an object of study. Indeed the relation of disinterestedness to science, already
present in Shaftesbury, shows the sort of contribution that these conceptions
of the aesthetic made to the disciplinary matrix and the basic modern conception of science. The idea that aesthetic phenomena fall outside the pur-
view of science is an artifact of a later, more specialized and more mechanical
science than that current in England or Germany circa 1800.

---

3. Walt Whitman, "I Hear America Singing" (1860), in Whitman, p. 174.

CHAPTER 5

Red, Gold, Black, and Green

Black Nationalist Aesthetics

Various of the themes we have approached thus far appear again and differently with regard to the Black Nationalism of the twentieth century, which I associate above all with the Marcus Garvey movement. It may be that if Garvey, who appointed himself Provisional President of Africa, had succeeded in creating his black nation, he would have ruled it by authoritarian means. But as it stood, he used a version of romantic nationalism as a strategy for resistance. The meaning and the effect of romantic nationalism, like that of every artpolitical ideology, depends on the context in which it is deployed. Wagner's operas and Speer's architecture were dominant artistic forms with generous budgets and tremendous sweep. The arts generated by Black Nationalism, however, were rigged up by poor people and pitted against the dominant political and aesthetic systems. But what is remarkable is that the arts of Black Nationalism—above all, reggae and hip hop music—have had more effect on world culture than a hundred Wagners or Speers. Partly this has to do with their subaltern origins—as it were, they well up from below—and with the power of improvisation. Indeed we could think of Garvey himself as taking romantic nationalism and riffing on it, turning it, investing it with a different set of aesthetic contents, and, to a remarkable extent, transforming the world with it.

In my view, liberation movements often follow a particular trajectory. They begin in definition and unification: by constructing an oppressed group as essentially homogeneous, endangered, and exploited together. Thus feminism began by purporting to speak for women's experience; the gay rights movement originated as a call to unity and the definition of a homosexual identity. This is sometimes called "strategic essentialism," and often entails a revaluing of imposed identities; one might, for example, embrace "bitch" or "queer." There has to be a moment of consolidation and mobilization and identification. This is, if you like, the nationalist moment, and the elements out of which these identities are forged are centrally aesthetic. The movement needs its insignia; it needs the materials of identity: narratives, professions, images. Black Nationalism forged an identity out of African cultures, slave rebellions, third world revolutions, prophecies. In the process of the representation and dissemination of these materials, the identity gets pluralized or becomes complex, and the movement both pervades the wider culture and undergoes dilution as the identities it defines are put into question. The activities of representation, dissemination, and pluralization are in many cases fundamentally works of art, and that is true of Garvey-style Black Nationalism, a peculiarity in this case being that the dissemination was almost unbelievably successful or pervasive, as one might see from the music of Bob Marley or Public Enemy.

The Marcus Garvey movement of the 1910s and 1920s is often called the largest organization of African diaspora peoples until that point. And it is often regarded as well as a failure: it dissolved in the financial meltdown of Garvey's Black Star shipping line and in a vendetta against Garvey by the U.S. government, spearheaded by J. Edgar Hoover, issuing in Garvey's imprisonment and deportation. But though it did not directly give rise to an enduring mass movement or repatriate significant portions of the diaspora to Africa, it had infinitely rich ramifications, specifically in religion and the arts. In the Caribbean one result of Garveyism was the religion of Rastafari, which informs the whole history of Jamaican recorded music—most famously, of course, the roots reggae of Bob Marley, the first third world superstar and a symbol of liberatory hope and marijuana abuse for generations. In North America Garveyism gave rise, among many other things, to the Nation of Islam and the ministry and political organization of Malcolm X, as well as the Five Percenters (or Nation of Gods and Earths), which have influenced American music profoundly. The importation of Jamaican musical practices into New York resulted in the musical style known as hip hop, like reggae a major dimension of world music ever since, with political as well as aesthetic ramifications.

Although music has been the most recognizable aesthetic heritage of Garveyite Black Nationalism, that political movement contains all possible aesthetic expressions, which in turn make connections between religious, political, and aesthetic spheres in an exemplary way. Indeed these spheres are indistinguishable on the ground, a fact that Black Nationalism displays continuously. Garvey himself developed the red, gold, and green (and sometimes black) Black Nationalist flag and color scheme; if one walks down the streets of any city in the world, one is likely to catch a glimpse of it on people's clothing. He wielded color per se as an artpolitical weapon, celebrating "blackness" and trying to change its valence in Western arts and imagery as a symbol of ignorance and annihilation; the Nation of Islam and many others have developed this theme systematically. Garvey denounced hair straightening and skin bleaching products marketed to black people, a theme later taken up by Malcolm X and others, and developed an aesthetic of the Negro body as a political site. Hairstyles such as dreadlocks and even the Afro (and hence, e.g., the "Jewfro") derive from the same sources. The Garvey-influenced religions developed a series of iconographies that have likewise penetrated everywhere, from the Lion of Judah to the faces of Malcolm and Marley to the esoteric symbolism of the Five Percent Nation. Languages, dialects, and slangs employed by and deriving from Black Nationalism, such as the "Dread Talk" of Rastafarianism as well as hip hop slang, have remade the poetry and the vernacular of English and other languages. Graffiti, associated with hip hop, has changed the physical environment of cities and been appropriated into advertising and typestyles.

The Garvey movement coincided closely with the Harlem Renaissance, and its themes were mirrored by many figures in that movement, notably Zora Neale Hurston (also a Garvey skeptic), Countee Cullen, Arna Bontemps, and many others. Langston Hughes developed what might be thought of as a Black Nationalist poetics: "We younger Negro artists who create now intend to express our dark selves without fear or shame. If white people are pleased we are glad. If they are not, it doesn't matter. We know we are beautiful. And ugly too" (Hughes, p. 50). This statement was welcomed ecstatically by, among others, Garvey's wife, the activist Amy Jacques Garvey (see Van Deburg, pp. 57–58). The vernacular literature of Hughes, Claude McCay, Jean Toomer, and others was the literary embodiment of black pride and a celebration of black dialect.

Race Theory and Ethiopianism

As romanticism, nationalism, and modern democracy arose in the late eighteenth century, Thomas Jefferson, among many others, suggested that a solution to the problem of American slavery might involve a repatriation of African Americans to Africa. In the early nineteenth century, the American Colonization Society pursued this approach, which eventuated in the founding of the Republic of Liberia in 1822. Both Jefferson and the colonization movement were explicitly racist, holding that white and black folk could not live together successfully. Indeed the great abolitionist William Lloyd Garrison wrote a book attacking the colonizationists as racists and slavers, but even such statesmen as Henry Clay and Abraham Lincoln entertained the idea seriously. It is not surprising that the idea also captured the imagination of some African Americans: after all, their departure from Africa had not been voluntary. In the spirituals and church services of American slaves, "Zion" or "the promised land" of the Israelites became implicitly identified with Africa. A number of black repatriation movements, such as those of Henry McNeal Turner and Chief Alfred Sam, took some hold in the late nineteenth and early twentieth centuries. And even later in the twentieth century there was some contact between Black Nationalists and white racists: Marcus Garvey endorsed segregationist Senator Theodore Bilbo's repatriation bill in the late thirties, and persistent rumors had Black Nationalist leaders—including elements of the Garvey movement and the Nation of Islam—meeting with members of the Ku Klux Klan and the Nazi Party to try to institute the physical separation of the races (See Essien-Udom, pp. 51–52; Cronon, pp. 186–87).

Although Marcus Garvey was born in Jamaica (in 1887 in Saint Ann's Bay, the same area from which Marley originated) and spent a good deal of time in Panama and elsewhere, while later influencing anticolonialism in Africa, it was of course in the United States and specifically in Harlem that he caught the imagination of hundreds of thousands of people in the late 1910s and early 1920s. He did this with a racialist rhetoric that derived in turn from German nationalism and the thought of such nineteenth-century racialist thinkers as Gobineau, who taught that each race of man had a particular origin and a particular destiny, embodied in its thought, its politics, and above all in its arts. In Gobineau and in the Black Nationalism that made use of this tradition (for example, the early thought of W. E. B. Du Bois), the concepts of "race" and "nation" were run together: race might be conceived as the biological trace of national geography, expressed in mythology and the arts. Each race had its spirit or genius, its contribution to make to world civilization.

Indeed, one way to characterize much of the thought, particularly in Germany, that segued from Enlightenment to romantic was its enthusiasm for collective consciousness, present in such extreme degrees in Rousseau, Hegel, Herder, and Marx, for example, that the fundamental locus of consciousness is removed from the individual human body and lodged in collective entities, including nations and races. It is this thought—of historical actors smeared over many human bodies and generations—that articulates the idea of race which was wielded as a weapon in genocides, but also in movements of resistance and autonomy. The arts of a given people, race, era, and so on became one conspicuous and decodable expression of its collective consciousness. Such a thought drives even "empirical" or scientific programs up to the present and stands at the origin of anthropology.

The black race, or "the Negro," or the nation(s) of Africa were often conceived in this structure to be repositories of a particularly aesthetic consciousness, a thought fully expressed by Gobineau. Obviously, racial theory of this type—racialism for short—is potentially racist, and every stereotype of every people, including every negative stereotype of black people, is inscribed somewhere in the various expressions of the theory. But just as obviously there are resources in racialism for a reversal, as Du Bois's (from here) bewildering 1897 essay "Conservation of the Races" makes clear. (Du Bois had been educated, in part, in Germany.)

> The history of the world is the history, not of individuals, but of groups, not of nations, but of races, and he who ignores or seeks to override the race idea in human history ignores and overrides the central thought of all history. What, then, is a race? It is a vast family of human beings, generally of common blood and language, always of common history, traditions, and impulses, who are both voluntarily and involuntarily striving together for the accomplishment of certain more or less vividly conceived ideals of life.[1]

This is a pretty good statement of nationalism as applied to race, though Du Bois distinguishes the two. If every race has a destiny, then every race finds a justification for its intrinsic identity in the unfolding of world history. The members of a given race are supposed to have a common origin, a common character, a common message to carry to the world, and if that were so, it should be a matter of pride to black folks to be black.

When black folks turned this notion to account, the result was often termed "Ethiopianism," in accord with the historical use of "Ethiopia" essentially to mean Africa as a whole, and with the biblical passage "Princes shall come out of Egypt; Ethiopia shall soon stretch out her hand to God" (Psalms 68:31). This passage was quoted or paraphrased in African American writing

---

1. W. E. B. Du Bois, "The Conservation of the Races" (1897), in Du Bois 2, p. 817.

at latest by the early nineteenth century. For the Rastafarians it made particularly vivid the crowning of Haile Selassie as Emperor of Ethiopia as a turning point in history or a harbinger of the judgment and the redemption of black people. Du Bois, in *Souls of Black Folk,* finds this expressed in the American Negro especially in music. He called Negro spirituals "the most original and beautiful expression of human life and longing yet born on American soil" (Du Bois 1, p. 156). Even Frederick Douglass—who had little time for the cosmic essentialist theories of race—had said much the same thing. This is both a stereotype and a reversal of the stereotype or its strategic deployment in a liberatory ideology, typical of almost all black appropriations of racialist theory: the music of Africa and the African diaspora—captured in the image of the talking drum and in the notion of natural rhythm and the ability to dance, along with an accompanying innate faith, soul, or religiosity—was both a limitation and a liberation, a contribution of the Negro to the world, like the supposedly innate philosophical consciousness of the Teutons or the commercialism of the Anglo-Saxons. "Black Nationalism" makes use of race theory as a way to unify black folks, and in particular it imagines for them a nation, a common origin in Africa, from which unfolds a common destiny embodied in cultural expressions, often crystallized in the concept of repatriation. These expressions are sources of pride and also potentially vehicles of cultural construction, ways to forge a unity among, in this case, a despised, enslaved, and exploited people: the suggestion of a glorious destiny even in the midst of a degraded history.

Garvey managed to wield this thought in an unprecedented mobilization of the black race; he did it with great dignity, accessibility, and flair; wielded racialist theory as a potent form of liberatory propaganda aimed at average black folk of the Americas. Here, from a speech Garvey gave at the Universal Negro Improvement Association (UNIA) convention of 1924, is a characteristic formulation of Black Nationalism that crystallizes the common elements of all such movements in the twentieth century, secular and religious:

> The Negro wants a nation, nothing less, nothing more, and why shouldn't we be naturally free, nationally unfettered? We want a nationality similar to that of the English, the French, the Italian, the German, to that of the white American, to that of the yellow Japanese; we want nationality and government because we realize that the American nation in a short while will not be large enough to accommodate two competitive rivals, one black and the other white.... As we deliberate on the many problems confronting us...let us not lose control of ourselves; let us not forget that we are the guardians of four hundred

millions; let us not forget that it is our duty to help humanity everywhere, whether it be black or white.... So, let no prejudice cause us to
say or do anything against the interest of the white, or the yellow man;
let us realize that the white man has a right to live, the yellow man has
a right to live, and all that we desire to do is to impress upon them the
fact that we also have a right to live. (Garvey, p. 109)

This is an inspiring and decent vision, and Garvey made it inspiring to millions in part by pointed, self-conscious, and eclectic spectacle. The images of
Garveyism are above all Garvey himself in grand Napoleonic uniform—as
Wilson Jeremiah Moses describes it, Garvey "affected the airs of an Austrian
archduke" (Moses, p. 143)—and the street parade that combined oratory, music,
mass participation, and spectacular clothing into a racial-martial-celebratory
festival. He configured symbolisms of Africa, of Masonism, of religion, of
science and medicine, of circus into coherent syntheses that called forth an
ecstasy of celebratory identification. Garvey's was a political aesthetics of
genius, the ramifications of which we still inhabit.

Garvey himself had been raised in the Catholic Church, and even as he
exploited the religious as well as the nationalist elements of his own spectacle—
his image as Moses, his status as a prophet with all its rhetorical implications, his
self-forged title and uniform as Provisional President of Africa—he was never
quite comfortable declaring his movement to be religious or to be a religion.
Nevertheless, he helped found the African Orthodox Church, which remained
a firmly Christian denomination, at the same time hinting at the blackness of
Jesus... or even of God. This was a racialist interpretation, which even Garvey
understood as symbolic. Garvey's biographer E. David Cronon writes of the
first bishop of the African Orthodox Church, George Alexander McGuire:

From the first... Bishop McGuire urged the Garveyites to "forget
the white gods." "Erase the white gods from your hearts," he told his
congregation [in 1921]. "We must go back to the native church, to
our own true God." The new Negro religion would seek to be true to
the true principles of Christianity without the shameful hypocrisy of
the white churches. Garvey himself urged Negroes to adopt their own
religion, "with God as a being, not as a Creature," a religion that would
show Him "made in our own image—black."... During the opening parade [of the UNIA convention of 1924] through the streets of
Harlem, U.N.I.A. members marched under a large portrait of a black
Madonna and Child.... "Then let us start our Negro painters getting
busy," the Bishop declared, "and supply a black Madonna and a black
Christ for the training of our children." (Cronon, pp. 178–79)

It is obvious that this is not the only possible response: one might also reject Christianity in its entirety and engage in one or another form of religious invention/repatriation. If the "white race" was associated with Christianity—and of course Christianity had a role in the historical oppression of black people, if also in their liberation—then the racial genius might demand its own autonomous religious expression. Frederick Douglass's most vituperative attack on slavery had been against the religious hypocrisy of slave masters who professed Christianity: "I love the pure, peaceable, and impartial Christianity of Christ: I therefore hate the corrupt, slaveholding, women-whipping, cradle-plundering, partial, and hypocritical Christianity of this land" (Douglass, p. 97).

Garveyite Religions

As Garvey faded from the scene (he died in the U.K. in 1940, after at least a decade of decline for his movement), his followers began to preach various mystical interpretations of Garveyism. Indeed the mystical aspects of race were always implicit in racialist theory, and were exploited on the other side by Hitler and many others. A number of astonishing scriptures that mentioned Garvey were produced by black mystics of the twenties and thirties, such as the *Holy Piby* of Robert Athlyi Rogers, an Afro-Caribbean working in Newark ("Therefore, Athlyi yielded him a copy of the map, and declared Marcus Garvey an apostle of the Lord God for the redemption of Ethiopia and her suffering posterities" [Rogers, chap. 7]). Another example is the surreal spiritual poem *The Royal Parchment Scroll of Black Supremacy* by Balintine F. Pettersburgh. The much older text of the *Kebra Nagast,* which narrated the story of Solomon, the Queen of Sheba, and the religious history of Ethiopia and its line of emperors, was revived as an ancient source for Afrocentric religion. Rather remarkably, most of the texts of the Afrocentric religious movements emerged from the intersection of the Caribbean and North America: Rogers came from Anguilla. He founded a church based on his inspired scripture, which taught the destruction of Babylon and a "black Zionism": repatriation to the promised land. Pettersburgh originated in St. Thomas. Here's a slice of *The Royal Parchment,* which tradition has it was dictated by Petterburgh in an inspired state:

> Black Supremacy is the Queen of Ethiopia's Triumphant Resurrection.
> Africa's DESIRE is to Rebuild Solomon's Temple, but Solomon, is not BIG
>   ENOUGH, nor his FATHER DAVID to dictate to the Monarch of Dread
>   Creation.

I am Building a World's Super Capital for The Church Triumphant,
The Black Supremacy at the World's Dam-Head.
I am the Master Builder of Continents, and Countries, DYNASTIES and
Kingdoms on this Earth PLAIN. I am The Perfect Royal Head of This
World, The Root of Creation.
King Alpha and Queen Omega, The First and The Last. (Pettersburgh)

The Pettersburgh and Rogers texts provided the basis of the first properly
Rastafarian scripture, *The Promised Key* by Leonard Howell.

In the United States one Garvey-oriented religious tendency, also perhaps
originating in Newark, moved toward Islam. Some elements of Islam had
been preserved in African American culture by slaves of North African origin, and Islam provided an—or perhaps the obvious—alternative to Christianity as a monotheism that could be associated with people of color. Black
Masonism also provided a connection to Islamic ("esoteric") symbolism. An
originary movement was the Moorish Science Temple, founded in Newark
and then moved to Chicago by the Noble Drew Ali (Timothy Drew) during the disintegration of the Garvey movement in the late twenties (though
perhaps Drew Ali had been working toward it since the mid-1910s). The
Moorish movement derived explicitly from Garveyism, and even as it taught
the flatly heretical view that Drew Ali was Allah incarnate, it regarded Garvey
as a prophet. Drew Ali, too, had a flair for spectacle; he wore a feathered fez
that paid tribute both to the mysticism of the Middle East and to Drew's
American Indian ancestry. He taught that "so-called American Negroes"
originated in the Middle East, and that Islam was their "natural" religion.
He also produced a Garveyite scripture, *The Holy Koran of the Moorish Science
Temple of America,* which proclaims:

> In these modern days there came a forerunner, who was divinely pre-
> pared by the great God-Allah and his name is Marcus Garvey, who did
> teach and warn the nations of the earth to prepare to meet the coming
> Prophet; who was to bring the true and divine Creed of Islam, and his
> name is Noble Drew Ali: who was prepared and sent back to earth by
> Allah, to teach the old time religion and the everlasting gospel to the
> sons of man. (Drew Ali, chap. 47)

In a structure that was repeated many times, the Moorish Science Temple
devolved into schism, with Drew dying, probably in Chicago in 1929, after a
series of schismatic shootings. Various followers claimed to be his reincarnation, and thus Allah.

The Nation of Islam was apparently founded at around this moment by
W. D. Fard, also an avatar of Allah, a somewhat ghostly door-to-door salesman

active in the Detroit area in the early 1930s, whose teachings were, after his disappearance, taken up by Elijah Muhammad (Robert Poole). According to various sources, Fard was one of a number of people who claimed to be the reincarnation of Drew Ali, though the connection was denied by the Nation of Islam.[2] Indeed, so elusive a figure is Fard that one might be forgiven for doubting his existence. In a Chicago police report from 1935, the leader of the Nation of Islam is identified as "Wallace Fard... or Elijah Muhammad," as though these were the same person (quoted in Essiem-Udom, p. 44). Whatever the case, whereas Drew and even Garvey had preached the equality of the races, Elijah Muhammad preached black racial supremacy, saying that the white race had been the result of a breeding experiment by an ancient evil scientist. He taught also that the black race was God incarnate and whites a race of devils. This notion could be taken literally (sort of), or as a metaphor for the evils that Europeans had visited upon the world: imperialism, colonialism, slavery—in short, genocide.

The Nation of Islam recruited widely in prisons, where it found Malcolm Little (Malcolm X), who became its greatest preacher and organizer, an exemplar of its severely ascetic discipline who explicitly began to apply the teachings of the Nation to current political situations of the fifties and early sixties. Though Elijah Muhammad denied being influenced by Garvey—which is ridiculous—Malcolm's formative experiences had been in the Garvey movement, in which his parents were fairly major figures in Detroit, and in the service of which, according to Malcolm, his father had been executed by the Ku Klux Klan. Malcolm left the Nation of Islam in 1964—disillusioned by Muhammad's sexual and financial antics—converted to orthodox Islam, and founded new religious and political organizations. The Nation of Islam underwent a number of schisms in the sixties and seventies, as Elijah Muhammad's son Wallace led much of the group toward orthodox Islam. The original teachings were revived by Louis Farrakhan, a preacher who had been trained by Malcolm, though Malcolm's family held that Farrakhan had been involved in Malcolm's assassination.

Another Nation of Islam preacher in Harlem in the mid- to late 1960s, Clarence 13X (Clarence Smith Jowers or Father Allah), founded the Five Percent Movement (that is, 5 percent of us, or of them, will be redeemed), also known as the Nation of Gods and Earths, which dispensed with some of the ascetic and authoritarian aspects of the Nation of Islam. Indeed, Father Allah set up headquarters in a bar (the Glamour Inn) and was known as

---

2. It is worth saying that all sources that connect Fard directly to Drew Ali may derive from Arna Bontemps's and Jack Conroy's book *They Seek a City,* and ever since the scholars may have been corroborating one another.

an excellent professional gambler. He did time in prisons and the notorious mental hospital at Matteawan. "Gods" were black men, "Earths" black
women, while children were referred to as "Stars." The Nation of Gods and
Earths absorbed many of the texts and teachings of the Nation of Islam, but
also has as elaborate a set of original teachings as any of these groups, including systems of numerology, a mystical interpretation of the alphabet, and a
system of astrology. Starting out militant, the Five Percenters eventually tried
to bring peace to New York and worked in the late sixties with the mayoral
administration of John Lindsay to keep Harlem relatively calm, for example,
after the death of Martin Luther King Jr. Though it declined with Father
Allah's shooting death in 1969 (again, and typically, the circumstances are
obscure), the Nation of Gods and Earths revived dramatically in the seventies
and eighties, and spread over the boroughs of New York and then all across
the country. It revived the "Circle-7" symbol of the Moorish Science Temple,
adding a sun, moon, and star motif. The Five Percenters have carried their
message above all through hip hop music, where their astonishing hermeneutics is ubiquitous and functions almost as a cipher.[3]

All of these groups postulated historical origins for the "lost-found" tribe
of American Negroes; all of them taught repatriation in some form, physical,
spiritual, or metaphorical; all of them took races seriously as historical actors
and preached racial pride; all of them saw a glorious racial destiny for people
of African descent; all of them conducted active ministries among the poor,
the addicted, and the imprisoned; all of them, as can be seen by these themes,
venerated the memory of Marcus Garvey as a precursor, a Moses, a John the
Baptist.

During the same period in Jamaica a similar set of Afrocentric theological traditions developed, based in part on indigenous and African-inspired
religious systems such as Obeah, and in part on various forms of Christian
mysticism. Robert Athlyi Rogers founded a small Ethiopianist sect in Kingston in the 1920s. Garvey returned in the late twenties after his exile from the
States and became a major local figure in Kingston, though again without
an explicitly original religious orientation. Garvey, however, had apparently
said that a king would appear in Africa and lead black people out of their
Babylonian captivity.

In 1930 Ras Tafari Makkonen, supposedly a descendant of the biblical
Queen of Sheba, was crowned Emperor Haile Selassie of Ethiopia: "King

3. The definitive history is Knight.

of Kings and Lord of Lords, Conquering Lion of the Tribe of Judah." This news caught the imagination of the entire African diaspora, including a street preacher named Leonard Howell, a Jamaican who had known and followed Garvey both in New York and in Kingston. According to Hélène Lee in her remarkable book *The First Rasta,* Howell's friend Annie Harvey, who had been connected with the "black Jews" or "Israelites" in Harlem, attended Selassie's coronation in Addis Ababa. She brought back a photograph of Selassie "enthroned as the Prince of Peace." Howell began to circulate copies of this photo, along with the purported biblical prophecies and the words of Garvey that he connected to Selassie on the streets of Kingston (Lee, pp. 56–61). Howell's street ministry was the origin of Rastafarianism, which was in full swing by the mid-1930s both in rural Jamaica (especially Saint Thomas parish on the eastern part of the island) and in Kingston.

It was a remarkable religion, if nothing else, for its eclecticism. It was explicitly "Zionist," teaching that Ethiopia was the promised land and that the diaspora would be miraculously reunited in Africa, under an interpretation of the Hebrew Bible. Howell composed *The Promised Key* in prison in the mid-thirties, incorporating passages of *The Holy Piby* and *The Royal Parchment Scroll of Black Supremacy,* and published it under the "Hindu" name Gangunguru Maragh, or "Gong" (Bob Marley was later known as Gong, and his record company was Tuff Gong; his son Damian is "Junior Gong"). Hinduism, including the cult of Kali, had been imported into the island with Indian laborers in the mid-nineteenth century, and provided Rastafarianism with much of its ceremonial and aesthetic, including the use of ganja (Kali or Collie weed) as a sacrament, dreadlocks—a hairstyle reminiscent of Indian ascetic sects—and the vegetarian diet that became known as "ital" (Lee, pp. 97–101).

In 1935 Italy invaded Ethiopia, an event easily framed as the last battle between Babylon and Zion. Italian propaganda invented a worldwide conspiracy among black people to kill white people, supposedly headed by Selassie and called "Nya-Binghi." Bizarrely, when this screed was republished in Jamaica, it became almost a scripture, and led to the founding of a more violent strand of Rastafarianism (Howell, under the influence of Gandhi, preached nonresistance) (Lee, pp. 91–94). Eventually "nyabinghi" became the name both of a radical Rastafarianism and of the ceremonial drumming style (often using three drums, an African motif) at Rasta groundation ceremonies, and subsequently of a subgenre of reggae music that hewed close to ceremonial styles.

In 1939, after stints in prison and the mental hospital as a political prisoner, Howell founded a community in the hills of Saint Catherine parish, known as the Pinnacle, which practiced the worship of Selassie as the living god, and also began systematizing Rastafarianism in terms of groundation ceremonies and ganja as sacrament (also as a cash crop). Perhaps five thousand Rastas were resident in the immediate area (according to Lee, p. 137). The Jamaican government raided the Pinnacle a number of times. In 1954 the authorities destroyed more than a million marijuana plants and seized piles of cash (Lee, pp. 189–92). In 1958 the compound was burned. Thousands of Rastas scattered into Kingston and Spanish Town, where they practiced their ceremonies in "yards" or small public spaces in ghettoes such as Trench Town.

Under the influence of Jamaican music, starting in about 1960 Rasta doctrine was carried to the whole world, and gained adherents in many places, notably Africa. Haile Selassie visited Jamaica in 1966, where he received an astonishing welcome offered to the living god. He set aside a tract of land in Ethiopia, Shashamani, to host repatriated Rastas and diasporic Africans. The Rasta movement faced a crisis in the seventies, when Selassie was deposed, and when, a couple of years later, he was reported to have died. This many Rastas regarded as impossible and as a lie of the Babylonian media.

Like the "Black Muslim" movement, Rastafarianism taught that Garvey was a prophet, that the black race would be carried to the promised land, and that it had a grand historical destiny. In addition, it taught explicitly that "Babylon" (at first the British colonial government, then the Jamaican state, then the system of white/Western oppression as a whole) must fall. Rastas attempted to "chant down Babylon," or literally bring the end of the system by singing and drumming. They employed the red, gold, black, and green as a symbol of black redemption. And both north and south, the movements were apocalyptic: they anticipated the end time.

Like black Islam in the United States, Rastafarianism taught (in the words of Bob Marley) that "mighty God is a living man": that people must make their heaven or hell on earth, now, in this life. Both African American Islam and Rastafarianism, that is, are, as we might put it, "immanentist" religions; they reject pure spirit and affirm the essential embodiment of both people and god. "'The Holy One' is God in person and not a spirit!" wrote Elijah Muhammad in *Message to the Blackman in America* (Muhammad 1, chap. 4), referring no doubt to Fard, as Marley to Selassie: "we know and we overstand, that mighty God is a living man" (in the song "Stand Up for Your Rights"). That, of course, has revolutionary political implications, as we seek redemption not after death but here and now: redemption is identified with justice. Indeed the spiritual orientation of Christianity was associated in both movements with oppression; it justified patience and capitulation, promising a reward after death. But as Peter Tosh and Bob Marley said: "If you know what life is worth, / you will look for yours on earth. / So now we see the light, / and stand up for your rights."

Jamaican Music

From the beginning, Rasta ceremony was marked by chanting and drumming. And from the beginning of Jamaican recorded music, around 1960, the Rasta elements were central. Count Ossie, who ran a Rasta commune in eastern Kingston, appeared on one of the first Jamaican-recorded hit songs, "O Carolina" by the Folkes Brothers. The record was also one of the first to move toward the beat that became known as "ska," which has informed a number of revivals since, such as the "Two-Tone," a specifically interracial style of the late seventies in Britain associated with punk bands such as the Specials and Madness. A later stateside ska revival in the 1990s produced a number of hit songs, as well as enduring pop stars such as the Mighty Mighty Bosstones and No Doubt. Indeed members of the foundational ska group the Skatalites, such as Dizzy Moore and the great trombonist Don Drummond, had also played in Rasta ceremonies or groundations. The nyabinghi style played by Ossie, based on African-revival "burru" drumming, probably dated from the thirties, and involved three drums (the bass, the funde, and the repeater, African ceremonial styles), along with whatever instruments were to hand, and chanting or spoken-word lectures or meditations on slavery, Garvey, African repatriation, Selassie, and so on. The best document of this style and ideology is the album *Grounation* (an alternate spelling) by Count Ossie and the Mystical Revelation of Rastafari, recorded in the early 1970s, in which the connection of groundation ceremonial music to ska, rock steady, and reggae is developed with beautiful coherence, and the music is presented in conjunction with Rasta prayers for peace and brotherhood and meditative developments of esoteric Rasta doctrine. But from the very start, Jamaican recorded music featured recognizably Rasta themes and drum styles in such songs as "Babylon Gone" by Winston and Roy, and "Another Moses" by the Mellow Cats (Barrow and Dalton, p. 24).

Ska blended American R&B, which could be heard in Jamaica on radio stations out of New Orleans and Miami, with a distinctive lurching beat originally associated with a dance craze. The featured instruments were horns, though the style was defined by its rhythm, like the styles that followed, and established the tremendous emphasis on drum and bass that has characterized Jamaican music—and hence the music of the world—for much of the last fifty years. The teenaged Wailers began their career in the ska era as a vocal trio consisting of Bob Marley, Peter Tosh, and Bunny Wailer. At the start,

Rastafarianism was still a controversial and repressed religion, and though many of the musicians were involved in it to one extent or another, the Rasta themes were for the most part slightly disguised under images of lions or possibly Christian spiritual motifs such as the promised land or Judgment Day, traditional since Negro spirituals in slavery. Much ska was primarily instrumental, which made thematic subterfuge otiose, and some early artists were Christians (such as Toots and the Maytals), or even Muslim (as in the astonishing Prince Buster). As subsequent developments would show, however, these religious strands were not necessarily regarded by their practitioners as ultimately incompatible. A whole strain of Christian Rastafarianism developed, associated with "Jesus Dread" Yabby You and the Ethiopian Orthodox Church, to which Marley converted before his death.

During the hot summer of 1966 the beat began to slow down. Partly because the large ska-style band was an expensive proposition, the horns were to some extent sheared away, and emphasis shifted to what would basically be a rock band: guitar, bass, drums, and vocals. The style that eventuated became known as "rock steady," and it has provided the foundation for Jamaican popular music ever since, which has continuously sampled or reproduced its rhythm tracks. Rock steady as a dominant pop style lasted a bare two years. It produced a number of great singers in an American soul mode, and also began to introduce explicitly racial and political themes, as in "Young, Gifted and Black" by Marcia Griffiths and Bob Andy (originally by the American singer Nina Simone). Desmond Dekker had worldwide hits with "007" and the obviously Rasta-inspired "Israelites." Rastafarian theology became an ever more explicit theme in the rock steady era.

Jamaican music of this period was presented largely by sound systems, in which huge speakers were set up in fields for outdoor parties. These featured not bands but deejays spinning records. Some of these deejays themselves became stars by playing brand-new or unknown records (the main Jamaican record producers, such as Clement Dodd and Duke Reid, ran sound systems), and by "chattering" into and out of the record, as American R&B deejays were wont to do. As deejays such as King Stitt and Count Machuki became better known than the recording artists they were playing, producers started experimenting with issuing the B-sides of singles without vocals, so the deejay could do an extended chatter or "toast." Eventually they realized that multiple versions of songs could be successful commercially: the vocal version, the version with the vocal removed, and finally the deejay version, in which they recorded the deejay chattering over the instrumental or with some vocals in almost a call-and-response pattern. The first deejay to become a Jamaican recording star was U-Roy, who by 1970 dominated the Jamaican charts.

As I say, producers in the late sixties also began to experiment with the instrumental versions, kicking the vocal in and out, adding echo or reverb effects by re-recording over the initial tracks (all on tube equipment). These "dub plates"—the greatest technician of which was King Tubby, who owned a stereo repair shop in Kingston—became a fad in themselves and presented the possibility of another score with a single song, as well as a perfect context for deejay versions. Tubby stripped rock steady rhythms down to the drum and bass and rebuilt them with a kind of cosmic insouciance, conceiving his handmade recording equipment as a musical instrument in itself, a fundamental innovation that has ramified through world pop music ever since. Much of this was improvised as a set of cost-cutting measures. Rather than putting a band in a studio, producers would recycle the same riddims again and again, creating generations of hit songs from a single recording session. But in its conception of appropriation, recycling, and continuous reinterpretation and recontextualization, it also brought world pop music into the postmodern era.

One question that arises in dub and in many other contexts is technology as a form of subordination, a form of resistance, and an instrument of aesthetic expression. We might think, for example, of the gun. Like many technologies, the gun is designed in relation to the human body, as, we might say, a prosthesis: the pistol-as-hand or rifle-as-arm. And of course the gun as an enhancement of the body's capacity to kill has been central to power in modernity, a key to the slave trade, colonialism, genocide, or just the everyday policing that represents the small-scale or pedestrian saturation of our lives by the state. Yet the gun has also provided a mode of resistance; one can't conceive of an "unarmed" insurgency or guerrilla band. The gun, as it were, exceeds its intended application as prosthesis of power and is also the instrument or even the very body of the resistance. It introduces and enhances forms of order, but it simultaneously and in complement induces chaos. That chaos in turn drives the technology of the gun and its ammunition, the projection of the body into other bodies, the penetrative purpose that is the real power of the gun, its trajectory from my body into yours which expresses the gun's actual power. We introduce ever newer generations of the gun to enforce order on the ever-spiraling chaos. The gun is the principle of order and the whirlwind of alien, homicidal/suicidal strangeness, the essence of both rationality and insanity at one and the same moment in one and the same place.

If we think of technology in its conceptual structure—or, as Heidegger might put it, its essence—as purposiveness, we can begin to conceive the problem and the hope it embodies. The idea of technology is the idea of controlling our environment and one another in accordance with some telos, of bending the world and one another to, or including one another in, our will. This of course divides the world into subject and object, animate will and the inanimate reality over which it wants dominion. This, we might say, is in one sense the origin of the human individual, of the phenomenological detachment of the body from the environment and from other human bodies. But it is of course also the continual compromise of the individual, now nested in a power structure that proceeds through it or that manifests itself within it as it environs it in instruments. The gun is an assertion of integrity or even invulnerability, a defense of the body that increases the space it occupies in potential, the carving out of a defended space that asserts and preserves the body as an individuated object. That is, the gun individuates the body by asserting its identity with the space around it, by increasing its scope beyond the skin and into the space beyond, or even into the bodies of those who might occupy this space. The gun is an instrument of self-assertion or defense, but also in both directions a demonstration that the body does not end at the skin, that the skin can be penetrated and the body can be projected into surrounding space.

Technology typically has this multivalent or contradictory effect. It increases the integrity of bodies or expands that integrity: of the human body, of the state or corporation, of the specific inanimate thing. To move from violence into art, the technologies of control, of systematic generation of and pursuit of purpose, always also enhance the possibilities of improvisation. Improvisation is one way to "turn" or deflect technologies, one way to show their excess to their own essences, or to mount a demonstration that they have no essence, that each instrument packs within itself or entails excesses to its conceived purposes. Each assertion of control is also an atmosphere of improvisation or makes possible arts previously unimaginable, as new weapons articulate new insurgencies by accident.

Dub music is a technological music in the sense that although its materials originate in the music-making of guitarists, drummers, and so on, what makes the music dub is the technological intervention in the song by the "engineer." The engineer proceeds, first, by subtraction: removing vocals and dropping instruments out, then bringing them back in. And by enhancement, adding echo effects or reverberations that create a sense of vast space and then close it down, project the sound into an imaginary world and then collapse that world back in on itself. And by addition: of beeps or snatches of other songs, often in a different key, an explicitly foreign element disrupting or fragmenting the structure, creating a fractured surface.

One effect of dub is to break down the integrity of "the song," and dub's expansion and destruction of the song is now common coin in the world's popular music. Like American pop, Jamaican music of the 1960s presented the listener with integral songs suitable for radio play, three-minute temporal organisms characterized by internal "narrative" order: verse/chorus, verse/chorus, bridge, chorus. The basic way these songs were presented was, again, on the sound system, at outdoor parties or dancehalls where the system operator would set up a speaker system and a deejay would spin records. They began by playing American jazz and R&B records in the fifties. By the early sixties, when Jamaica achieved political independence from the U.K., the sound systems were spinning Jamaican ska records, which, like subsequent Jamaican waves such as rock steady, reggae, and ragga, in turn colonized England, Canada, and much of the rest of the world.

King Tubby improvised dub versions of tracks brought to him by various producers. He used engineering effects to create shattered soundscapes that would be comprehensible to people already familiar with the song. He would throw or drop a reverb unit, for example, to create crashing echo effects. He would pull pieces of the vocal and deejay versions into and out of the mix, or delete the bass, suddenly pushing it back in in a way designed to create a different atmosphere for sound system dancing. Now a single song could support an indefinite number of versions, at once an economical strategy for reducing overhead and a profound compromise of the very idea of a song. Some songs have sustained dozens or hundreds of versions from the rock steady period to the present, been extended to whole sides of LPs or provided the vaguely recognizable underpinnings of entirely new generations of vocal, deejay, and dub versions.

In the seventies dub became a Jamaican industry that was to be emulated in many ways all over the world. In the United States, disco producers made "extended mixes" so that people could dance for ten or fifteen minutes at a time to, say, Le Freak. Hip hop masters such as Kool Herc (in the Bronx, but raised in Jamaica) started versioning or "sampling" previously recorded funk and disco records and putting rappers over them, first at parties, and then on separate singles. These various uses of sound technologies (the turntable, the mixing board) had never been conceived by the people who invented them, but they have been absolutely central to world popular musics since the seventies.

One aspect of these practices is that they introduced new dimensions of improvisation, in the sense of both using technologies in unintended and unpredictable ways and playing with them as a jazz player plays with his horn: by feel, as it were. Improvisation is in some sense opposed to the conceptual framework of technology, which relies on the systematic administering of means toward a predetermined end. Both the ends and means were put at stake by dub producers: songs undermined, combined, indefinitely extended or suddenly cut off in midstream. Michael Veal, in his wonderful book *Dub: Soundscapes and Shattered Songs in Jamaican Reggae,* writes:

> Given the heavy demand for dub mixes from sound systems preparing for weekend dances, it is important to realize that these mixes were improvised on the spot.... Most dub mixing was done on Friday evenings, when producers deposited their master tapes with engineers, and sound system operators gathered at the studio so that each could be given a unique mix of a currently popular tune. Under these circumstances, an engineer might create dozens of mixes of a given tune in one remix session.... [E]ngineers had no way of preparing a mix beforehand; they usually improvised their way through dozens of mixes of the same track. King Jammy's approach was typical of most engineers: "I don't plan it before I get into the mix, it just comes creatively. I don't plan like, Okay, I'm going to take out the bass at two minutes or whatever. It's just instant creativity."... Using the mixing board as an instrument of spontaneous composition and improvisation, the effectiveness of the dub mix results from the engineer's ability to de- and reconstruct a song's original architecture while increasing the overall power of the performance through a dynamic of surprise and delayed gratification. (Veal, p. 78)

Every new dimension of technology brings with it the possibility of creative misuse; you can throw it at the wall and see what happens. As the world becomes more subject to control, it exceeds or undermines the mechanisms of that control, or pulls them into a subversion of themselves.

Technology territorializes the world, maps it, surveils it, brings more and more of it into the scope of comprehension. But people appropriate technologies in all sorts of bizarre ways, often with transformative effects, as dub music transformed world popular music. Then of course such developments are themselves colonized, comprehended, exploited, driving a new series of technological innovations (for example, in this case, digital sampling). Dub and digital sampling undermined such ideas as intellectual property or the integrity of the work, its authorship, its origin, which in many cases became untraceable or impossibly complex. These ideas then have to be reconstructed or elaborated at different levels, with different effects, which are in turn encoded in new technological means of definition and elaboration. Then of course these are in turn subject to misuse: they will be torn apart and turned to re-use and beyond use in sequence.

Jamaican recording and remix studios, which created many of the most radical technological innovations of modern popular musics, were primitive by the standards of cutting-edge Los Angeles, London, or Nashville recording facilities. No one is going to take a beautiful expensive new piece of technology and see what happens when you drop it. In superseding the technologies available to King Tubby or Scientist, recording technology suggested that those technologies were trash, detritus, which opened up a space of freedom for their exploration. As it were, the technologies are made into pre-technological authentic equipment, hand tools or acoustic instruments; they are disinterpreted, we might say, underdetermined and hence enriched, as in the use of Xeroxing in punk graphic arts. Or we might say their determination and interpretation had lapsed, so there are no longer right or wrong ways to utilize them. They are rendered over into improvisational environments. Lee Perry famously buried unprotected tapes around his studio and then used the weathered, degraded material as masters. He treated his tapes with rum, smoke, and urine, among other things, obscuring the distinction between natural and technological processes.

What circulated from the studio to the island, from the island to the world, were snatches of a torn-up revolutionary consciousness, a black nation in disintegration and recohesion. Veal speculates that the reverberations and echoes of dub mixes were a symbol of the yearning for and disintegration of the African origin thematized in the original Rastafarian-oriented lyrics and nyabhingi drum styles. Echo is a sonic representation of multiple repeated diasporas where the music circulated—Africa/the Pinnacle/Kingston/London/Toronto—where at each point the origin is lost and recovered, reconstrued, reasserted, mis- and displaced.

Technological innovation itself relies on this process of the reinterpretation of its own history. The cutting edge is arid, yanked out of the human context, but is continually being recontextualized in the human from below. The first world provides its last-generation technologies to the third world or the internal third world pockets within itself, then skims off its artistic improvisations; controls the third world and depends on it to live; takes its resources and re-exports them as trash; then re-imports them as art and reinterprets the art in technologies. And so on.

From rock steady emerged roots reggae music, built on the same pulsing beat that served as Rastafarian gospel music. The cult of Marcus Garvey was a dominant theme, spearheaded, as it were, by the chanting of Burning Spear's Winston Rodney:

The image of Marcus Mosiah Garvey...
He's the first black man
Who brings black civilization universally...
Marcus Mosiah Garvey say:
Man you cannot get no words

True make words, make words
Be creative, be creative,
Come, let's talk about the image.

Burning Spear's album covers featured images of Garvey, which also appeared on flags and in murals throughout Jamaica.

As political art and political speech, reggae was carried around the world by the Jamaican (double-)diaspora, in particular to London, New York, and Toronto. Here is a scripture by the Jamaican-British band Steel Pulse:

Rally round the flag
Rally round the red
Gold black and green

Marcus say, so Marcus say
Red for the blood
That flowed like the river
Marcus say sir Marcus say
Green for the land Africa
Marcus say
Yellow for the gold
That they stole
Marcus say
Black for the people
It was looted from

They took us away captivity captivity
Required from us a song
Right now man say repatriate repatriate
I and I patience have now long time gone
Father's mothers sons daughters every one
Four hundred million strong
Ethiopia stretch forth her hand
Closer to God we Africans
Closer to God we can...
Liberation true democracy
One God one aim one destiny.

This is an anthology of quotations from Garvey's speeches and writings.

Such artists as Max Romeo issued a long string of Rasta hymns, underlain by the drumming of Rasta masters such as Horsemouth Wallace. A particularly interesting synthesis was developed by keyboard player and dub master Augustus Pablo, whose "far east sound" combined serene, hypnotic reggae with elements of Hindu chants and Jewish klezmer, an eclectic spiritual orientation with rich and specific political implications even in pure instrumentals.

The early records of Marley and Wailers, like Romeo's and many others', were constructed by Lee Perry at the Black Ark studio in Kingston. Once Marley signed to Island Records, Chris Blackwell reconfigured the Wailers into a showcase for Marley's voice and into something like a touring rock band rather than a studio construction. Marley himself had been assigned by Rasta leader Mortimer Planno to be a missionary to the world, a mission in which he succeeded to an extent almost beyond belief. At this point Bob Marley is perhaps the most recognizable pop music icon throughout the whole world, and has inspired a variety of liberatory political movements with songs such as the profoundly beautiful "Old Pirates (Redemption Song)." The political turn taken by punk, as represented by such groups as the Clash and Rancid, emerges from this tradition. In a particularly appropriate development, reggae has become one of the dominant popular forms in Africa, under the auspices of such singers as Alpha Blondy of Ivory Coast and the late Lucky Dube of South Africa. Indeed a coup in Ivory Coast was in part credited to or blamed on Blondy's music, which carries a message of universal brotherhood delivered in French, English, Arabic, and Hebrew. There are Rastafarians throughout the continent and throughout the world.

The death of Haile Selassie in 1975 presented roots reggae and Rastafarian religion with a crisis. Marley's death in 1981 was also disastrous for the form. These events and the influx of cocaine into Jamaica, the introduction of digital recording technology and in particular digitally constructed rhythms, as well as a number of other factors, led to a disintegration of roots reggae in Jamaica in the eighties. Jamaican music moved toward dancehall or ragga styles and "slackness," or obscene lyrics. Nevertheless, the roots tradition in rhythm and lyric themes have also been in continual revival in Jamaica and all over the world ever since.

Hip Hop

Hip hop was born by an importation of Jamaican musical culture into New York City in the mid-seventies. DJ Kool Herc (Clive Campbell), generally acknowledged as the first hip hop deejay, grew up in Jamaica, going to sound system shows. In his definitive history of hip hop, *Can't Stop Won't Stop,* Jeff Chang writes: "The blues had Mississippi, jazz had New Orleans. Hip-hop has Jamaica. Pioneer deejay Kool Herc spent his earliest years in the same Second Street yard that had produced Bob Marley. 'Them said nothing good ever come outta Trenchtown,' Herc says. 'Well, hip-hop come out of Trenchtown'" (Chang, p. 22). In the Bronx, Herc deployed the twin turntables of Jamaican and American deejays, extending the "break" or drum/instrumental passages on disco and funk records to make them more danceable. The basic idea of constructing new songs from the remnants of old recordings on the fly was Jamaican in origin, and opened the creation of music to a different set of people with different skills. Grandmaster Flash began employing "rappers" to do his talking, in the fashion of Jamaican chatters such as U-Roy and Big Youth, so he could concentrate on turntable heroics of his own invention, especially "scratching" or moving the record back and forth under the needle to produce a rhythm. Herc and Flash were party acts, and the rappers who appeared with them delivered party rhymes that encouraged participation ("Throw your hands in the air, and wave 'em like you just don't care"). The deejay Afrika Bambaataa began drawing some of the political implications, forming a community association in the Bronx to ameliorate gang struggles and police brutality: the Zulu Nation. The child of Caribbean immigrants, Bambaataa started sampling Malcolm X speeches over his rhythm tracks.

Hip hop from the start was essentially a system of all the arts. Its "elements" were deejaying (now associated with turntable manipulation), rapping, breakdancing, and graffiti: movement and visual arts were intrinsic from the outset. Indeed graffiti has been one of its most potent political and aesthetic expressions, as "writers" "take space" or vie with officially sanctioned ways in which the urban environment is articulated and adorned. This often involved the explicit defacing of monuments or advertising, for example, though the greatest graffiti gallery was the New York subway system. We might add that hip hop gave rise to clothing and hairstyles, starting with sweat suits and adidas, but later including designer lines such as Sean John. For a time double-dutch jump rope was also considered a hip hop discipline, for one thing to include the girls. And hip hop in all its arts gave rise to practices of renaming in accordance with aesthetically defined personal identities; few rappers or writers used their full given names, but rather transformed them into poetic identities such as Zephyr or Futura. The films of Spike Lee and others might also be connected to hip hop aesthetics.

As I say, at the beginning, hip hop was a party style, but Black Nationalist political themes began to be woven into the lyrics from a fairly early point, for example, in the records of Run-DMC. By the late eighties Black Nationalism became a dominant theme of hip hop in the work of such seminal acts as KRS-One and Public Enemy. Sampling was a weapon in the artpolitical war, as speeches by people such as Malcolm X, Louis Farrakhan, and Khalid Muhammad (the radical Nation of Islam preacher) could actually be incorporated into the ever more complex sonic structures. The teachings of the Nation of Gods and Earths were explicit from an early moment, for example, in the work of ur-rappers the Cold Crush Brothers, who never recorded but can be seen performing in the indispensable graffiti film *Wild Style*. Kool Herc says: "A lot of Five Percenters…used to come to my party.…[Y]ou might call them 'peace guards,' and they used to hold me down" (Knight, p. 177). In fact much of the best-known hip hop slang or patois derives from Five Percenter teachings. One hears the phrase "dropping science," for example, continually. The term "Word!" or phrase "Word up!" which has entered the language, derives from the Five Percenter declaration "Word is bond." The term "bombing" as applied to graffiti and "da bomb" to mean any good thing probably originate in the Five Percenters' practice of "bombing" one another with "knowledge of self" (Knight, p. 178).

The work of Public Enemy was particularly potent in this regard, and Chuck D, Flavor-Flav, DJ Terminator X, and "Minister of Information" Professor Griff created hyper-aggressive hip hop that presented Nation of Islam and Black Nationalist ideologies in an extremely compelling way, constructing a sonic equivalent for a militant ideology on albums such as *It Takes a Nation of Millions to Hold Us Back* and *Fear of a Black Planet*. The stage presentations were filled with paramilitary imagery; Chuck D dressed in black with uniformed bodyguards scanning the crowd, while Flavor-Flav presented a jester figure or a bit of comic relief. Flavor-Flav famously wore giant clocks to ask the political question "What time is it?" It's time. Past time. The rapper-poet-memoirist-novelist-activist Sister Souljah—whose supposedly anti-white lyrics became an issue in the 1992 presidential campaign in an argument between Bill Clinton and Jesse Jackson—also emerged from the PE nexus.

Here are some of the lyrics from Public Enemy's "Prophets of Rage":

I'm like Garvey
So you can see, B,
It's like that, I'm like Nat [Turner]
Leave me the hell alone
If you don't think I'm a brother
Then check the chromosomes
Then check the stage
I declare it a new age
Get down for the prophets of rage.

It's knowledge of yourself
That you're needin'
Like [Denmark] Vesey or [Gabriel] Prosser
We have a reason why
To debate the hate
That's why we're born to die
Mandela, cell dweller, Thatcher
You can tell her, clear the way for the prophets of rage

Public Enemy was the biggest act in hip hop circa 1989. They associated themselves with the Nation of Islam, drew on its argot for their lyrics while the DJ, Terminator X, sampled Farrakhan and Malcolm. And Public Enemy has influenced political hip hop around the world. NWA and Ice-T on the West Coast were strongly PE-influenced.

Hip hop in the nineties became a dominant pop style under the auspices of Dr. Dre on the West Coast and Sean "Puffy" Combs on the East, among others, who developed a melodic, loping style underneath lyrics about sex, cash, and substance abuse. This style, which became known as "gangsta" rap, was pointedly apolitical, though it said nasty things about the police. Nevertheless, the political and Black Nationalist strains continued in "underground" hip hop. In particular, followers of the Nation of Gods and Earths turned in some of the most seminal and interesting material of that era, including records by Big Daddy Kane, Brand Nubian, Mobb Deep, and Poor Righteous Teachers. This strand became commercially potent under the auspices of the massive hip hop collaboration/nation Wu-Tang Clan and its many offshoots. Meanwhile, some of the most esoteric imagery associated with the Nation of Islam, Rastafarianism, and the Nation of Gods and Earths found its way onto the records of less commercial artists, such as Jedi Mind Tricks, Aceyalone, and Immortal Technique, who made some of the best and most absorbing hip hop records in the history of the style. A typical and outstanding Gods and Earths act is the California duo Self Scientific, who on "Love Allah" sum it up as follows: "News flash, the black man is God, no doubt."

Graffiti and Language

Foucault and Deleuze, among others, have pointed out that language, and in particular written language, is an instrument or form of power, a thought at least as old as Vico. One suspects, indeed, that to some extent written language was developed to preserve and disseminate the decrees of rulers, as well as to keep records of debts and violations. It is hard to see how one would set up or preserve an elaborate hierarchy, a proper state, without a written language; and though tribal cultures have had a variety of inscriptional tools, they've rarely had anything like hieroglyphics, or written Chinese, or Sanskrit, or English, unless they were subjected to them. Indeed the rise of the state— systematic power worked on a large territorial scale, eventually global—coincides with the development of written language and is inconceivable without it. Much the same might be said of the huge religious hierarchies associated with Judaism, Islam, Christianity, and Hinduism. These have relied to one extent or another on the mystique of text, and a monopoly on its interpretation or even on sheer access to it, as in Catholicism in relation to Latin, for instance. The God of monotheisms, conceived by analogy to human rulers, expresses himself in text, as to Moses: gives laws. World capital also proceeds in the same way, more or less. Advertising is largely incomprehensible without text; the idea of franchise, the recognizability of Wal-Mart, trade regulations, the transfer of funds, even which crops are planted where, all depend on textual forms. Science depends on repeatability of experiment, which in turn presupposes careful written description. Technology is cumulative in virtue of its textual encryptions. All forms of systematic power, we might say, are text-heavy, are forms of sentencing.

Deleuze and Guattari distinguish between "major" and "minor" languages; the former (such as French or standard English) are instruments of power, the latter (such as, to use two of their examples, Québécois and Black English) instruments of resistance. But their point is more complex than that. In fact nobody speaks standard English; slang and ephemeral idiom make their way into everyone's speech. And likewise the minor language depends on the standard forms, which it puts in play, adapts, reverses, or sets spinning.

> If a language such as British English or American English is major on a world scale, it is necessarily worked upon by all minorities of the world, using very diverse procedures of variation. Take the way Gaelic and Irish English and any number of "ghetto languages" set American English in variation, to the point that New York is virtually a city without a language. (Furthermore, American English could not have *constituted* itself without this linguistic labor of the minorities.) (Deleuze and Guattari, pp. 102–3)

That is, the major language *lives in* its minor variations, or feeds on its own destruction.

> The problem is not the distinction between major and minor language; it is one of becoming. . . . Black Americans do not oppose Black to English, they transform American English that is their own language

into Black English.... Conquer the major language in order to delin-
eate in it as yet unknown minor languages. Use the minor language to
*send the major language racing....*The notion of *minority* is very complex,
with musical, literary, linguistic, as well as juridical and political references. (Deleuze and Guattari, pp. 104–5)

We might add that the aesthetic, linguistic, legal, and political aspects are
inextricable.

I have already mentioned the centrality to hip hop and graffiti of processes
of renaming; we ought also note their centrality to Black Nationalist religious
expression. Rastafarians have achieved a minor language, based largely on
remaking the word/syllable "I," used in many contexts, notably the plural
pronoun referring to African peoples: "I and I," the name of a nationality and
of oneself. The Nation of Islam replaced the "slave names" of black people
with the marker "X"; Clarence 13X was the thirteenth Clarence converted
at the Harlem Mosque. Elijah Muhammad writes:

God offers you His own name. Every attribute of His name means
something glorious, worthy, and something of divine. Not one of his
names can be interpreted other than something of divine, but you have
the name of the devil: Johnson, Williamson, Culpepper, Hog, Bird, Fish
and what not. These are nothing but common devil names. Your Bible
teaches you that in that day, God will call you after His own name.
They must have the name of the beast taken away from them and given
the name of God, before they could ever see the hereafter. Well, this is
the time. You hear my name called Muhammad. Go check the devil's
dictionary. Read the meaning of it, and he will bear witness to me that
it means one that is praised much and is worthy of praise. It is the name
of God. (Muhammad 2, p. 88)

We might also point out that African American musical styles have elaborately practiced renaming, and also presented and driven Black English. The
slangs associated with jazz and hip hop, for example, are extremely elaborate,
and have to some extent been codified in dictionaries. Hip hop is, among
other things, a patois or minor language, centrally invented by the Nation
of Gods and Earths, whose teachings are always presented as codes for reinterpretation of the major language, constantly presenting new idioms to be
decoded.

Our environment bristles with rules expressed in signage. Or consider
the tax code, and try to conceive of a system of taxation in anything like
the modern sense without written language. "Standard" English is written

English as issued by authoritative outlets: the *New York Times,* for instance, or books published by Knopf. And standard English is a node of power and a flashpoint for power struggles about such things as multilingual education, "official" languages, ebonics. Ebonics is a pretty good example of the whole thing: an oral tradition holding out against written standard English, preserving tribal anachronisms, taking standard English and ripping it up or reconfiguring it, playing with the dictionary to create cultural spaces in the context of elaborate caste systems and power hierarchies. The standard written language, indeed, has a certain monstrous dead weight, enshrined in the *Chicago Manual of Style* or the *OED,* always a step behind the living word as it emerges from people's mouths, bearing with it the whole weight of history and law: slow, cumulative, growing behind us inexorably. It yields a great profusion of expressive tools, but it also canalizes our expressions through forms of power.

Children are subjected to the written language in the most literal sense. Their education is compulsory. We force their eyes to the linear form, discipline them to it. Much of their "socialization" consists, first, of learning to read, and second, of what they read and what we say about what they read and what they write: the five-paragraph essay—topic sentence, body, conclusion—rigid as possible. The public school is a textual environment, even more replete with written instructions and other messages than the rest of the settled world. The text is the primary vessel of the "shared culture," "our" history, "our" Constitution and codes of law; it's a primary tool by which this "us" is forged, to whatever extent it is forged.

Text is conceived to be abstract. All the kids in class have "the same" book, thought of as an essence subsisting simultaneously in indefinitely many spatial locations. "The rule of law" is an interesting phrase—odd, actually. It attributes power to an abstraction, offloads it from the human body or even any concrete object of any kind whatsoever. It's the repeatability, the reinscriptive or reprintable or cut-and-pasteable incessant power of the type: the true presence and authority of the Platonic form. "The text" itself is nowhere and hence everywhere; it floats around us like a spirit environment, and flows through us, too. Foucault talks about bodies as "zones of inscription," and no doubt the very firing of our neurons has taken on a textual form.

If the basic functions with regard to authority of the text are performed by its rigidity—its repeatability from context to context, apparently without alteration of information—the prestige of the text is essentially a function of its ontological status as an abstraction. This connects it with "mind" in a Cartesian or Platonic sense, and on a social scale with "civilization": mind bloated precisely to the size of a political state. Indeed the ontological prestige

of any given object in European history is essentially connected to the degree
to which it is conceived to be nonphysical = spiritual. The savages who are
excluded from the written word/world are insistently, pointedly physical.
This is still our mythology of race, for example. It's not really all that false
about them; it's false about us, since our own status within the hierarchy rests
on a metaphysics for which there can be no evidence. There is, of course, a
long history in the West of iconoclasm, but understandably as well there is
a long history of logoclasm—burning books, rubbing out the laws, defacing
signs, and so on—and perhaps the logoclastic tradition is a bit more alive at
the moment than iconoclasm, which has an anachronistic flavor.

At any rate, logoclasm, or the eradication of text, is only one possible
response. Others work from within, and rest on acts that compromise the
abstraction of the text. Preeminent among these, I suggest, are poetry and
graffiti, textual arts that are also at their essence the concretizing of text.
Poetry and graffiti insist that, more or less like everything else that exists, text
is particular and physical, that it cannot be separated from the occasion and
location and the bristling particularities of its inscription.

Poetry relentlessly emphasizes sound; at a minimum it needs to be read as
imaginatively spoken. All the traditional formal elements of poetry—rhyme,
meter, alliteration, line breaks that correspond to pauses, and so on—are
incomprehensible outside of a conception of text as a representation of the
spoken word that allows for the reproduction of spoken language on particular occasions. It originates in bardic traditions of the spoken word and returns
us to them through textual media.

Rap is a particularly insistent and innovative example. Its medium is the
recording of a particular voice speaking its poetry in music. Rap is in fact a
fascinating phenomenon here for many reasons. For one thing, it reconnects
the spoken word explicitly to music, both as its context and in its actual performance, which is often a compromise between singing and speaking (Nelly,
for example, or for that matter the "singjay" reggae style of such figures as
Eek-a-Mouse). We might say it is Homeric. It is not, as much pop music
remains (though this is less and less the case under the influence of hip hop),
the recording or simulation of the recording of an antecedent performance
(a paradigm here would be the Lomaxian "field recording" of folk music;
another is the rock band, which continues recording under a performance
model), but something that relies on recording as explicitly its material and
medium, made initially on turntables and then through digital sampling.
Here we might consider the techniques employed by Beck, for example.

Hip hop occupies a site interstitial to text and oral tradition; it is mechanically reproducible, but what is mechanically reproduced is the voice. It has

an immediacy that pure text lacks—more trace of the body, we might say—and it uses the forms of ebonics and various other slangs and dialects. Not surprisingly, it is a site of power struggles. Derrida has rejected the view that the written text is a representation of spoken language, and that much seems basically right to me: text is its own animal, though as I say, it can perform on occasion as a representation of speaking. And it emerges at least as much from pictorial as oral communication, in the hieroglyph or ideogram. In its fully alphabetic form—rigidified and regularized or militarized, disciplined into the line or march of one-way communication—it is fundamentally distinct from both picture and sound. But the hip hop disc or MP3 is something of a unification of spoken word and publication, now a translation of spoken word into digital information, which is both an apotheosis of text in its effortless reproducibility and an undermining of text as pure abstraction.

Graffiti, though it often employs images, is fundamentally a form of writing, and indeed graffiti artists refer to themselves as "writers." The medium of much of it is the name, the re-name. The name itself occupies an uneasy or ambiguous zone of the language. When philosophers such as Russell, Wittgenstein, Quine, and Kripke have given accounts of reference, or the relations of words to the world, they have had special difficulties with names and often had to confer on them a special status or to develop particularly elaborate accounts to work them into the wider theories. Evidently what a word like "chair" refers to, and the process by which it comes to refer, is somewhat different from the case of a word like "Crispin." Doing any responsible or interesting account of this distinction or its history would take us far afield, but a couple of points might be pulled out for mention. Russell tried to account for names on the model of his logical theory for general terms or predicates and the existential quantifier. This reverses a long history—explicitly rejected by Wittgenstein in the *Philosophical Investigations* in relation to a quotation from Augustine, but stretching at least to Plato—in which general terms or predicates were accounted for on the model of names. Saul Kripke and Hilary Putnam, among others, have attacked Russell's view. Kripke's account is sometimes called "the causal theory of proper names." According to it the referential function of proper names is radically distinct from that of predicates, which perhaps can be given some sort of Russell-style account. Names, by contrast, originate in specific dubbing ceremonies (like when my Mom dubbed me "Crispin"), and are rigid across possible worlds.

Obviously if you don't get all this and you want to, you are going to have to tackle the extremely rich history of twentieth-century analytic theory of reference. But what it amounts to for present purposes is this: the relation between a person and her name is a particularly vivid relation, or a particularly intimate relation, or a particularly concrete relation so far as relations of words to the things to which they refer goes. Learning to use the term "chair" correctly is a triumph of the human abstractive capacity because you are learning to construct and deploy into your mental economy and public communicative space a "kind" or universal or Form. But the dubbing ceremony and the use of the name that is parasitic on it proceeds from a specific speech act in the presence of a specific object: it is a concrete utterance on a particular occasion. Then the transmission of the name proceeds by a series of these concrete interchanges in specific oral or written repetitions. The name, we should say, is the least abstract zone of the language, the most specific and concrete of its applications.

In graffiti, the name and the act of dubbing are seized and simultaneously undermined. Most graffiti artists dub themselves with the name they use in their work. In part this is an attempt to undermine the use of names in the legal system and modes of surveillance, to create a persona that worms its way underneath the forms of textual power. The idea is simultaneously to be hard to identify by power and massively famous outside it, to manufacture an unofficial name that does not appear on the birth certificate or other documents and then to broadcast it as far as one possibly can (to "king a line," for instance, or "go all-city") in a culture underneath the official one. And the means of broadcast are not, essentially or initially, publication or the infinitely reproducible abstract textual form but a perfectly concrete inscription: a version of the name that is completely space- and time-bound, unlike our imagination of published text, which floats free of all dimensionality. The tag is actually made of paint, unlike the word "chair," which is not actually made of anything. And insofar as it is text, it is name, which means that it lives in some particularly concrete relation to what it names. I wonder, for example, whether you feel this with regard to your own name: that it is the text closest to you, that you and it exist in a particularly intimate relation—more intimate, for example, than your relation to words that might pick out your gender, or your race, or the place where you live, and so on, though all those words "apply" to you. This is why practices of renaming such as we have briefly examined are practices of re-identification, of creating a self that evades existing power structures, an extra-Babylonian self.

The art history of typography exists in a rather uneasy relation to the general idea of text in the West. Typography treats words as concrete objects, focuses on their inscription in particular spaces. People have expended tremendous energy on typography. Part of this expenditure can be given a kind of ideological reading: the purpose of it is to create maximum transparency to reading, to make the abstraction as effortless as possible, to enable you to forget that you are a particular body looking at a particular page. But people also get caught up in the sensible qualities of type, its beauty or the appropriateness of its shape for expressing its meanings. There is an aesthetics of text as visual array as well as significance. These two functions—the sensible and the semiotic—are complementary, but also often enough in tension, because while the semiotic function of text tries to draw you away from the concrete interaction you are having with the screen or page, the sensible can be trying to draw you back into it, or to mediate the meaning through the concrete sensible interchange. Indeed one might point out that it is impossible to present written text without typography: that written communication requires concrete inscription in one form or another. Typography, we might say, can enable mind, but it can also operate within a nostalgia for embodiment. This is true of other "arts of the book" as well, such as papermaking and binding, internal and external design. It is true of Web design or the design of street signs.

One of the places where we experience the interaction of the sensible and the semiotic most vividly is indeed in signs and advertisements. Different typefaces can be central to the semiotic effect. You tilt the type right, for example, to convey the idea of speed or the future. You resort to blackletter to enforce a sense of tradition or persistence. Or you use the plainest sans-serif lettering you possibly can to give yourself a "no-frills" aura, which promises that things are inexpensive, and so on. Probably in every case the communicative trace of written text is effected in a collaboration of typography (or calligraphy) and semiotics. Another way to put this is that the two are not on any particular occasion separable, an example of the conceptual structure of this book. You could discuss the "message" separately from the physical qualities of the inscription or the aural qualities of the utterance, but a message can be embodied only in a particular inscription or utterance with a particular visual or aural quality.

An "idea" might be separate from its inscriptions, but it requires aesthetic embodiment in particular forms to be expressed on any given occasion. The "type" appears only in its "tokens"; it must be sensuous. Even in cases where maximum transparency to meaning is the intention, that itself takes up a place within the semiotic interchange that occurs around the inscription. Every inscription is necessarily a concrete object, a specific object with particular sensible properties; and though these may not be cognized on a certain occasion and may exist in tension with, as it were, text's conception of itself, it is always part of the situation, part of the constructions and the disintegrations of meaning. Berkeley argued against Locke's theory of general ideas—essentially conceived as a variety of mental image—that it was impossible to imagine a dog, say, that was neither a dachshund nor a pit bull not a mongrel, whose hair was neither long nor short, that was neither black nor white nor brown, small, large, or in between, and so on. Any image of a dog in the mental economy of anyone necessarily had a variety of specific features apparently extraneous to the status of the idea as the general idea applying to all dogs. The same is precisely true of text: its generality and abstractness are qualified on every particular occasion by a bristling collection of concrete sensible qualities.

Graffiti style is strongly related to the art of typography; indeed, many graffiti artists have invented a repertoire of alphabets, created in their black books and deployed on trains and walls. In addition they have appropriated lettering styles from advertising, comic books, and many other sources, which they have adapted to their purposes. But it is also worth pointing out some of the differences. Typography proper inhabits—at least apparently—a more abstract zone than graffiti, which is even more insistently focused on the particular inscription. Typefaces are expressed as a series of types open to mechanical reproduction. Certain typefaces become standard, and this is a reflection of the basic purpose of most typography: to enable standardization and to apply to any number of specific texts in their indefinitely wide dissemination through publication. Graffiti alphabets, by contrast, are always aimed squarely at entirely specific inscriptions. They retain a handmade quality; they are guides for the hand in producing specific works. The works themselves are paintings and partake of the ontology of paintings: that is, they are specific physical objects. Destroy a copy of *Ulysses* and the novel persists; destroy the Mona Lisa, the actual specific physical object, and the work is extinguished. *Ulysses* is pristine, as perfect now as at the moment it was completed; the Mona Lisa, like all particular physical objects, ages and alters in time.

The twentieth century, of course, saw a thousand intersections of picture and text, and thousands of objects that were not clearly one or the other or that were both. That is true of graffiti with special intensity. It inhabits a particular zone between the picture and the text as rap inhabits a particular zone between the text and the spoken word. Graffiti is essentially the name as particular painting, the text drawn into a physical ontology, a complete merging of type and token. Perhaps this is in part a revival of the forms of writing current before the technology of print, a kind of reincarnation of the scribe. This is true in more ways than one. It is no coincidence that printing coincides roughly with the Reformation, whereas scribe traditions could be associated with texts used for hermetic or even secret purposes in a society of illiterates. The scribal text involved a connoisseurship of visual form and had a magical significance, a particular power that has been lost in the world of continuous publication and compulsory education. Essentially texts were reproduced for particular people, their functions and even legibility limited to certain individuals and interpersonal formations.

The history of graffiti text can in part be written as a history of unintelligibility. The early work—by and large dedicated to the fame of the writer—presupposed legibility as well as a fairly conventional set of lettering styles, especially "bubble" letters. But with the advent of "wild style" graffiti in the early eighties—embodied in pieces rather than tags or throwups—letter styles started to become more and more elaborate and less and less easy to read. This is usually accounted for as a shift to a kind of "code" analogous to the most slang-ridden varieties of rap; the idea was to mark off those who could read the lettering as a special group with its own language. To some extent this is certainly true, and one can of course learn to decode various lettering styles, or to associate them with particular crews or writers even where one can't decode them. Indeed wild style graffiti was fairly quickly taken up into actual typography and signage styles. But further developments took some writers well beyond any attempt at legibility and into a kind of purely visual play with the word, a systematic fragmentation or disintegration, often arrayed in a perspectival three-dimensional space that was essentially pictorial rather than linguistic. Such developments would certainly be hard to employ in advertising.

The book *Taking the Train* produces a record of the great graff artist PHASE 2's styles over the decade from 1972 to 1982, as reproduced in his black book (Austin, pp. 184–85). Each of the ten steps reveals a loss of legibility. At the sixth, I would have to look at the thing for a while to decode it. At ten, it wouldn't matter how long I looked. In the last few versions, the name seems to be more and more torn up; by the last, it is in shreds.

In the case of PHASE 2, at any rate, this process is magnificently conscious. Joe Austin quotes him as follows:

> I'm absorbing and devouring language in its co-existing state and creating something else with it.... The English language isn't much, especially in its current state. By comparison (to Chinese and Japanese) it's like a dot. Why not go beyond that and just create an alphabet or language? You can't put a limit on communication or how one can communicate; you've always got to look further; that's how style expanded in the first place.... If they really need Western thought, why don't they examine the Greek myth of the alphabet? Cadmus sowed

dragon's teeth and they sprang up as armed men. Greco-Roman letters were rudiments (regiments) for an imperial, militarized world—social realities that still curse us. (Austin, p. 114)

This presents the linguistic approach of graff at its widest scope. First, it connects it with the ideogram and an explicit critique of the alphabet. But the content of that critique is of special interest: it connects alphabetic languages to military and state power in its very structure or visual appearance as something lined up and regimented: thought conveyed as a military maneuver, disciplined in a military style, like the rows of Germans arrayed before Riefenstahl's cameras.

Any book that reproduces contemporary graffiti shows that the process of deconstructing the text—at once venerating and destroying it—has proceeded ever since the early 1980s at the latest, and has reached a point of astounding refinement and variety. It is now accomplished by virtuosi, people as immersed and skilled in their craft as Raphael was in his. There has never been a more elaborate art of text, and there has never been a more elaborate interruption of text. One other element in this, which is also incorporable in the more casual tag, is the intentional use of the drip (poster by Shane Jessup: "DRIPS ARE TOTALLY HOT RIGHT NOW"), emphasizing at once the physical presence of wall and paint. Often you have the sense that you could read what the thing says, except the drips have made it impossible: the word is flowing down the wall, melting or liquefying in the reemergence in dry form of its liquid origin. Many such works, we might say, *depict* drips, as do the comic book versions of gestural painting by Lichtenstein.

It is likely that many of these developments can be accounted for by analogy to well-established structures of mainstream art history. And in fact, about the same time as wild style graffiti appeared, graffiti merged to some extent with mainstream art history. Artists such as Dondi, Zephyr, and Futura started working on canvas and showing in galleries, while many graffiti artists also started doing legal murals. Such developments—along with the increasing hand skills of writers as they matured—encouraged a culture of virtuosity and an avant-garde structure in which the point was to surpass rather than merely imitate or venerate one's forebears. In addition, these shifts accompanied a shift in basic values from quantity to quality. Where before, the point might have been to do the maximum number of tags, which would form the basis of the writer's fame, now the source of fame could also be the writer's artistic ability and stylistic innovations. Before that time (and to some extent this remains true), graffiti deployed more a craft guild structure than a romantic/modernist/avant-garde ideology. What was privileged was not the genius or the masterpiece but the labor. This is often true of arts that are actually in process and vital rather than being monopolized by professionals. And it's a revealing juxtaposition because the two worlds (avant-garde and graffiti) were in parallel in the same city. But at any rate the art boom eighties had a bit of an intersection with the graffiti world, which predictably though unfortunately had more of an effect on graff than on Jeff Koons, who could have used a dose of work ethic, commitment, and craft. And though the incorporation of graff into SoHo art turned out to be a brief fad, and galleries dropped artists within a couple of years for the most part, it did manage to help set graffiti spinning in some new directions.

Graffiti went from being words to being pictures of words, and then being the simultaneous massive elaboration and tearing apart of words. The work expresses both a veneration of text and a very direct hostility toward it: the act of celebration is also the act of destruction. Surely while the typographic and other writing arts have included bits that were extremely elaborate and even hard to parse, there has never been a moment before in the history of text in which illegibility was so explicitly thematized, celebrated, explored, and exploited. Sometimes lettering is consumed in flames, or blown sky-high, or dispersed by the wind, or taken in a hand and shaken out of comprehensibility. Text is merged into picture, but then also compromised toward pictoricity or shaken out of its status as text almost altogether. Nevertheless, the sheer fact that text is involved is preserved: that's not usually the question. The name is still evidently present, only it's buried, sliced, blendered, flipped, folded, twisted, disassembled, and put together again in a different order, as dub treats the song.

Written language has a future, if we do. It's obviously in flux right now. One might mention hypertext and other ways that linearity is being exploited and compromised. Graffiti, I'm suggesting, shows one way that language is being altered and created, one with particularly antiauthoritarian implications. But like hypertext too, it is constantly being reappropriated into essentially authoritarian systems such as the avant-garde art world and corporate design culture. It is also undermining these worlds.

Graffiti started out as a crime, and graffiti proper (as opposed, for example, to post-graff design style) remains a crime. The idea of art as a crime and a subversion of order is a rich one historically but has rarely been quite so pointed. Graffiti is explicitly at its root an antiauthoritarian art, and that fact has informed its history, its look, its practitioners, its surfaces. In short, the medium is incomprehensible without the crime, or: the medium is crime. The fundamental impulse of graffiti is the antiauthoritarian impulse. What I'm arguing is that this is not only a matter of the sheer fact that the stuff is illegal; it's not just a matter of racking paint and running from the cops. It's inside the form and content of the art itself. This of course is not surprising, and the fact that the fundamental impulse of any given work of art is in some sense visible on its face is typical rather than the reverse. In this case it drives forward a saturated sign system of revolution that attacks the state and the schools by attacking the word, while also reclaiming the word or claiming a place in authority—claiming the power to remake the word and hence the world. We could say that this is an attempt to revamp or rearticulate authority, to read it through a new set of codes, to take control of it and bounce it back and play with it, make something of it instead of merely knuckling under to it. It's an attempt to take language back.

The political life of a culture is conducted in the fine arts and under the sponsorship of the state and its representatives, as we have already seen and will see again, particularly in architecture. But it is also conducted in the popular arts, which present modes of resistance in which the aesthetic and political elements are inextricable. Of course, African American popular musics were the popular musics of the world for much of the twentieth century: blues, jazz, swing, bop, rock 'n' roll: all of these are fundamentally African American styles, whereas ska, reggae, and hip hop are Afro-Caribbean-American. The youth subcultures of the second half of the twentieth century—greasers, mods, hippies, punks, antiglobalization anarchists—have been largely identified by and configured around music; despite the basic failure of such subcultures to remake entirely the politics of Western culture, their political effects were incalculable. And the treatment of language as an aesthetic site has been a central motif of both political power and resistance to that power.

CHAPTER 6

Arthistorical Themes

To some extent the idea of art history as a distinct discipline has inhibited the understanding of history, and even as the discipline is always working to put high art into a cultural context, it is always pulling it out of history into a practice of connoisseurship or expertise as well, by definition isolating art as a distinct sphere. Indeed we might think of art history as a correlate of political science; the definition of the discipline is implicitly a set of isolations or limitations on methodology. These limitations will have to be broken in layers, and of course the idea of political aesthetics is potentially just as limiting; if it ever generated a line of discourse, it would have to be undermined or transcended in its turn. None of these is a comprehensive structure, and in fact no structure could actually be comprehensive. Nevertheless, in the context of art history and political science, political aesthetics represents an opening. "Social" or "sociological" histories of art—for example, the work of Albert Boime—often perform the immediate economic reduction, just as though this were 1848. A reasonable alternative is captured in the term "material culture": an investigation into the shaped environment that would encompass anthropology, art interpretation, political history, and so on.

Art History and Political Science

I conceived the methodology of this book initially as a fusion between political philosophy and art history. It struck me that the skills of the art historian—looking at the real shape of real things and decoding its significance—could be trained on the subject matter of political science: political systems, ideologies, constitutions, relations. But although there is, for instance, plenty of art history about revolutionary art (French neoclassicism, for example), there is too little art history about the texts and actions of the French revolutionaries. On the other hand, directly political expressions already occupy art history or the study of material culture. One cannot but be struck by the aesthetic objects spun off by political regimes, some of which dominate whole cities or landscapes, the works of those who wield the power of taxation, we might say: the pyramids, cathedrals, capitols, stadiums—the wonders of the world. As I tried to develop such rough notions of synthesis into something comprehensible, I began to focus on political aesthetics as an alternative or supplement to political science, ranging (roughly) over the same subject matter but filling in gigantic lacunae. That is, the subject matter of political science (political systems, ideologies, constitutions) was to be treated in its aesthetic aspects.

The idea of a political science originates in a moment within the academy in which virtually every discipline was aiming for scientific status. In the late nineteenth and early twentieth centuries, science was conceived as the only legitimate epistemic procedure, and other disciplines were legitimated through an approximation to science. Philosophy, for example, went through an extremely anxious period circa 1890–1920 in which it attacked itself—particularly in its idealist moments—as woolly, without certain results or concrete effects. "Analytic" philosophy and the sudden explosion of work in symbolic logic were responses to this professional crisis (Sartwell 2). And this, too, is the period of the maturation of the social sciences, of which, I suppose, political science is one, or several. If political science were to shift or broaden to include political aesthetics, this would no doubt show something about the academy of our moment.

As a discipline, political science is a bit of a congeries, and its subspecialties hardly overlap, from political theory to quantitative demographics to political economy to international relations to studies of rhetorical effects to biographies of leaders. And surely the question of how far political life can be explained scientifically—or what that means exactly—is an open one. But the preference for science could itself be understood to some extent to be an aesthetic preference. Science is among other things a prose style: precise, clear, filled with stipulated technical terms, third person, nonnarrative, building a theory brick by brick. (This is not to say that science is *merely* a prose style, of course.) In philosophy, the need for clarity or the backlash into clarity was fueled by the sheer speculative nature of German idealism—by its epistemology—but also by its profuse and tenebrous prose. Above all, Russell did not write like Hegel.

At the same moment that the social-scientific disciplines in their modern matrix were constituted, the arts were extruded; this extrusion was constitutive both ways around, and is central to what we call modernism in the arts. Art history itself, however, had to make peace with a scientific-academic conception of history, as well as with its amorphous, ambiguous, rich, and maddeningly elusive and replete subject matter. But in any case it had to be conceived as a specialized academic discipline, entailing its detachment from the subject matter of political science (though they are always also being resynthesized), despite the fact that in art history's origins in Hegelian philosophy of history, art and politics are joined at the hip.

The data of art history or material culture, considered in its widest scope, concerns what Jacques Rancière has called "the distribution of the sensible": it is an aspect of the arrangement of real things in the world, as are, say, economics and politics. But the distribution of the sensible is foundationally aesthetic in the sense that it embodies the arrangement qua arrangement: aesthetics is necessary to trace the contours as a whole.

> I call the distribution of the sensible the system of self-evident facts of sense perception that simultaneously discloses the existence of something in common and the delimitations that define the respective parts and positions within it. . . . This apportionment of parts and positions is based on a distribution of spaces, times, and forms of activity that determines the very manner in which something common lends itself to participation and in what way various individuals have a part in this distribution. . . . Plato states that artisans cannot be put in charge of the shared or common elements of the community because they do *not have the time* to devote themselves to anything other than their work. They cannot be *somewhere else* because *work will not wait*. The distribution of the sensible reveals who can have a share in what is common to the community based on what they do and on the time and space in which this activity is performed. (Rancière, p. 12)

For Rancière, the distribution of the sensible is not some inmost mystery of being; it is precisely the fact that we distribute people into professions and objects into locations and hence shape a polis. The question ultimately is how we physically arrange the world and move through it. Ask yourself whether the shape of the social as sensible admits of exhaustive scientific description, and you'll see why political theory must avail itself of aesthetic criteria. There could be other reasons to do political theory, such as elucidating matters within various frameworks. But for a description or an evaluation of the contours of the whole, you would do well to go to aesthetics. Obviously, however, the question of how the sensible actually gets distributed is a political question, while the question of the actual state of this distribution at a given time is an aesthetic question, and I think that the genetic and formal accounts are best juxtaposed or collapsed into a single explanation.

Origins

I have presented political aesthetics as being concerned with the aesthetic aspects of constituted political systems, regimes, ideologies. But it is necessary to think about the aesthetics from which political systems emerge as well as the aesthetics they embody. For example, the national or tribal identities on which political identities supervene or are represented as supervening are in their essence aesthetic systems. A paradigmatic case is the idea of a "German nation," which in the nineteenth and twentieth centuries dictated a series of border shifts, political alliances, and military actions: redistributions of the sensible. Habermas among others has written about how this identity was discovered or manufactured by folklorists and historians such as the Grimm brothers, who consciously identified or generated a myth cycle, a vernacular literature, and a set of folk arts in which this national identity was said to consist (Habermas).

Many national identities seem to rest on "national epics," a poetics of identity, as in Homer, the epic of Gilgamesh, Exodus, the tales of Arthur. And national identities rely foundationally on languages and artifacts that embody an aesthetics and draw people into a sort of imaginary and real unity. A similar history tries to identify or manufacture an American character by weaving together a canon of texts and objects: portraits of Washington and Lincoln and their memorial architectures; Mount Rushmore; the figures and the writings of Emerson and Whitman; the tale of the pilgrims; the dramatic gastronomy of Thanksgiving; emblems of eagles and flags; Hank Williams and Snoop Dogg; Louis Armstrong and Robert Johnson; an imagined New Orleans or the Empire State Building; representations of the *Maine* and Pearl Harbor and 9/11; Iwo Jima. Gender or racial differences, likewise, are understood at their heart aesthetically, by the different roles or practices of different genders or races in storytelling, cookery, the crafts and professions, and so on. Any even rudimentary explanation of the differences between black and white culture in the United States, for example, would have to make reference to different systems of folklore and the arts, or tales of aesthetic origins. We trace the roots of African American popular music to West Africa, or trace an aesthetic of "sparkle and shine" from African ceremonies to American bottle trees (see Thompson). Gender, we might say with Rancière, is a distribution of the sensible. The idea of a woman as the nurturer in the private home not only entails various modes of interior decoration, the production of craft objects such as quilts, and the preparation of food, but also helps create the architecture and layout of subdivisions. Then a feminist critique of such arrangements—or a demographic shift of women into the workplace—entails a redistribution of the visible kinesthetic material world.

Political arrangements respond continuously to such identities, or embody them. I don't want, however, simply to say that political systems derive their distribution of the sensible from some pristine aesthetic state of nature; in some sense aesthetics and politics are equally primordial—as we have seen. Each is shaped by the other throughout. The shape of things reflects relations of power; the aesthetic and the political are structurally analogous, one might say, or contiguous and hence inverted images of each other, and so on. The political shapes and is shaped. Stare at the Pyramids or at a skyscraper or at a one-room schoolhouse or the Department of Justice website and ask yourself what it shows you about power, or about design. But then ask what what it shows about design shows about power, and what what it shows about power shows about design.

Certainly political systems use preexisting aesthetic resources, materials that are already saturated with meaning, and reinterpret and redeploy and develop them. Indeed every political system arises in a variety of existing aesthetic as well as political contexts, at an art historical moment, with certain productive strategies or capacities, a context in which a given symbol or symphony is comprehensible or the reverse, in which its meaning is developing and from which its meaning can be plucked. Even when they try, political systems cannot originate a formal or stylistic language from scratch. One might think of the arts of the Soviet Union: though its leaders shut down their own high modernists, they availed themselves of an existing vocabulary of realist painting with a history in leftist European politics. But they also tried to remake, redesign the landscape, in agriculture and industry. Every five-year plan was an aesthetic plan as well as a set of production goals, or at any rate had aesthetic entailments. The very attempt to institute a centrally planned economy makes that economy subject to evaluation according to its design features and renders a "free market" economy—or whatever it was that the communist economy opposed—subject to new sorts of aesthetic description.

We might think of political systems as hermeneutical systems, engaged in an interpretation and reconstrual of preexisting texts, arts, identities. A political system arises amidst a vast aesthetic detritus, and it attempts to mount a coherent interpretation, and hence redistribute and remake the sensible and the psychological world (to a limited extent). This can be extremely conscious, as in the various run-throughs of American history that you get at the Smithsonian Institution: the Museum of American History, the Museum of the American Indian, and so on. Or it can be inchoate and as it were fully naturalized; this is simply who we are. But the specification of who we are is a selection and reconstruction of the cultural junk in the midst of which the political hermeneutics finds itself: partly a narrative, partly a picture, partly an architecture, partly a song, and so on. Obviously each such interpretation is the site of controversy, or is subject to whatever political forces can affect the condition of the state and the culture. One of the functions of the state is to narrate an art history and hence forge and falsify a contemporary distribution of the sensible. And again, even the negation of art history as a proper discipline for the state, as in Marxist regimes, forges an aesthetic, and forges it out of the existing detritus; it tells the story as economic, with a thousand obvious design or narrative entailments.

Such political/economic structures as the five-year plan or the policy of rapid industrialization or a mobilization for a war effort or a housing program or a nationalized health care system or trade agreements or border policies remake the environment and have design implications and embodiments. We could say that central economic planning of the sort employed by all versions of the modern mega-state is always landscape architecture as well as whatever else it is. It affects everything from the color of the sky to the shape of the hills to the cuisine of the home. And, for example, the extreme sudden fashion for environmentalism in the face of the global warming "crisis" is also an aesthetic commentary, and the glorification of "nature" or of the wild in, for example, John Muir or Thoreau or Wordsworth or Rousseau is foundationally an aesthetic system, preference, and critique, bound up with all the features of romanticism as a system of the arts. The national park system is an aesthetic corollary of this point of view: landscapes shaped by landscape paintings and literary descriptions, even as the landscape paintings and literary descriptions are shaped by the land itself and by a history of its depictions—pictorial and poetic conventions from perspective to oil paints to iambic pentameter, but also political action and policy.

High industrialism and the machine have an aesthetic cult as well, seen for example in futurism, or the work of Charles Sheeler, but much more pervasively expressed in the machine landscapes themselves that these artists depicted. These may appear to be entirely anti-aesthetic, but that only shows our post-postromantic recommitment to the "natural" as an aesthetic category in everything from parks to cosmetics, clothing to cuisine, gas station architecture to cleaning products. "Suburbanization," for example, or "regentrification" is driven by economics and politics (and race, and gender), perhaps, but of course both are saturated with aesthetics: the suburban subdivision, house, and rectangular lawn may strike one as banal, but they are embraced (or rejected) for aesthetic reasons; they define or articulate a space in accordance with a notion of how things should look. Within the domestic interior a thousand objects and arrangements capture an aesthetic ideal, or ideals of various sorts, even as that interior is bathed in media: music and television drama and sport and comedy. A simple history of the most commonplace American architecture from outhouse to strip mall to McMansion would, of course, implicate a complete cultural and political history.

Taxonomies and Periodizations

The idea that economic periods are also art historical periods is obviously not new, and any Marxist would of course say as much. But in relation to Marxism we ought at least to get worried about the base-superstructure model. I seriously assert that the aesthetics drives the economy as much as the other way around. On the one hand, "late capitalism" is an art era, like "the Restoration" or "the Counter-Reformation," or "the Second Great Awakening," or "the republican revival." On the other hand, "the baroque" and "modernism" and "the Golden Age of Greece" are political and economic and religious eras. Collapsing these distinctions enriches them all, but perhaps enriches them to the point of chaos, and any decent art historian would grope after taxonomic principles of artpolitical history.

I suggest as the first move in developing a taxonomy of artpolitical systems that we take them as representing either power or resistance to power. I do this not because the concept of political aesthetics demands it, or because I see issues of power as the only real issues. I do it because political power, or political oppression, and resistance to them are *for me* the central issues of politics and political philosophy. Other purposes and other predilections will call out different ordering principles. In the case studies presented in this book, I explore two dominant and two resistance-oriented aesthetic systems: fascism and republican neoclassicism on the one side, and Black Nationalism and punk on the other.

Now, the opposition between art that serves power and art that resists power is complex, and probably any artpolitical orientation is liberating for some, threatening to others. So while I sometimes present this distinction from my place in the sky as clear or exclusive, I am aware that it is tremendously complex on the ground. The revolutionary aesthetics of one generation may be the establishment tropes of the next, though one would expect certain sorts of transformations. Typically, civil rights or peace movements reproduce gender oppression. Nevertheless, there are whole "subaltern" aesthetic systems, minor languages and vernacular poetries, ethnomusicological histories of minorities, tribes, peoples who have faced oppression over a long period of time. From an artpolitical point of view many of these traditions are exemplary: they make aesthetics a weapon of resistance or a negotiation with power or both. The histories of women's work such as the fabric arts and cookery are still being written. The African American arts emerge from and transform a context of slavery and apartheid; think of Bob Marley's reggae or Immortal Technique's hip hop. These liberation movements can also harbor repressions of other subgroups; each person's relations to the power structures is multifarious.

As I have argued, dominant artpolitical systems are always threatened with death, in virtue of their own resistance to temporality; and every dominant political system seeks permanence, and seeks to achieve and express permanence through the arts. The systems try to ensconce themselves, settle in for the long haul, which is why they tend to like marble and steel. Resistant artpolitical systems or anti-systems, however, are volatile; they contain a principle of movement, an essence of life. Dominant and subcultural artpolitical systems hence enter into a dialogue. The dominant system uses the subcultural system to retain a semblance of life, while the minor systems depend on their own co-optation to motivate new changes. One example of this that I have explored is the music of Bob Marley. Starting as patois expressions of ghetto resistance from the third world, his songs are taken up by Babylon, and now "One Love" is the jingle of the Jamaican tourist bureau. Of course, what folks are listening to in Kingston now has been transformed ten times since Marley's death, and if you wanted to make your next record sound fresh or alive, you'd do well to head to Jamaica on aesthetic safari. Your appropriation of the style (or, let's say, Gwen Stefani's appropriation of the style) is part of what will demand the next wave of strange and offensive sound from the Kingston studios.

At any rate, power/resistance is just one of many possible provisional taxonomies of artpolitical systems in political aesthetics. The taxonomies that will be of particular interest will as it were work at the intersection of art historical and political chronology, seeking links between political and aesthetic styles. On the one hand, it would be a nice idea to keep the question open as to whether the name of a period or movement originates in the arts or politics of the era. I think of Foucault's use of the term "classical era" for, let us say, 1760–1800, in French politics, legal theory, medicine, painting, and so on. On the other hand, the familiar periodizations in either discipline must be up for grabs, and there is, for example, no properly Nazi period of art, even if there is an elaborate Nazi visual style. Or perhaps abstract expressionism and minimalism are aesthetically opposite practices to a certain extent, but with similar political locations and preoccupations; the artistic style varies independently of the politics. Perhaps they both emerge from an art school–trained New York avant-garde, for example, so that even as they battle each other aesthetically, they correspond politically in some sense, or occupy a similar niche that is outside the mainstream political transactions of their culture. You could sketch your own principles of artpolitical taxonomy— individualist/collectivist—or fundamentally in terms of conditions of produc- tion: technologies and economies, perhaps. Or Western/non-Western, Chinese/ not-Chinese, classical/anticlassical, democratic/totalitarian, or whatever you require for the project at hand. Of course we could try tripartite or more elaborate structures rather than dualisms as well, and of course we should.

The point would be to write the history of politics as though it were, or to the extent that it is, an art history. Then we would develop stylistic cri- teria, chronological narratives, and specific methodologies about which we might debate. This, it is to be hoped, would have some refreshing ramifica- tions. We might, for example, throw into question from this point of view the traditional taxonomies of both political science and art history. Once we try to construe political systems aesthetically, we might doubt, question, or ignore traditional ideological distinctions (communism/democracy/fascism/ anarchism), and art historical stylistic distinctions (classical/baroque/rococo/ neoclassical). Or we might reemphasize such categories and display some of their hidden content, enrich our conception of these categories by looking at their implications from the other perspective. Interestingly, for example, the architecture of mid-twentieth-century state urban planning looks remark- ably similar under Marxist and capitalist regimes. This points to hidden similarities in the ideologies that might explain the similarity of concrete outcomes (the theories emerged simultaneously in the eighteenth century, represented in Smith and Rousseau, and both use economics and its means- end rationality as a philosophy of action and history). A "stylistic" history of politics would comport only roughly with the traditional methods of sorting political systems and ideologies.

The language of art history is already riddled with political terms and turns of phrase—revolutions, movements, avant-gardes, and so on—not to speak of the language of power, mastery: the idea of transforming a world, as the transformed world emerges from the giant head of Michelangelo or Beethoven. One reason for this may be the origins of the discipline of modern art history in Hegel's philosophy of history. It is, for Hegel, politics that most clearly drives history, or is most clearly the rational working-out of God's will in time; the arts are added as more than an afterthought, but always in correlation with political eras, events, and figures. For Hegel, of course, all the aspects of history must be coordinated; a Hegelian philosophy of history entails the legitimacy of political aesthetics. Marx tells a story in which productive economy is the ground of taxonomy and the narrative structure. But we might point out that the ways we tell histories are always up for grabs, and the models for and engines of history must be the subject of controversy as well as the events we narrate. One never knows when a sudden juxtaposition of methods or disciplines will produce a flash of light.

For example, in *Political Style: The Artistry of Power,* Robert Hariman uses a cross-period taxonomy, sorting political styles into "realist," "courtly," "republican," and "bureaucratic." He defines political style itself as "a coherent repertoire of rhetorical conventions depending on aesthetic reactions for political effect." I think this definition is far too narrow, in that its foundation is rhetoric, and the subject matter seems to be the art of persuasion or manipulation through aesthetic effects. But Hariman's treatments of examples are far richer than this restriction of the subject would indicate. For example, in his exemplary discussion of the absurd court of Haile Selassie, he discusses everything from clothing and architectural styles to the ways the function of courtiers are defined and resisted. At any rate, here is how he sets out the essence of each of his four forms:

> The realist style [which Hariman associates with the political philosophy of Machiavelli] radically separates power and textuality, constructing the political realm as a state of nature and the political actor as someone either rationally calculating vectors of interest and power or foolishly believing in such verbal illusions as laws or ethical ideals.... The courtly style is centered on the body of the sovereign, displaces speech with gesture, and culminates in immobility. This style has little purchase institutionally in modern societies but seems to be particularly resurgent in mass media representations of political events. The republican style develops a model of oratorical virtuosity for public performance in a parliamentary culture. This model includes an appreciation of verbal technique, a norm of consensus, the embodiment of civic virtue, and a doctrine of civility that exemplifies the difficulties

facing contemporary liberalism. The bureaucratic style organizes the communicative conventions that together constitute office culture, including jurisdictional definition, hierarchical structure, the ethos of the official, and the priority of writing. As this style operates, it places everyone in a symbolic drama of assimilation that is the dominant form of identity in the late modern world. (Hariman, p. 4)

I might hang a few remarks on this amazingly rich map. First of all, it immediately exceeds the ways we'd usually think about "rhetoric" or even "aesthetic effect." The style emerges from and encompasses the basic ethical values deployed in each type of system, and the sorts of subjects it creates; its narration of history and identity; its centralization or displacement of text, costume, organizational shape, and so on. Second, Hariman's discussion, nuanced as it is, makes a fundamental synchronic move at its outset: it deemphasizes historical developments, finding commonalities of styles across eras. In this it both recapitulates and simplifies art historical methodology, wherein "the classical" or the "mannerist" or "the Gothic" keep reappearing but in profoundly altered shapes explicable in terms of specific historical and stylistic developments. I would say Hariman's isolation of each style is a useful first move, but that ultimately the different expressions of "republicanism," say, have to be distinguished and historicized as much as they must be displayed in their commonality. But Hariman's technique does not preclude that at all.

My own taxonomy, which begins by sorting artpolitical expressions into those that serve or constitute power and those that resist it, arises from both a political and an aesthetic agenda. And if power and resistance to power sound like fundamentally political categories, my argument is that they are also fundamentally aesthetic. I want to understand and condemn the artpolitical systems of power and to understand and celebrate the artpolitical expressions of resistance. I am an anarchist, and this shows in the basic treatment of cases. I do also think that this sorts the terrain in an interesting way and in a way responsible to the data; the artpolitical systems of power have certain features in common (gigantism, for example) and that so too do those in resistance (roughness, unfinishedness). The matter is complex and difficult, as becomes obvious as soon as one starts dealing with cases across eras and cultures. But it feels to me like a bit of leverage, and it might contribute in the long run to my anarchist political argument.

However, I want to insist on a distinction between political aesthetics as an area of inquiry and my particular program within that area. There could easily be programs that, for example, take the opposition from which I begin and merely reverse its norms, so that the art of power is preferred to the art of resistance. I daresay this is the usual case; it is the traditional orientation of the discipline of art history, for example. One might think here of the equation of civilization with the state, or the association of many of the greatest monuments of art, from the Great Wall and the Pyramids to the paintings of Michelangelo or Velázquez, to the symphonies of Haydn, with political power. Or as I say, the taxonomy could be entirely different. What is required is not to adopt a particular position but simply to take the aesthetic aspects of politics fully seriously, to treat them as intrinsic, to hold that no explanations in the realm of politics are complete without treating of these aspects and showing them to be connected to or rather inherent within all the other aspects of the political situation. In such inquiries the meanings of terms such as "aesthetics" and "politics" should, of course, be up for grabs as well.

Art and Power

Let me briefly try to justify the power/resistance taxonomy. To an astonishing degree, the material remains of cultures—and hence how we understand these cultures—are bound up with political power. The aesthetic products of the nondominant groups have for the most part been expunged. But of course every ancient Chinese peasant laid out her hovel in some particular way, and no doubt ornamented her place and herself to whatever degree or in whatever fashion she could; this appears to be a fundamental human impulse, visible in every suburban home and every shantytown. But what survives are "monuments": art history is tilted toward gigantism. The arts are a constant site of political contestation, and the victors shape the environment until they get whomped by history in their turn. Often they try to create indestructible, eternal objects. These can of course only be the result of political/economic power on a gigantic scale that enables a regime to pour labor and materials into such projects, as well as into patronage systems and other ways to shape the distribution of the sensible. This is true of the Egyptians, true of the Nazis, true in Saddam's Iraq or imperial France.

The narrative of the arts of Europe from, say, 400 to 1400 is the narrative of the patronage of the Catholic Church and of the expressions of its ideologies, even if these expressions are remarkably varied and sometimes subversive. One should expect, I think, a whole raft of subaltern art histories as well: blasphemous and heretical paintings, the immolation of altarpieces, sudden outbreaks of paganism, or local internal revolts of the church. Certainly the events themselves are part of the narrative of the church's own history, but the material traces are obscured. We should never forget how the history of political power shapes and falsifies art history by what it preserves and what it destroys. It is all too easy for the discipline of art history to become a mere trace and servant of political power. Writing the history of atheism or anarchism, for example, is not possible because of what happens to atheists and anarchists, to the point where one might doubt that there were any European atheists in the Middle Ages. I suggest that you already know that such a position would be absurd. If you don't think the Catholic Church would generate a raised eyebrow or an exasperated rolling of the eyes from the cynical at any moment of its history, you're not really familiar with our species.

This is as true or more true with regard to literary remains, and the ancient texts that we preserve, we must believe, are the texts authorized or employed by political power: Homer in Athens, the Hebrew Bible, the texts associated with Confucius, the Code of Hammurabi, and so on. The farther back we go, in many ways, the more oppressive, the more the only traces that remain are the traces of the institutions that built and preserved the objects and texts. The preservation of texts and objects is also subject to accident, and which ancient texts or buildings survive has to do with fire and earthquake, as well as with war and the decisions of rulers. It has to do with waves of iconoclasm and idolatry, which are then superseded by further waves. But in any case, one of the primary factors in a work's survival and its promotion to classic status is the political context in which it was made and the succession of political contexts in which it is preserved and interpreted.

This entails that art history is political history. What remains to us is to a stunning extent the art of empire, of nation, of—in short—the state. The arts of resistance are, by comparison, fragile and ephemeral, dangerous to retain, display, preserve. In simple terms, they emerge from much smaller budgets. They have what we may think of as a human scale in comparison to the superhuman monumentality of state and church and corporation, designed to exalt powerful persons and institutions, to help them transcend time. Think of the difficulty of studying the arts of the Huns or Visigoths, as opposed to those of imperial Rome. Well, barbarians have no arts: a ridiculous, impossible conclusion. The distribution of the sensible is no less pronounced or profound among nomads than in the capitals of empires, only quite intentionally it is erased when they are. The arts of the nomad are by definition ephemeral. Finding anything out about them is going to be next to impossible—or speculative, at any rate—whereas any tourist can deal with millennia of monuments in Rome.

Of course, power itself is complex and equivocal, and if one looks seriously at the variety of visual expressions of Catholic theology, one is struck by the variety among different eras, regions, or even individual artists in the same era and location. One is struck, too, not only by the stultifying orthodoxy, enforced if necessary by burning at the stake, but also by the theological tensions and confusions, contradictions and equivocations. That is, neither power nor resistance to power is a simple thing, and it is often at the sites of its contradictions that resistance emerges or from which it whispers. Imperial architecture has its interstices: Rome is a set of monuments but also a sprawling chaos of dwellings and alleys, a system of catacombs. Indeed the more gigantic the aesthetic ambition, the more gaps are created for concealment and resistance, the more meaningful the graffiti and the harder it is to catch the perpetrators.

Pitting graffiti against empire, or against commercial capitalism, is a pretty useless exercise in some ways, not likely to result in the fall, which requires ravening hordes of pissed-off barbarians rather than the pretty impotent internal critique of teenagers. But graffiti can also be a powerful sign: this apparent unanimity is not universal; we still have not been thoroughly processed or controlled, and we maintain an aesthetic sensibility that allows us still to shape our environment to some extent; we have not lost control completely of our own lives and world. The arts of resistance are pretty modest by the standards of the empire, until such moment as the resistance succeeds and begins its march into world history, remaking the built environment and starting to tear down or reinterpret and adapt the monuments of the former regime, replacing them with its own.

Classical and Baroque

To conceive the first division in artpolitical taxonomies in terms of power seems to privilege the political over the aesthetic categories. But I might quickly as an example assay another solution: I suppose I grew up on Wölfflin, and I watch Western art history traverse the classical/baroque dyad repeatedly in varied forms. I am using these terms in a general or extended sense, so that we trace in artpolitical history a profuse iconography, a bewildering array of apparently arbitrary signs or delight in elaboration; then a response as to surfeit, a stripping away to essentials, a mass and dignity, a rational systematic simplification and clear coordination of elements; then repetition, boredom, and again the gradual elaboration, the resort to delight in surface or even whimsy, the sense of luxury or at least emphasis on pleasure, the individual expression of idiosyncrasy; then again an ascetic backlash of self-control. Each iteration of this process would be somewhat different from the one before, informed by the previous versions, emerging in a somewhat different artpolitical moment for somewhat different artpolitical reasons. Hence archaic Greek/classical Greek/Hellenistic; Gothic/Renaissance/baroque/rococo/neoclassical; expressionist/minimalist/eclectic; and so on.

Classical and baroque are visual styles, but they are also pervasive cultural moods; they are epistemologies of reason or faith, ethics of austerity or hedonism, economies of luxury or restraint of various kinds. They also provide vocabularies in which political regimes express themselves or to which they are in some sense identical at particular locations: architectures of capital cities, the forms of patriotic festivals on the one hand or on the other hand of protests or revolutionary movements. To mention one example, consider the work of Boucher in its depiction of luxury goods and persons as a real economic situation or budget, as a court-sponsored political statement, in relation to slavery or to monarchy. The French court in the eighteenth century had luxury but no dignity, and it produced signs of that everywhere in a way guaranteed to cause a "classical" reaction and a political response that remake the vocabulary of images and architectures. The critique and transition are moral, epistemological, economic, religious, encapsulating in material forms the entire situation of a culture. When Winckelmann exalts the classical—beyond all reason, I would say—he's working a political as well as an aesthetic angle, or perhaps actually helping define the factions who enter into the power struggles that eventuate in revolution. And people immediately understood Winckelmann's exaltation of the antique as a political discourse. That accounts for its pervasion throughout European intellectual culture. It was a critique of modernity, and not just for its bad statues, but for its bad statutes. Winckelmann did not cause the French Revolution, but he captured a moment in its momentum: he embodied that moment in an aesthetic.

In the West, the heritage of the classical is an inexhaustible artpolitical theme, one that I engage over and over in this book. To embrace it, reject it, revive it, interpret it: these are aesthetic actions that are central to Western political history, as they are to Western art history. Why this should be is a question I don't feel I can adequately address; I'm not sure I think it can be adequately addressed. It may be the almost arbitrary promotion of certain signs as a way to organize one's thinking and making, as in the godhead of Jesus; it could as easily have been Fred who founded a major religion lasting thousands of years. Perhaps we could have used the austerity of the Pyramids and Egyptian aesthetics generally or something else in a similar way, but we didn't. The classical as a historical theme certainly correlates with the identification of Western thought in a variety of disciplines—philosophy, science, literature—with origins in the Greek world. Every return to the classical is a return in imagination to the foundation, to the origin—the ethical, epistemological, political, and artistic basis: the Elements, in the Euclidean sense. One thing about the classical: it is from the start an extremely self-conscious system that can be defined in part mathematically, which immediately draws to itself a whole interpretive discourse that is not present in various other candidates for dominant Western aesthetic systems.

At any rate, the question of what the classical is and who has a claim to it persists even through the Middle Ages, in the form, for example, of the relation of the classical to paganism. The aesthetic shifts are theological, as is the rejection and the return of classical learning. The classical is a (or even the) defining trope of Western political and artistic history. This weight is almost unbearable or absurd, and of course entails that the classical, even understood in terms of fundamental proportion and rationality, has been put to multifarious and contradictory uses.

Modern political science owes its origin to one such flourishing of the classical, in Machiavelli and Renaissance humanism. Machiavelli's authorship, indeed, is perched at a nice angle: it reveres and pushes beyond classical political discourse into a hardnosed political materialism, giving Democritus and Lucretius the political expositors they never seem to have enjoyed. No doubt this was already a mood by the time Machiavelli wrote; one sees it in the painting and the governmental systems—the revival, of course, of republicanism, or republicanism of a certain variety—of that moment as well. One transformation of this variety of classicism is the hardnosed commonsense realism so notable in even the most fantastic or fabulous thinkers from the British Isles (Berkeley, for example), which eventuates in the atmosphere of Hobbesian reactionary materialism. The "scientific" part of political science emerges with the conception of man as a rational contractor or an economic agent. His actions are explicable because his motivation is simple, always the same: material self-interest in Smith, Marx (whereas in Machiavelli, as in Nietzsche, the driver was power). Political economy, one might say, is a commercial venture. At any rate, it supposes that there are springs of and descriptions of human action by which it can be rendered as rational and predictable.

The continual cyclical or spiral revival, the widening gyre of the classical, is bound up with a constellation of fundamental artpolitical ideas: reason and faith; republicanism/empire/tyranny; austere realism and fantastic elaboration; humanism as against theocentrism; humanism and, later, empirical science as against scholasticism; progressivism or a sense of time as a narrative structure as against a static or circular time. These ideas sound pretty abstract, but you can do the archeology: this made cities and roads and factories; cathedrals and farmsteads; Congresses and cornfields; skyscrapers and explosions. Of course, the aesthetic that is connected with all of these developments is neither simply the cause of nor simply an effect of the material situation in all its myriad bristling particularities—economic, political, religious, technological, epistemological, military—but they mutually, simultaneously cause each other. The aesthetic dimension is a dimension of interpretation of the surrounding situation, but it is also the shape of that situation, or a global description at the level of utmost generality and of the most concrete physical stuff.

Idolatry and Iconoclasm

I think the extent to which the Reformation and the Counter-Reformation, and for that matter Catholicism itself, are to be understood as essentially aesthetic movements is far underappreciated, even if accounts of these events almost always resort to works of art and acts of iconoclasm as emblems. They are treated as signs of the underlying doctrinal—that is, linguistic—differences. People study the artistic expressions for the light they shed on events, or the events for the light they shed on the art, but what we need to do is begin with the hypothesis that the political, aesthetic, and religious expressions are not, in fact, distinguishable in any given embodiment. Luther and his cohorts, of course, were repelled by the corruption, hypocrisy, and decadence of the Catholic Church; Luther's trip to Rome in 1511 has often been specified as the origin of his disaffection: for the rest of his life he blisteringly ridiculed the pointless luxury and the decadent cosmetic arts of the "Whore of Babylon."

The largest lines in the church budgets were for the arts: from the dome of St. Peter's to the Sistine Chapel, from the mega-cathedral in every major European city and its contents to the Vatican Treasury. Indeed one cannot but be struck, even at this late date, by the extreme aesthetic systems on which Catholicism rests: its amazing profusion of imagery, of Christ, Mary, the saints and patrons of the church; the astonishing outfits of its pontiffs and cardinals; the Spanish and Mexican Churrigueresque. It is a familiar point that the Catholic Church communicated with medieval Europe by imagery, but that is a bit impoverished: it communicated by creating a continual multimedia aesthetic extravaganza, a completely enveloping aesthetic environment in which people were continuously basted.

In your basic art history survey, one is taught that the imagery used by the Church was a means of conveying doctrine to the illiterate. This may be true, but leaving it there is extremely tendentious; it separates the religious expressions into the textual dogmas and a series of visual emblems, analogues, or representations of those dogmas. This begs the question in favor of what we might call a textualist approach to religion and to politics: the text is the underlying reality that the picture represents. This is rather an odd structure, actually, as pictures are initially conceived as imitations not of texts but of objects. And as literacy has increased, the use of imagery in Catholicism has persisted. But it is also a traditional structure, as in depictions of the Homeric heroes. At any rate, to throw the images into a historical account in the role of a kind of manipulative or propagandistic superstructure on the real teachings—always captured in text, always reconstructed in historiography as text—simply cannot be an adequate interpretation. The use of images by priests, by cardinals and popes, by saints and kings is absolutely central, and the texts are as often interpretations of the images as vice versa.

Now, by contrast, the role of scripture in Protestantism is central. There is a quite conscious turning away from images to text that is demonstrable in the central Protestant teachings, and Luther's translation of scripture is a pivotal moment in his ministry. (And so is the Lutheran hymnal, which gives collective articulation to a shared religious and aesthetic emphasis.) The role of text in Judaism and in Islam to some extent motivates the aniconic emphases of at least portions of those religions, and the story of the wars between and the alliances of text and image is the story of culture. It would be worthwhile to throw music in here as well, to explore the infinitely rich connections and oppositions between image, text, and melody.

When Luther talked about the corruption of the church, or called the pope "Anti-Christ," he was delivering, centrally, an aesthetic critique, and the most immediate distinction between a Catholic and a Protestant church is that the Protestant church is aesthetically minimalist, unpretentious, and hence, among other things, more democratic. The first impulse is to strip the church of its ornament. This critique is at once aesthetic, economic, political, and spiritual. The Reformation was accompanied by a popular wave of iconoclasm—an aesthetic/political/religious/economic tide of revulsion directed at paintings and sculptures—and I daresay as the Reformers burned the altarpieces, they did not distinguish between their act of art criticism and their act of religious expression. They immolated at once the hierarchy, the wealth, the pantheon of saints, and the visual style.

We might think of the result in, for example, the design cultures of radical Protestant sects, such as Shaker furniture and architecture, but also Shaker leadership structures and economy. If you want a perfect contrast, oppose an eighteenth-century Quaker meetinghouse to a Gothic cathedral. The Reformation in the widest sense of the term, or as I am generalizing it, was a "neoclassical" movement, and indeed explicitly urged a return to the theology of Augustine and Paul: Greek in their own way with just a hint of Attila, descending with his ravening hordes on Rome. But the Reformation at its radical moments strips the ornament down well beneath even classical dignity to absolute utilitarian simplicity, complete rejection of ostentation, an a priori bonfire of the vanities that simply never admits them. It is an intensely aesthetic program or atmosphere, and Shaker communities created environments of incomparable order and beauty, sublime in their simplicity, clear in their usefulness, perfect in their craft, an apotheosis resting on humility. If the Shaker village has precursors, they are the Franciscan monastery and the plain peasant architecture of the northern European village: a political, economic, and aesthetic signifier, fully or perhaps even more intensely present in communities that became prosperous and could have tricked (perhaps "pimped" is the word I'm groping for) their places out however they liked.

Idolatry in one form or another is a fundamental aspect of political power. From the visage of the beloved leader to the flickering pomp of state as depicted on television, the image is at least as central as the text in political history. This is true in, for example, the Roman Empire, in which the hilarious promotion of the emperor to godhead consisted almost entirely of a set of images that made him analogous to Jupiter, or lent to the image of the emperor the aspects and devices associated with divinity in its multifarious forms. This, I think, would both anger and amuse your average barbarians, and the revulsion at the wealth, the insane hubris, and the political strategy might bring them down from the steppes in an avenging mob of hyper-violent art critics. Later, such barbarians might throw down a Reformation. It is often argued that the place of religion is filled in the modern world by art, an unfortunate notion on many grounds. First of all, religion proper hasn't actually faded. And second, if art is a religion, it is the religion of a tiny minority of well-heeled precious aesthetes. But the state is a pagan cult, a system of textolatries and idolatries, and the image of Lincoln or Kennedy, inflated to gigantic size and stuck into a pseudo-Roman temple, is a major tourist attraction. Children are introduced to the cult early through the noble visages adorning their textbooks and schoolrooms, on coins and bills.

One appreciates the very existence of Mount Rushmore in this regard, taking a hill holy to the Lakota and blasting it into gigantic presidential heads. For one thing, this displays the tight relation of idolatry and iconoclasm, as the act of artistic creation is itself a profound act of destruction. It is apparently a ceremonial act among the contemporary Lakota to form a human chain, so that someone can piss over the edge onto Teddy Roosevelt's nose. The Lakota have no way to rival the absurdity of a mountain/sculpture; what they have is a set of iconoclastic responses, at once political, religious, and art critical, funny and ephemeral, inappropriate and just.

At any rate, we could think of idolatry and iconoclasm as religious/political strategies or rhetorics. But it will not surprise you at this point that I think the matter runs deeper than that. The revolutionary does not destroy the images of the ruler as a political statement any more than he executes the ruler as an aesthetic statement; the iconoclastic impulse drives the revolutionary as much as does the textually expressed political agenda. As Mao said, revolution is "an act of insurrection by which one class overthrows another," but it is also a tea party: an elaborate act of art criticism. Only if the political system could be in principle disassociated from its representational content could the act of revolution be distinguished from its aesthetic correlates.

If every state is idolatrous, every revolution is iconoclastic. The French Revolution lopped the head off not only the king but also simultaneously his statues. It defaced his portraits and burned his outfits. The Russian Revolution did the same with the tsar, and to some extent with the icons of the extremely icon-heavy Russian Orthodox Church. The American Revolution involved dancing around "liberty trees," burning colonial officials in effigy. Unsuccessful revolutions can break idols and leave it at that, but successful revolutions must construct a new idolatrous cult. Were it perfectly clear that the people running the new state were actually people instead of noble colossi, their power could not be justified. That is, I assert that the state in its essence is a cult of images. This is as true of modern democracies as of ancient empires, with one major development. Texts, especially constitutions and laws, fill some of the functions typically associated with images in political history, and the rule of little gods is replaced to some extent by the rule of little marks on pieces of paper.

Text, Power, and Material Culture

With this development, however, text takes on various features of pictoricity. The Constitution of the United States is a textual structure or "type" that appears in many places simultaneously, but it is also an image, a calligraphic "We the People." Early versions of it are venerated, placed in vitrines and preserved assiduously, very much as though they were unique illuminations. In the veneration of a written constitution, the document is poised between an iconic and a linguistic sign system. In such an atmosphere, various traditions of iconoclasm are generalized to textual items. Burning copies of documents does not have the same power as burning a leader in effigy, or scratching out the eyes of his portrait, or even burning a flag, but it resonates nevertheless. A famous case is William Lloyd Garrison, who argued that the Constitution recognized slavery, called it "a pact with the devil," and traveled about publicly burning it. Such text/images pull the text toward particularity or emphasize its particular inscriptions as physical objects that can actually be destroyed. In some ways, indeed, we might think of copies of the Constitution as pictures of the original document. The type/token distinction with regard to texts is somewhat like the relation of picture to object (I am not saying they are the same relation). Then to burn a copy of the Constitution would be like burning the Constitution "itself" in effigy. One thing that makes a picture a picture of a particular thing is various dimensions of isomorphism: the shapes of depicted and depiction are parallel or similar.[1] This is precisely the case with texts and in part accounts for two inscriptions being inscriptions of the same text: they are isomorphic in some dimension, even if letter forms, for example, can vary widely. If there were ever an American revolution so thorough as to attack our form of government fundamentally, or start a new history, it would begin by immolating not only the memorials in Washington, D.C., but also the contents of the National Archives, as Shays's Rebellion and many others began by burning mortgages, deeds, and other legal documents. That might or might not literally be iconoclasm; but our gods are partly textual, and their images are particular inscriptions.

Indeed, the cult of text itself emerges in part from the Reformation, which lionized scripture and rejected imagery (to some extent). If the Reformation gives you the Shakers on one end, it also eventuates in the educational systems that generated the Enlightenment, that yields a Locke or Voltaire, the secularism of a Jefferson, or even Marx's materialism. It is ironic, then, that in this process text becomes picturized, though of course this is a process that can be found throughout religious and political art, as in INRI and so on, and when you begin really to examine the pervasiveness of text in what are usually conceived to be religious images, you note that the two modes frequently or perhaps typically appear in concert or are not firmly distinguished. The account of the icon as a text for the illiterate is complemented by the account of text as a picture for the literate. But of course text is picturized in a thousand ways because it has to be converted into concrete inscription or utterance (in the case of utterance, the analogy would be to music rather than icon). Religious imagery often incorporates words, but calligraphy, typography, and graffiti, among other arts, involve developing elaborate pictures of abstract texts. Of course in various linguistic systems, such as hieroglyphs or Chinese characters, the distinction between word and image breaks down altogether. And while the alphabetic languages do deploy the distinction and even make it a fundamental ontological and epistemological tenet, concrete inscriptions

---

1. This is of course a controversial assertion, but it seems right to me. It has been beautifully defended in Hyman.

in these languages are continually working to throw it into question, as we have seen in the case of graffiti.

As I have said, I regard the moment as ripe to refocus the discussion of political systems and ideologies from texts to other modes of formulation. But it is also necessary to resituate texts as aesthetic objects, and thus connect them more carefully to the other dimensions of political expression and embodiment.

Texts are, we may say at a first stab, immaterial objects, ideal objects, abstract objects. Garrison burned the U.S. Constitution over and over, which would have been impossible if the Constitution were, on the one hand, a material thing, or if, on the other hand, it were a purely imaginary or fictional thing. Of course the Constitution could not have been burned at all if it were merely an abstract object. And of course if it were a material object made of ink and paper, he couldn't have burned it now and then, here and there; once it was consumed, it would have ceased to exist. Burning the Constitution is not exactly like, for example, burning someone in effigy, an imaginary act of violence performed on a surrogate. The Constitution is present in its particular inscriptions in the way the human person cannot be in effigies or representations. The inscription instantiates the actual structure of which the Constitution consists, in its entirety. Each accurate inscription of it is equally it, and is equally not it, in a way no mere visual representation of its object is or is not its object. The texts of a people, we might say, are its immaterial culture.

It would be possible to be skeptical about the existence of texts entirely, or to go through various nominalistic conniptions in the attempt to elucidate the type/token–structure/inscription relationship. It is also possible to give various political readings of the ontology of text in the West, and of the privileging of abstract objects in relation to various oppressions and liberations. Who has access to text is a political matter; prohibitions on teaching slaves to read were also attempts to keep slaves from the realm of the human, as the pro-slavery politician understood humanity: engagement of mind with a universe of abstractions. The Catholic Church practiced and enforced a monopoly of text, embodied in the monk-scribe, which signaled an exclusive access to the spiritual—that is, more-than-material—realm. Indeed the use of dead languages in Catholicism and Judaism, for example, turns texts into fundamentally formal/aesthetic objects or music: it leaves us with the sound itself as the only object of spiritual experience, playing in the gap between the sensuous and the spiritual. Luther's Reformation was an unleashing of vernacular text made possible in part by printing. The rise of democracy was a rise of the accessibility of text, and Jefferson and many others associated citizenship, dignity, with literacy; steeping oneself in text coincided with a kind of ontological apotheosis that was also a political ascension.

To take the thing from the other angle—to accept for the moment an ontology of abstract structures and their concrete instances, or at least to acknowledge this as the practical ontology of our cultures—texts do institute material alterations in the world, and can have no effect if they do not. That is, each utterance of a text is a physical event, each inscription a physical object. Even the most abstracted textualist approach to political systems needs the intervention of the abstract in the material world to derive any actual political effects. This truth has myriad artpolitical dimensions. For example, the art of political oratory is partly an art of composition, of writing, but it is also a science of the aural and gesticulatory expression, manifested only on particular occasions: a performance art, a musical art in which speech is score, voice and body instruments. And the history of politics must be connected with the history of inscriptions, from incised monuments to broadsides, calligraphy to typography to Web design, newspaper distribution systems and cartloads of "Common Sense" rattling down roads around the colonies, burning books and smashing presses, prior restraint and pirate radio, intellectual property and cut-and-paste. One fascinating textual intervention in the physical world that I have explored is graffiti. But I also want to focus at least briefly on the history of typography.

It is a familiar point that typography has influenced and been influenced by the art historical moments at which it appears. There is neoclassical typography, based quite literally on Roman inscriptions and embodied in "roman" alphabets. There is romantic typography, giving print various emotional valences through distortion, or extreme design, one of many answers to classicism. There is dada typography, surrealist typography, modernist typography, postmodern typography. All of this has real behavioral effects, in commerce, in politics, in science or philosophy. And it is not just a matter of groping toward a form for antecedent thought or purpose; it is a matter of embodying thought and purpose, or introducing tensions and material interventions. There are typographies of the state: Carolingian, Internal Revenue Service, Government Printing Office, Little Red Book typographies. There are nationalist typographies.

For example, we might consider the centuries-long struggle between roman and blackletter ("gothic") scripts. As the humanists were reviving roman alphabets, Gutenberg and Luther were setting in blackletter. Here the idea of the "roman" was extremely highly charged and ambiguous, both an attack on the church for its mysticism and an assertion of the centralized power associated forever in the West with "Rome." Roman was a secularized script but also a reconstrual of secular power that centered it in the papacy. Skipping with historical irresponsibility into the nineteenth century, blackletter became a symbol of German uniqueness, a mode of presenting and embodying the German Volk in a written presentation. Otto von Bismarck said, "I do not read German books set in Latin letters" (quoted in Bain and Shaw, p. 14). Indeed it is still often asserted that blackletter is particularly appropriate to the German language, and roman for Romance languages, even as the victory of roman has been more or less complete. By the nineteenth century the blackletter-roman opposition took on a tremendous weight of meaning, political and otherwise: faith versus reason; Gothic versus classical; authority versus liberty (as articulated in classical liberalism); ornament versus transparency to meaning; old versus new; national versus universal; beauty versus truth; fantasy versus science, and so on. It is worth saying that this weight was laid on texts, but that of course any text could in principle be set in either style of type; that is, the form of the text carried an almost incredible semantic weight. The conception of typography as ideally simply transparent to an antecedent meaning existing in an abstract textual structure is itself, we might say, a roman conception, partly a matter of the typography embodying the text, as well as a factor in determining the type in which the text was set.

The Nazis insisted on blackletter typography for these reasons, then in 1941 discovered, for reasons that remain profoundly mysterious, that it was a "Jewish" script and banned it. (Possibly it has something to do with the name of one of the blackletter typestyles, Schwabacher, which sounds sort of Jewish, I guess. Possibly it also had to do with a reconception of Hitler's empire as a comprehensive cosmopolitan authority rather than [merely] a "Greater Germany.") But then blackletter was also revived in England under the auspices of "pro-Gothic" romantics such as Ruskin and Morris, as an aid to get out of or around modernity. It has been revived by neo-Nazi groups. It has also been revived as a beautiful display face for tattooing, in which the decorative aspects of lettering are appropriately emphasized. Indeed the body as a literal zone of inscription and as a literal support of visual art is an elaborate site of the intersection of text and materiality, a real refutation of the dualism between the abstract and concrete, mind and body.

Ben Franklin was a self-consciously classical printer, and though the Declaration of Independence and the Constitution were first hand-inscribed, when John Dunlap set them in type as broadsides, he did so in classical roman letters of chaste dignity. These broadsides have mutated into something like works of visual art, or at least particular artifacts whose value is not only in what they say but also in the visible embodiment of what they say. They are displayed in the way masterpieces of painting are displayed. The roman capitals Dunlap used were literally derived from monumental architectural inscriptions (Trajan), and it is often said that their basic forms derive from the column: the analogies to Jefferson's architecture, for example, are not speculative or merely metaphorical but based on real visual and historical connections. And the texts and the architecture each guided and intensified the interpretation of, the experience of, the other. Furthermore, the poetry of the Declaration was a model of the classical as understood in that period. Very few American printers of the revolution and early republic were setting in blackletter, but in any case a blackletter set of the Constitution would be incoherent, or pointedly ironic.

Almost every attempt to standardize scripts has been accomplished under the auspices of political authority, from Alexander to the Roman emperors, Charlemagne to the French monarchy, Stalin and Hitler. This in turn reflects the centrality of text in its physical embodiments to the very possibility of systematic political power: the function of text in record-keeping, taxation, criminal justice, maintaining the loyalty or at least capitulation of the populace. Stanley Morison, the great scholar of script and the designer of Times New Roman, connected the whole history of writing to political power, a basically plausible hypothesis. We should also, however, mark its uses in resistance, as shown even in documents such as the Declaration of Independence. But also in whole alphabets of resistance, scribbly alphabets of anarchism, improvised typefaces on strange websites, practices of logoclasm directed at state documents.

CHAPTER 7

Political Power and Transcendental Geometry

Republican Classicism in Early America

It is rather a remarkable fact that of the first three American presidents, two were distinguished architects, and Jefferson the most influential architect in our history, at any rate until the twentieth century. And if the Declaration of Independence and Constitution are our founding documents, they are built by analogy to our founding buildings and vice versa: the structures of American republicanism. The messages embodied in the documents and in the buildings are, however, intensely equivocal as between state power and individual freedom; American exceptionalism and provincial anxiety; starting anew and reinstating tradition; pride and humility; slavery and democracy.

Of the founders of the American republic, none had a clearer classical art-political program than James Wilson. Addressing the Pennsylvania ratifying convention in 1787, he said:

> It is...a fundamental principle of society that the welfare of the whole ought to be pursued and not of a part, and the measures necessary to the good of the community, must consequently be binding upon the individuals that compose it.... [W]hen we take an extensive and accurate view of the streams of power that appear through this great and comprehensive plan [the proposed Constitution], when we contemplate the variety of their directions, the force and dignity of their

currents, when we behold them intersecting, embracing, and surrounding the vast possessions and interests of the Continent, and when we see them distributing on all hands beauty, energy, and riches, still, however numerous and wide their courses, however diversified and remote the blessings they diffuse, we shall be able to trace them all to one great and noble source, THE PEOPLE. (Bailyn, 1:797, 802)

This coordination of elements as a route to comprehensive conception—clarity of organization in the sense of comprehensibility of each part in terms of a whole, and that as a conception of beauty—is the heart of the classical, in different ways, in ancient Greek philosophy, in Italian Renaissance painting, and in the dignified and unified neoclassical American architecture of the late eighteenth and early nineteenth centuries, among many other outbreaks throughout intellectual, aesthetic, and political history. The whole emerges from the parts or "supervenes" on them, but also transcends them; the center of the classical is the imposition of rational form on matter (for Wilson and the rest of the founders, the people), a perfect coordination of integral elements. Wilson's "force and dignity" crystallize a neoclassical artpolitical ideal.

One thing to notice as well is that the classical political order Wilson describes is capable of indefinite expansion, that it will in Wilson's vision bestride the continent. So pure is the classical ideal that it is apparently indifferent as to size (though I have already traced its outer limits in Speer's architecture), and parallel lines behave as Euclid stipulates no matter how far apart they may be; indeed every line in a classical conception is a trace and a segment of infinity. The most classical classical ideal in political philosophy is no doubt the republican ideal—which is really the context of politics proper—as defined in philosophy for the first time by Aristotle, after its practice in Athenian aesthetic democracy was well established. It seeks coordination of disparate elements: classes, professions, talents, citizens, slaves, women, foreigners. But the classical aspires through rational poetics to a perfect universality, neutral simultaneous comprehension: empire. That Periclean Athens was an empire, that the Roman Republic was a prelude to the conquest and administration of approximately the known world, is comprehensible in terms of the classical aesthetic system itself, though in its expansion it lands in self-contradiction. The austerity and comprehension of the classical aesthetic system give it the flavor of a denominator of all disciplines, of all understanding; the classical ideal is system per se: autonomy of parts and their holistic comprehensibility within a graspable schematism and hierarchy of potentially comprehensive extent. The idea of rhetoric is at the heart of the classical political conception, and the art of persuasion makes use of a concept of consensus, strives toward an ideal of unanimity or universality achieved by rational means and chaste poetry.

In his classical vision of the American republic, Wilson of course draws on an artpolitical tradition. Nowhere is the classical as a political ideal better expressed than in Leonardo Bruni's panegyric to the city of Florence, which for a time he administered along republican lines:

> As this city is to be admired for its foreign policy, so it is for its internal organization and institutions. Nowhere else is there such order, such elegance, such symmetry. For just as there is a proportion among strings which, when they have been tightened, produces a harmony from the different pitches, than which there is nothing sweeter or more agreeable to the ear; so all parts of this prudent city are so tempered that the resulting whole commonwealth fits together in a way that brings pleasure to the mind and eyes of men for its harmony. There is nothing in it that is out of order, nothing that is ill-proportioned, nothing that is out of tune, nothing that is uncertain. Everything has its place, and this is not only fixed, but correct in relation to the others. Offices, magistrates, courts, and ranks are all separate. But they are separated in such a way that they are in harmony with the whole commonwealth. (Bruni, pp. 116–17)

Classical and Neoclassical

In practice the nature and heritage of the classical are contested throughout Western history since the Hellenistic period, or rather from the moment of its inception, even more politically and aesthetically than philosophically. Classicism provides the vocabulary of the Roman Republic and Empire; the indispensable backdrop of Augustine and Aquinas; Petrarch and Napoleon; medieval Islamic scholarship and the paintings of Poussin; the Nazis and Newtonian physics; the proto-romanticism of Winckelmann and Goethe; the philosophy of Spinoza and the architecture of the United States Constitution. This in part derives from political theory as a prestige economy. Pedigree is prestige: the Chinese retailed stories of the Yellow Emperor in order to justify the political system of a particular moment; mere antiquity is authority. The classical, at least in imagination, stands at the source of our tradition and has the authority of the origin. (This is not to say that antiquity is the only source of the prestige of the Greeks.)

One would be foolish to think that "the classical" means the same thing in every case of its deployment, and one is forced precisely by the amazing variety of moments, places, and ways that the classical has been revived to believe that there is something in the forms themselves of the classical that is particularly open to interpretation, appropriation, adaptation, distortion. Most aesthetic vocabularies—even the most potent—have been used in fewer and less equivocal ways; or rather, no aesthetic vocabulary in the West has ever been used in more or more equivocal ways. But we should also be alert to the zones where the classical vocabulary might indicate real connections between the meanings of apparently disparate phenomena. We might wonder in each case why the people practicing that mode turned precisely to the classical, or adapted it, rather than grabbing something else off the shelf of forms or explicitly striking out in some new direction.

It is a familiar point, which we have already explored, that public architecture, and to some extent private architecture, is an expression of political power. Indeed Vitruvius begins his treatise on architecture with a fawning dedication to Augustus, and finishes his introduction by saying:

> Since, then, I was indebted to you for such benefits that to the end of life I had no fear of poverty, I set about the composition of this work for you. For I perceived that you have built, and are now building, on a large scale. Furthermore, with respect to the future, you have such regard to public and private building, that they will correspond to the grandeur of our history, and will be a memorial to future ages. (Vitruvius, p. 5)

Vitruvius, that is, presents monumental classical architecture as a form of communication with both the contemporary world and the future. In this, of course, the Romans were successful. The communication with the future is of course also a communication with the present; it indicates that the political situation or system is permanent, and thus might as well be accepted. This in turn is part of the prestige of the origin as that which persists eternally or makes a universal claim. But in the classical this becomes fully explicit. Euclid is eternally valid, and no philosophy makes a more pointed claim to the universal than Plato's.

Vitruvius goes on to formulate the classical canons of Roman architecture, which now certainly appears within the political frame he has generated. His formulation of classical aesthetics is paradigmatic.

> Now architecture consists of Order, which in Greek is called *taxis*, and of Arrangement, which the Greeks name *diathesis*, and of Proportion and Symmetry and Decor and Distribution which in the Greeks is called *oeconomia*.
>
> Order is the balanced adjustment of the details of the work separately, and as to the whole, the arrangement of the proportion with a view to a symmetrical result....

Proportion implies a graceful semblance; the suitable display of details in their context. This is attained when the details of the work are of a height suitable to their breadth, of a breadth suitable to their length; in a word, when everything has a symmetrical correspondence.

Symmetry also is the appropriate harmony arising out of the details of the work itself; the correspondence of each given detail among the separate details to the form of the design as a whole. As in the human body, from cubit, foot, palm, inch and other small parts comes the symmetric quality of eurhythmy. (Vitruvius, pp. 26–27)

Heinrich Wölfflin, in *Principles of Art History,* gives a formulation of the classical aesthetic drawn from the Renaissance; the ideas are similar but not perhaps identical.

The central idea of the Italian Renaissance is that of perfect proportion. In the human figure as in the edifice, this epoch strove to achieve the image of perfection at rest within itself. Every form developed to self-existent being, the whole freely co-ordinated: nothing but independently living parts. . . . In the system of a classic composition, the single parts, however firmly they may be rooted in the whole, maintain a certain independence. It is not the anarchy of primitive art: the part is conditioned by the whole, and yet does not cease to have its own life. For the spectator, that presupposes an articulation, a progress from part to part, which is a very different operation from perception as a whole. (Wölfflin, pp. 9–10, 15)

Obviously there is no reason to consider a description at this level of generality more as an aesthetic than as a political outline, or for that matter than as a form with regard to whatever subject matter you might name. "The classical" is a peculiarly rich or open category in this regard. Wölfflin opposes the classical to the chaotic on one side and the completely unitary on the other, a Greek taste if ever there was one. In comparison to a Gothic church or a Hindu temple, the classical structure is unified, coherent, whole. In comparison to, for example, a pyramid or an *ensō*—the Zen calligraphic circle—the classical structure is varied and plural. Aristotle criticizes the *Republic* on the grounds that it is too unified, whereas the *Republic* criticizes democracy on the grounds that it is not unified enough.

The classical, then, can be characterized by what precedes and what supersedes it; it understands itself as a mean. It is preceded by the primitive, the Gothic, the expressionist; it is superseded by the Hellenistic, the mannerist, the baroque, the romantic, or again the expressionist or even the primitive (or in this case the primitivist: the primitive as a self-conscious aesthetic choice). The romance and tragedy of the classical is that it achieves repose, a true resting place in time, but that it is never permanent. This of course is as true of the classical republic as it is of the classical period in art history; it achieves and thematizes its own ephemerality even as it works in eternity. It knows itself to be universally valid and subject to decay. The classical is what is always threatened by decadence, just at the moment of its greatest achievement, its perfection, as in the transition from High Renaissance to Mannerist painting. In giving persons a place of aesthetic rest, it tends to produce boredom; in its overweening rationality it pushes people toward perversity or at any rate overt emotionalism; in its exalted nobility it shows people their intellectual and moral insufficiencies and hence produces resentment. Its perfect coordination of parts is an image of an organic polis, or is a totalitarian transformation in accordance with a preconceived system; it is always subject to romanticism and revolution.

When Adams, Jefferson, Wilson, and other founders conceived of the problem of government, they thought of it as a problem in classical aesthetics. The question was about an intrinsic and comprehensible relation of parts to whole, and the various conceptions or designs of this relation determined the taxonomy of going political positions at the most general level, with the emphasis placed on the whole or central government by the party of Adams or, further right, Hamilton, and the emphasis on the integrity of the parts by Madison and Jefferson. What the differences slightly concealed was that in conceiving the question as to how part and whole could be integrally coordinated, they all shared a set of classical presuppositions. Jefferson:

> The way to have good and safe government, is not to trust it all to one, but to divide it among many, distributing to every one exactly the functions he is competent to. Let the national government be entrusted with the defense of the nation, and its foreign and federal relations; the State governments with the civil rights, laws, police, and administration of what concerns the State generally; the counties with the local concerns of the counties; and each ward direct the interests within itself. It is by dividing and subdividing these republics from the great national one down through all its subordinations, until it ends in the administration of every man's farm by himself; by placing under everyone what his own eye may superintend, that all will be done for the best. (Jefferson 1, p. 32)

It might be presumed that the question of a coherent ordering of integral parts into a comprehensible whole is always the problem of government.

It was conceived that way by Plato and Aristotle, but it was not conceived that way by the Huns, or the Khanate, or the tsars, or the anarchists. It was not conceived that way by Marx or Khomeini. That is, it is one conception among many, and it is a classical conception.

Rhetoric and Writing

Eighteenth-century Europe and European North America sustained a literal cult of the classical, so extreme as at times to be comical in its veneration of everything Greek and Roman and its devaluation of everything since, with the exception of the High Renaissance. This cult is expressed in its most unremitting form by Winckelmann. One of its central moves is the connection of ancient writing to visual arts; the same aesthetic is detected in each, and the implication is that the prose and visual rhetorics ought to be revived, which was certainly accomplished, even as each revival was also an extension and a falsification. Winckelmann writes:

> In all human endeavors impetuousness and inaccuracy appear first; poise and exactitude follow, and it takes time to learn to admire them. Such qualities are characteristic of great masters only, whereas for learners the violent passions are even advantageous. The noble simplicity and serene grandeur of Greek statuary constitutes the true distinguishing mark of the finest Greek writing, that is to say the works of the School of Socrates, and it was these same qualities that contributed to the greatness of Raphael, which he attained by imitating the ancients.[1]

As in Wölfflin, Winckelmann's treatment characterizes the classical in extraordinarily general terms that might apply to everything from prose to architecture to political systems: "poise," "exactitude," "noble simplicity," "serene grandeur." Notice too that Winckelmann treats the idea of the classical as a mature style that rejects the characteristics we might associate with the archaic, the Gothic, the romantic, and so on. These aesthetic movements are comprehensible in terms of the classical, but for Winckelmann, it too in terms of them. With regard to Greek and Latin, Thomas Jefferson wrote, "To these we are certainly indebted for the rational and chaste style of modern composition which so much distinguishes the nations to whom these languages are familiar."[2] Rationality and chastity are likewise qualities

---

1. Johann Winckelmann, *Thoughts on Imitation in Greek Painting and Sculpture* (1755), quoted Eco and McEwen, p. 38.
2. Letter to John Adams (1819), quoted in Richard, p. 27.

Jefferson attributed to the architecture that he admired and the architecture he produced.

A central feature of the classical that was in continual revival from the fourteenth century at latest, and that at least metaphorically can be said to encompass all the arts, is the very idea of rhetoric: the application of classical ideas to language, in political no less than literary discourse. When Petrarch conceived the idea of a return to classical models, he meant above all the models of classical writing, and he conceived this in direct connection with a political revival of Italy: "Who doubts that Rome could rise up again were she only to know herself?"[3] (a sentence, I might point out, that could have been produced by Mussolini). Indeed the Renaissance as a whole had explicitly political motivations in an Italy famous for its ancient glory and its contemporary impotence, still being smacked by barbarians and rebuilt with their Gothic architecture. In painting, the Renaissance story usually begins with Giotto or Cimabue, but of course the classical models of painting had by and large been lost to time and iconoclasm. If Giotto was "classical"—by no means an unproblematic assertion—his classicism was largely speculative. But Petrarch and Boccaccio could avail themselves of ancient languages and take as models ancient texts; the literary Renaissance was much more explicit than the visual for its first century or more. The rhetoric of Cicero, in particular, but also of Quintilian and others gave shape to the prose of humanism and of the Renaissance.

Erwin Panofsky to some extent traces the Renaissance in painting to the model of classical rhetoric. He describes the structure of Leone Battista Alberti's *Treatise on Painting:* "Alberti also adapted, however tentatively, to the painter's profession the categories of classical rhetoric: invention, disposition (changed to *circonscriptione* and *compositione,* and about a hundred years later replaced by *disegno*), and elocution (changed to *receptione de lume,* and about a hundred years later replaced by *colorito*)" (Panofsky, p. 26). The idea of a classical painting had essentially to be invented, and it was invented from sources in the other arts and in classical philosophy and what we might term Pythagorean mathematics. That is, it proceeded in terms of light, as in the Greek and in particular Neoplatonic identification of light with knowledge or with the source of the universe; and it proceeded by canons of rhetorical structure: the architecture of language.

The idea of rhetoric originates in the Athenian democracy, in which persuasion was of paramount importance for successful political and legal participation. Empires and totalitarian regimes in general have far less serious

---

3. Petrarch, *La Familiari* (ca. 1350), quoted in Panofsky, p. 18.

and urgent reasons to pursue rhetoric, because their public discourse is monologic; the real agent of persuasion is the iron fist or the overwhelming spectacle. Even in imperial Rome, rhetoric was conceived as a mode of participation in the vestigial aspects of republicanism, above all the Senate. Aristotle's rhetoric encompassed argumentation and persuasion as a whole, and deployed characteristic tripartite distinctions (*ethos, pathos,* and *logos,* for instance). The classical aesthetic in its entirety was wrapped up into these distinctions, and that aesthetic was transmitted to the various classical revivals above all in terms of rhetoric and in models of it known through writing. Latin and Greek were revived for their "nobility" and "grand manner": their simultaneous beauty (conceived as a classical architecture) and ethical essence or upshot, their seriousness and ethical exaltation. "Rhetoric is useful," Aristotle writes, "because things that are true and things that are just have a natural tendency to prevail over their opposites, so that if the decisions of judges are not what they ought to be, the defeat must be due to the speakers themselves, and they must be blamed accordingly" (Aristotle, 1355a22). That is, we're talking not about "mere" rhetoric or persuasion but about the art of persuasion with moral and epistemic upshots, as a key to science and law. Indeed the *Rhetoric* recapitulates Aristotle's ethics, his political philosophy, and his aesthetics.

Classical and Enlightenment

Things become more complex if we try to relate classicism to "the Enlightenment" in order to approach more nearly to the moment I'm addressing. Certainly the idea of secularism in epistemology, of reason as a source of knowledge, is in part the heritage of Renaissance humanism; it is what the renaissances found again and again in the Greeks. It also comports fairly well with Protestantism; Luther at one time anticipated that Erasmus would join him in his opposition to the Catholic Church. But many Enlightenment figures such as Adam Smith and Benjamin Franklin, or for that matter Diderot, were hard-edged empiricists of a kind wholly characteristic of modernity. Here we might array such figures as Bacon and Hobbes as predecessors; despite their own reliance on the classical tradition, they were essentially moderns, and did not understand themselves as fundamentally revivalists, in spite of their classical learning. One might think of the art of Hogarth, or for that matter of *Tristram Shandy,* essentially indifferent to classicism even in the midst of its revival. This empiricist development did not set itself against antiquity, exactly, but it was ultimately external to it. Or we might say it didn't need antiquity; it had methodology. These moments or moods—the classical and the Enlightenment (the empiricist or the pointedly modern)—run all over the eighteenth century, coalescing and diverging, as in the amalgamation of republicanism, contract theory, and anthropology in Rousseau, or the pre-neoclassical frippery of Robert Adam or Anton Mengs, or the eclectic commentary of Voltaire. And indeed such figures as Jefferson split time and consciousness between the Enlightenment in Paris, with its heavy classical admixture, and the Enlightenment in the British Isles, even as he split his political philosophy between Locke and classical republicanism.

Eighteenth-century classicism, that is, like each such revival, is conditioned by its context, which fixes the source of the need for or resort to the classical. If Raphael emerges in dialogue and tension with a pointedly corrupt Catholicism, for example, then Jefferson emerges in an atmosphere of scientism and skepticism, as well as in the death throes of monarchy and the rococo. Any of these things might leave you yearning for unity or "poise": in short, dignity.

Republicanism

At any rate, one of the basic traditions of one strand of classical political theory was what has come to be called "civic republicanism," based especially on sources about the Romans: Cicero to Machiavelli (including Bruni of course), with little outbreaks appearing throughout the Mediterranean basin over the centuries. A locus is late medieval Lombardy and Tuscany, where the city-republics struggled to maintain their independence between the Holy Roman Empire and the papacy, as well as various local tyrants. The texts that fixed this tradition as it emerged into the Renaissance were the Roman historians: Livy, Sallust, Plutarch, Tacitus. The ideas were accessible to and attractive to the basic humanist figures of the Renaissance, and provided the visual vocabulary in which the subsequent waves of classicism spoke, as in early- to mid-seventeenth-century French painting à la Domenichino and Poussin and then the late-eighteenth-century, properly "neoclassical," phase. In architecture we might mark the development as follows: the Greek temple/Vitruvius/Brunelleschi/Alberti/Palladio/Wren.

The Greeks and Romans had themselves romanticized their ancient republics, and each classical phase saw a revival of republicanism as it saw the revival of the Roman historians, who had themselves romanticized the Roman Republic as the acme of virtue and the origin of empire. "Classical" Venice and Florence were ruled as republics intermittently, at least on paper, from the late Middle Ages through the Renaissance, while the Dutch republics (1581–1795) and Geneva in the eighteenth century were also self-consciously organized classicist polities, always in the process of dis-integration and revival; always already the object of nostalgia. The republic is the perfect form of government for any renaissance: it was a golden age even during the golden age. Here we might connect the fad, in the current American empire, for biographies of the founding fathers of the American republic: their dignity, their virtue, their thoroughly republican style of leadership. The republic is the political condition from which the West has always degenerated, as the classical embodies the heights of art from which we are descended, fallen.

If there is a governing metaphor for the classical republic, it is an organism, and hence in my view the republican tradition in political philosophy must trace its origin to Aristotle, for whom the polis is natural and "prior to the individual." The polis, as it were, is the basic human individual; without it, a man is a god or a monster, not a human being. Recall Wölfflin: "Every form developed to self-existent being, the whole freely co-ordinated: nothing but independently living parts," a kind of cellular or biological account. The human body itself presents this aspect of the classical, which we might also call Stoic: it connects the order of nature with the order of intelligence, matter with mathematics. The Stoics identified Nature with Reason, an amazing and perverse and utterly classical idea that allows mimesis to be identified with knowledge. Classical architecture, until its imperial bloat, is given its basic size and proportions through a consultation with the body or by the measurements of an ideal body. The obsession with the naked human form, characteristic of the Greeks, of the Italian Renaissance, and of Winckelmann, yields not just classical emblems but a model of the relation of parts to whole: independence (articulation) and interdependence (coherence).

Panofsky observes, with regard to Manetti's treatment of Brunelleschi:

> The letter to Leo X explicitly states what in the meantime has become common knowledge as a result of Vitruvian studies, that those famous classical orders represented an architectural transformation and glorification of the human body: "the Romans had columns calculated after the dimensions of man and woman."
>
> This statement, manifestly based on Vitruvius' derivation of the Doric, Ionic and Corinthian columns from the proportions of a man, a full-grown woman, and a slender virgin, expresses the fundamental fact that classical as opposed to mediaeval architecture is—if I may use these terrifying expressions—catanthropic rather than epanthropic: dimensioned in analogy to the relative proportions of the human body, not scaled with reference to the absolute size of the human body. (Panofsky, p. 28)

And of course we might draw a variety of other conclusions: whereas medieval architecture was dedicated to God, classical architecture was dedicated to man. "Medieval architecture preaches Christian humility," writes Panofsky. "Classical and Renaissance architecture proclaims the dignity of man" (Panofsky, p. 29). (It is worth pointing out that medieval architecture preaches humility by overwhelming you with structures built by human beings; that it divinizes the human hierarchy of the church; that it humbles you by its overweening display of pride. The stuff was not actually designed or built by God.) That would make classical architecture congenial to humanists, of course, and to a rational deist and moralist such as Jefferson. It is also a political expression, since it refers above all to the design of public buildings, and moves from theocracy and monarchy to the dignity of the citizen.

American Republicanism

If I could identify a completely self-conscious systematic American republican political authorship in philosophy in order to summarize the tradition as a whole, it would be that of John C. Calhoun. In an extremely distinguished and profoundly problematic career as a statesman, Calhoun served as senator, secretary of war, secretary of state, and vice president; while trying to hold together the Union, he was the preeminent pro-slavery statesman of the first half of the nineteenth century. Late in life he wrote excellent philosophical treatises on politics, central systematic statements of American republicanism. The distance from the founding did him good: whereas the *Federalist,* for example, emerged as advocacy journalism, Calhoun cultivated a detachment from any particular set of events; that is, his late writings were self-consciously distanced philosophical disquisitions on American republicanism.

Calhoun was by his own account himself a revivalist of the classical era of the United States: the period of the founders, from rebellion to Bill of Rights. Already by 1840 the American republic was an exalted condition from which we had fallen, Washington and Jefferson the men of an ancient dignity and virtue that we needed to try to recover. Through those figures Calhoun approached an Aristotelian ideal of mixed government—the central political concept of John Adams, and more generally of the Federalists. Calhoun's republic was a government of interests rather than individuals, of professions or even guilds, classes, regions, and so on. That there is a states rights, pro-slavery undertow is obvious, and cannot be eliminated as a datum: both democratic Athens and republican Rome practiced slavery (as did Washington and Jefferson, of course), no doubt and unfortunately one reason why Calhoun found their republicanism congenial. In Book One of the *Politics,* Aristotle hesitantly drew the conclusion that some men are naturally slaves, some naturally masters. Such a doctrine is seen in attenuated form in the classical republican John Adams's obsession with natural aristocracy or inequality. Indeed slavery and war as related activities (prisoners taken in war constituted a significant portion of the slaves of Athens and Rome) taint the history of republics and are the occasion of their mutation into military machines and empires.

Nevertheless, Calhoun's organic and comprehensive republican vision is admirable in many respects and does not necessarily depend conceptually on slavery, though the sort of political participation required in the classical model is difficult without a leisure class. Calhoun attempts with the benefit of hindsight to rewrite the republican legacy of Patrick Henry and John Taylor of Caroline. He grew up in Greek Revival Charleston, and formulates his theory precisely by making "organism" a technical term, in a rather ingenious interweaving of "political science" (the term is Calhoun's), virtue ethics, and design culture. He writes: "What I propose [is] to explain on what principles government must be formed, in order to resist, by its own interior structure—or to use a single term *organism*—the tendency to abuse of power. The structure, or organism, is what is meant by constitution, in its strict and more usual sense" (Calhoun, p. 12). The "organic" conception of the polis derives from Aristotle and other ancient sources, and describes the canons of public architecture no less than those of governing arrangements. It is to some extent opposed to a Lockean polity of individual rights: this tension is inscribed throughout the founding and early republic, but Calhoun's authorship is the most squarely organic and republican of any historical American political thinker.

Calhoun's political philosophy is, we might say, pointedly classical, and the main point is to coordinate disparate elements into a comprehensible order. He thinks not primarily in terms of individual rights but in terms of a balance of forces that arrives at equilibrium. To cite Wölfflin once more:, "Every form developed to self-existent being, the whole freely co-ordinated: nothing but independently living parts": a summary of Calhoun's political philosophy. A balanced polity, he says,

> can only be accomplished in one way—and that is, by such an organism of the government—and, if necessary for the purpose, of the community also—as will, by dividing and distributing the powers of government, give to each division or interest, through its appropriate organ, either a concurrent voice in making and executing the laws, or a veto on their execution. It is only by such an organism, that the assent of each can be made necessary to put government in motion; or the power

made effectual to arrest its action—and it is only by the one or the other that the different interests, orders, classes, or portions, into which the community may be divided, can be protected, and all conflict and struggle between them prevented—by rendering it impossible to put or to keep it in action, without the concurrent consent of all. (Calhoun, pp. 21–23)

The fundamental political actors in Calhoun's system are not individuals but interests, or what Madison termed factions; the Calhounian polis is the site where these interests interact or press their claims.

In Calhoun's view, the disparate elements of the nation are not to be united; they are to be coordinated. Or more accurately, the integrity of each element must be respected, cultivated, emphasized; a complex and coherent structure is to be produced by an understanding of the integrity of each element. The vision is Vitruvian, Palladian. When Calhoun was vice president, he articulated the relation of the federal and state governments this way:

To realize [the American system's] perfection, we must view the General Government and those of the States as a whole, each in its proper sphere, sovereign and independent; each perfectly adapted to its respective objects; the States acting separately, representing and protecting the local and peculiar interests; and acting jointly through one General Government, with the weight respectively assigned to each by the Constitution, representing and protecting the interest of the whole; and thus perfecting, by an admirable but simple arrangement, the great principle of representation and responsibility, without which no government can be free or just. To preserve this sacred distribution, by coercing each to move in its prescribed orbit, is the great and difficult problem, on the solution of which, the duration of our Constitution, of our Union, and, in all probability, our liberty depends. (from the Fort Hill Address; Calhoun, pp. 375–76)

The imposition of coherent form by force and reason; the arrangement of disparate elements in a simple, rational arrangement; the conception of the whole as a distribution or proportion of elements and as a body or constitution: these are all classical conceptions that originate in the realm of the aesthetic; and they are ideas embodied in Jefferson's neoclassical architecture. Immense tensions or contradictions—between coercion and liberty, individualism and organicity, stasis and dynamism, city-state and empire—are wrapped up in the classical from the beginning, and are precisely what the classical both preserves and explicates, what it is and what it resolves.

There is a range of republican positions and aesthetics in early America: the poles are well represented by Adams and Jefferson. Adams's republicanism is more elitist or aristocratic, as well as more classical, Jefferson's more democratic or liberal. But they both endorse a mixed constitutional government; they both take man to be a political animal, suited by nature for sociality and polity; they both enjoin sturdy virtue and self-reliance, and so on. Both Adams and Jefferson are self-consciously founders of, as we might say, an ancient republic. Indeed the people who led the American Revolution were, almost to a man, devoted to the idea of classical learning to an at times almost absurd extent: every sentence another allusion to Plutarch, Cicero, or Sallust. In part this was characteristic of the cosmopolitan learned and diplomatic communities that they frequented, or fancied they frequented, from Charleston to Boston to Paris and London. And in part it might in fact have represented their social anxieties, particularly in the case of modestly born men such as Adams. Treating the classical sages as contemporaries, displaying their Greek and Latin: these were claims of people who were in some sense beyond provincial—colonial—to equality of status with the people occupying the center of the universe. But whatever the sociology, classical aesthetics provided the serious theoretical underpinnings of American republicanism, and it lent the founders a vocabulary in which to explain or display themselves to the outside world and debate with one another.

Adams's rejection of democracy and design for a "mixed" government, incorporating elements of monarchy (executive), aristocracy (senatorial), and democratic (representative) forms—which in effect became the constitutional conception—is completely, self-consciously classical in form and justification. Late in his life he summarized his views in a letter to John Taylor, a sophisticated advocate of agrarian democracy:

> An equilibrium of those "different powers" [is] indispensably necessary to guard and defend the rights, liberties, and happiness of the people against the deleterious, contagious, and pestilential effects of those passions of vanity, pride, ambition, envy, revenge, lust, and cruelty, which domineer more or less in every government that has no BALANCE or an imperfect BALANCE.... [I]n every one of [the old colonial forms of government] there had been three branches,—a governor, a council, and a house of representatives,—which, added to the eternal and unalterable nature of things, induced the legislators of those states to adopt new constitutions. (Adams, p. 409)

Adams's own design for the Massachusetts Constitution deployed such a model scrupulously. In all of his writings, the governing notion is balance; it's no coincidence that he capitalizes it in his communication with Taylor. The classical is here also connected to the "eternal" and "unalterable." Here the very ancientness of the texts he appeals to serves a rhetorical function, even as it reiterates the classical aesthetic's own obsession with bringing time to stillness: in Parmenides, Plato, and Euclid, for example. Adams's *Defence of the Constitutions of Government of the United States of America* is an immense work of republican scholarship, an edifice of elucidation and adaptation of ancient political and aesthetic systems.

Above all, classical texts, particularly in Latin, provided the models of American prose style. It was for its remarkable classicism—its purity, dignity, symmetry, and so on—that Jefferson's style was admired by his contemporaries and which led to his assignment to draft the Declaration of Independence, specifically to Adams's insistence that Jefferson undertake the task. Here one might later consider the remarkable modular essays of Emerson, each a series of ringing classical similes or aphorisms arrayed into periods. Indeed, though Jefferson and Gibbon were contemporaries, more or less, it is no exaggeration to say that American English of the late eighteenth century was more consistently classical than English English, which showed a tendency toward genre and even vernacular farce, a kind of nascent popular culture. The Revolutionary generation of Americans was in a self-conscious mini-renaissance of the kind one finds scattered temporally and spatially throughout the Mediterranean and the Atlantic basin, from Byzantium to Morocco to Spain to Ireland. Jefferson's architecture and his prose referred to previous outbreaks, to Palladio and Inigo Jones and Wren but not Bernini or Borromini. In this the Americans connected with the French preference for the classical, which became ever more emphatic as the century went on, even as French republicanism and American republicanism revealed their affinities and created a military and diplomatic alliance.

The distinction is that French neoclassicism arrayed itself against the precious and hedonistic aristocratic taste of the rococo, which can scarcely be said to have had a presence in the British colonies of North America. That is, French neoclassicism was driven specifically by a rejection of rococo art-politics, and so possessed a layer of self-consciousness that the Americans lacked, though of course Americans connected with the French in a rejection of actual aristocracy. Nevertheless, the Americans bowed to nobody in their devotion specifically to the classical texts; they appropriated from the British tradition and invented in order to forge sentences in English analogous to sentences of the classical languages. This gave the words a stern, moralistic tone, relieved by a touch of wit or a particularly euphonic turn of phrase. The syntax of English could not be the syntax of a classical language, but a passage of English no less than a passage of Latin could be a pure example of the syntax of its own particular language. One became alert to the architectonic or structural elements of prose and arrayed them with a supreme self-consciousness. The Declaration of Independence is a monument to this consciousness. Even so droll a writer as Ben Franklin, who had almost no organized education, delivered masterpieces of profuse concision in a style recognizable in Thoreau, Twain, Bierce, and Mencken, and in Strunk and White: American neoclassical prose.

We might trace the rhetoric of any of the design arts. An extremely clear example is "fashion." Actual resources are expended in the outfits of Marie Antoinette and her ladies, and actual resentments—not to mention beheadings—are engendered thereby: the design culture shapes the national budget and the political outcome perfectly concretely. But whoever is shopping and how, you could not have the aesthetic sensibility of a Marie Antoinette and be an Abigail Adams; the ornamentation of women is not an independent choice but an entailment of the political scheme. Or we might entertain the idea that the political scheme is an entailment of the manner in which women ornament themselves. Surely such things are as much the source of the republican rejection of monarchy as are the philosophies of Aristotle or Montesquieu, let us say. Is this repugnance moral, political, or aesthetic? What I want to entertain is the idea that these are not distinguishable on the ground, that each is always all.

If politics is the site wherein interests are negotiated and from which power is deployed—which is certainly the way it is understood by Calhoun, for example—some of these interests are best conceived not as straightforward considerations of wealth or status but, in connection, as aesthetic interests. Indeed the eighteenth and nineteenth centuries, in Smith and Marx, for example, thought of the political arena, or even life in general, as the pursuit of economic self-interest by whoever was deemed to be an actor: the human individual or social class. Everything else was seen to be a disguise or ideology through which these actors pursued their economic interests. Even if that is true, however, the question of political arrangements has to be partly aesthetic. You must achieve an arrangement that you can understand as conducing to those interests: a comprehensible and enduring structure. And the structure cannot be enduring if it does not to some extent coordinate disparate interests.

Classical republicanism could be understood to be one such structure of coordination, but any such structure is an aesthetic structure. The classical in the context of its continual revival since the Renaissance is also a rejection specifically of Christian theocratic solutions to such problems, to mystical architectures and profuse iconographies, which we might associate with the Gothic, for one example. Jefferson's separation of church and state is explicitly embodied in his public architecture. Gothic mysticism and exaltation are also an aesthetic of political power, remaking the environment under the authority of a God that exceeds human epistemic capacities; it locates at the heart of politics a mystery, which in itself can be satisfying to contemplate. The political, however it is construed, must issue in actual rearticulations of the environment. These in every case deploy an aesthetic that is related in one way or another (including perhaps by falsification) to the political ideology, in such a way that the aesthetic, economic, religious, and political dimensions of understanding are best conceived as a complexly interrelated system. Nowhere in history is this better understood or more explicitly explored than by figures such as Jefferson.

Jefferson's Architecture

Wrote Jefferson: "A Portico may be five to ten diameters of the column deep, or projected from the building. If more than five diameters there must be a column in the middle of each flank, since it must never be more than five diameters from centre to centre of columns."[4] Notice that the ideas are expressed invariably through proportions rather than, for example, absolute figures. Indeed "proportion" itself is identified in the classical tradition with beauty. It is used almost equivalently with "harmony" "measure," "fitness": notions so vague as to be applicable to any mode or medium of art; to personal comportment or governmental institutions; to ideas, equations, comedies, philosophies, organisms. And yet in every specific case one tries to put meat on these bones, with golden sections, doctrines of the mean, and so on.

Carl Richard, who has exhaustively researched the classical rhetoric of the early republic, writes:

> Jefferson was so immersed in the classics that they profoundly influenced his writing style, helping to produce the clarity and concision which stands as his trademark. Jefferson used the Roman historians Livy, Sallust, and Tacitus as models for oratorical writing. . . . From classical rhetoric Jefferson learned the three qualities which he deemed essential to good republican oratory. These were simplicity, brevity, and rationality. In his literary commonplace book Jefferson copied from the fifth-century Athenian dramatist Euripides this passage on

---

4. Jefferson to Madison, quoted in Richard, p. 47.

the virtue of simplicity in rhetoric: "The words of truth are simple, and justice needs no subtle interpretations, for it has a fitness in itself; but the words of injustice, being rotten in themselves, require clever treatment." (Richard, p. 29)

This nicely captures a self-conscious artpolitical construction that conceives architecture, writing, and politics as the same discipline: that is, American republicanism is conceived as an aesthetic system of which texts and buildings are central embodiments. The Declaration of Independence is a text of great dignity and chaste poetry, as well as a visual form, and surely its power derives partly from these aspects. Nor are they separate from the ideas being expressed. It is the dignity, humility, integrity, and poetry of independence that is both stated and expressed in the text in the same act, that is embodied in a music of words and a balanced design of government and a dignified calligraphy: simple, clear, and handsome. The design of government set out in the Constitution is an equilateral triangle, a paradigmatic neoclassical compositional motif, derived by Adams in particular from Montesquieu. If the design of the American government had eight branches, asymmetrically arranged so that some had more power than others and so on, it could not have the immediately compelling quality that it does.

Jefferson's state capitol in Richmond is generally held to be the first Greek Revival building in the Americas, and it is remarkable in its absolutely stark classicism, certainly unprecedented in the Western hemisphere. To Madison on September 20, 1785, Jefferson wrote:

Much time was requisite, after the external form was agreed on, to make the internal distribution convenient for the three branches of government.... We took for our model what is called the Maison quarrée of Nismes [Nîmes], one of the most beautiful, if not the most beautiful and precious morsel of architecture left us by antiquity. It was built by Caius and Lucius Caesar [that is, in the republic, which is certainly wrong], and has the suffrage of all the judges of architecture, who have seen it, as yielding to no one of the beautiful monuments of Greece, Rome, Palmyra, and Balbec.... It is very simple, but it is noble beyond expression, and would have done honor to our country, as presenting to travellers a specimen of our taste in our infancy, promising much for our maturer age.... [H]ow is a taste in this beautiful art to be formed in our countrymen, unless we avail ourselves of every occasion when public buildings are to be erected, of presenting to them models for their study and imitation?...You see I am an enthusiast on the subject of the arts. But it is an enthusiasm of which I am not ashamed, as its object is to improve the taste of my countrymen, to increase their reputation, to reconcile to them the respect of the world, and procure them its praise. (Jefferson 2, pp. 829–30)

Here we see the seriousness of Jefferson's commitment to architecture, but also the anxiety of the provincial. The public buildings that he had a hand in designing—and this would include the Capitol in Washington, D.C., and the White House (to which Jefferson added the colonnades), and by influence the presentation of the federal government on the Mall in Washington and the statehouses of most of the states—were designed to direct an interpretation of the United States to other nations, to make a claim to legitimacy. And they had a directly educational function, the effectiveness of which was testified to by the whole of Greek Revival American architecture.

Everything that Jefferson designed was an aesthetic critique of monarchy for its lavishness (which *is* its injustice: you dispossess the peasantry in order to toss another statue into the formal garden; the distribution is manifestly asymmetrical, irrational; wrong in the sense that it displays the regime's lack of virtue). Of course Jefferson fully participated in the contemporary French neoclassical moment, spending five years in Paris at its height. If the monarchy is decadent, unjust, luridly out of balance, this is not merely demonstrated in its design; it is embodied by its design; it is identical with its design. One way to frame the critique would be in aesthetic terms, another in moral, another in political, and these are all the very same critique: the monarchy and its specific expressions lack balance, proportion, measure, dignity, chastity. And the republican response is not merely reflected, for example, in the costume worn by a Jefferson—the clothing of a citizen—as president, as opposed to a Louis XVI; the clothing really is, substantively, the response, or part of the response. The British monarchy perhaps survived by toning the stuff down a bit, and there is something to be said for the notion that Jefferson himself was a bit the slumming aristocrat as citizen, a fashion in France at that moment: he conceived himself to be a kind of Roman senator.

An advocate of highly decentralized democracy, Jefferson did as much as any president with the possible exception of Polk to transform the United States into a continent-bestriding colossus, negotiating with Napoleon for the Louisiana Purchase and sponsoring Lewis and Clark's exploration of the West. His policy and his architecture made a claim for the United States as a world power, the first symptom of what was a centuries-long migration of world power to Washington. The classical again made its transition from Greece to Rome, and from republic to empire. Indeed it is often said that Jefferson was a man of contradictions, and not the least of these is that he portrayed himself through his public and his domestic architecture as a farmer and a framer, as a citizen and a king, a scientist, a scholar, a statesman, a "renaissance man" of the first water. His architecture was a fantastic self-portrait, forging a character that is both a radical egalitarian and a natural aristocrat. We could say that American civic architecture has followed Jefferson in this complex symbolism: projecting both power and forbearance, pride and humility. Perhaps the best crystallization of this aesthetic is Jefferson's retreat in Bedford County, Virginia, the home known as Poplar Forest, a truly perfect example of neoclassical domestic architecture based on the octagon, exquisite in its coordination, symmetry, balance, and symbolic content, a presentation of the private man as public figure and a humble power.

Complaining about the architecture of the early American republic in 1781, Jefferson gives a little classical catechism:

> The genius of architecture seems to have shed its maledictions over the land. Buildings are often erected, by individuals, of considerable expence. To give these symmetry and taste would not increase their cost. It would only change the arrangement of the materials, the form and combination of the members. This would often cost less than the burthen of barbarous ornaments with which these buildings are sometimes charged. But the first principles of the art are unknown and there exists scarcely a model among us sufficiently chaste to give an idea of them.[5]

Obviously Jefferson did what he could, and the classicism of Poplar Forest or the University of Virginia is notable for its humane scale, its dignity and rationality, both its ambitions and its self-abnegation in the face of necessity or for the sake of excellence: stoic with a touch of optimism. Of course the mathematical-sounding formalism, and its connection to the "chastity" of design, is a good description of a classical response to the Gothic or the rococo, a response that recurred with variations in Europe for at least five hundred years. The humanism of Jefferson's private architecture is taken up and contradicted in his public work on behalf of the state, where he aims for a dignity and conceptual power that makes a claim to legitimacy on a global scale.

Generations of high school seniors have come to Washington by bus and seen the very essence of the American state, and if they have been uplifted by the openness and rationality, they have also been intimidated by the power and wealth: Isn't this inspiring? and: Resistance is useless. Now, as Washington

---

5. *Notes on the State of Virginia,* in Jefferson 2, p. 279.

hunkers down into a security state in the face of the irrational religious extremism of Islamic terrorism, it is the intimidation that holds sway, and the openness of the buildings of democracy and the institutions they house and express is fundamentally compromised in the midst of a world designed to express it. Jefferson wanted the Rotunda of the Capitol building to be the "Hall of the People"; these days, once you pass through the layers of security and enter a world of hyper-intense surveillance, you might be forgiven for thinking that you are in a police state still expressing itself in republican tropes, a Rome indeed.

Again, one of the most conspicuous historical contexts of the dignity of the Greek polis and its chaste Euclidean arts is that, as a matter of fact, they were taken up and bloated by the Roman Empire. The danger of classical aesthetics as it has actually emerged in history is that it segues into imperial aesthetics. We wed classical lines with gigantism, rationality with infinite power, so the message is that resistance is ugly, irrational, and without prospect of success. (This is of course a simplification; central features of American classicism—notably the dome—were certainly of Roman origin, though there associated with the republic.) Napoleon avails himself naturally of the neoclassical aesthetics of French republicanism, though he must inflate them exponentially as to scale. I suggest to you that a visit to Washington, D.C., is a beautiful, or at least kind of impressive, illustration of this transition. The agrarian republicanism of a Jefferson is now simulated in massive edifices that pay tribute to continent-bestriding wealth and world-bestriding military might. Washington teaches through the arts the inspiring story of American democracy and freedom, and also teaches that those who resist will be erased, that you are dealing with a set of gigantic implacable institutions toward which all the world's resources flow like the Nile. The capital city pays tribute to both our war dead and our tax resister, the latter by a priori erasure, by an extremely concrete demonstration that Shays's Rebellion or the Whiskey Rebellion just didn't work out. If the past is any guide, the city will someday be a picturesque ruin: rotting, inhabited by roaming decadent predators.

In one way the empire is the natural aesthetic inheritor of the republic. I'm not sure whether this is merely a historical coincidence relying on the Roman, French, and American or even German cases (Weimar Republic to Nazi empire), or whether there really is something inherent in the republican aesthetic that leads to extreme expansion. One thing we might say is that in a way Euclid is constant as to size, and an edifice the size of a modest residence or of the world as we know it can equally instantiate the golden section. In working up the curriculum for the University of Virginia, Jefferson placed "military and naval architecture" in the department of pure mathematics.

Military architecture embraces fortification and field works, which with their bastions, curtains, horn-works, redoubts etc. are based on a technical combination of lines and angles. These are adapted to offence and defence, with and against the effects of bombs, balls, escalades etc. But lines and angles make the sum of elementary geometry, a branch of Pure Mathematics: and the direction of the bombs, balls, and other projectiles, the necessary appendages of military works, altho' no part of their architecture, belong to the conic sections, a branch of transcendental geometry. Diderot and Dalembert therefore, in their Arbor scientiae [the taxonomy of the disciplines in the *Encyclopédie*, the "systematic diagram of the human sciences"], have placed military architecture in the department of elementary geometry. (Jefferson 2, pp. 1441–42)

We might call this the pure mathematics of budding empire. This 1820 letter to Adams proceeds immediately to Greek etymologies.

The classical, that is, is both a "transcendental geometry" and a weapons system, and the rational environment it produces harbors the possibility of an immense destruction. Euclid is both a set of pure concepts and a way to calculate the flight of missiles. Nevertheless, I do not want to be understood as saying that the artpolitics of American republicanism is a purely oppressive system; it is equivocal, and preferable on innumerable grounds to a European-style monarchy, or a communist or fascist dictatorship. But American republicanism is no less an aesthetic system than are fascism and National Socialism, and that should make you think twice about the idea that the aestheticization of politics is a necessarily totalitarian idea. Politics is necessarily aesthetics, though not always as self-consciously as it is in a Jefferson.

Conclusion

Political Styles and Aesthetic Ideologies

What I want to bring out of the case studies—besides what I hope is their intrinsic interest—is something of an inductive demonstration of the legitimacy and usefulness of political aesthetics as an area of inquiry. With regard to political phenomena, the specialization of disciplines has resulted in huge ranges of data omitted or marred by confusions and arbitrary limitations. First, the distinctions between political and aesthetic realms, and thus between political science, art history, philosophy of art, and political philosophy, are unsustainable on the ground. Or at least the subject matters are profoundly enriched by being brought into proximity and juxtaposition. Second, political systems of both power and resistance—ideologies, constitutions, state arrangements, and social arrangements alternative to the state—are aesthetic environments. They centrally include texts, but they are also systems of visual arts, musics, decorative arts, architectures, design cultures, festivals, clothing styles, body modifications, and so on. The texts themselves benefit from consideration in their aesthetic aspects, and need to be for the moment deemphasized so that a fuller appreciation of what political systems are can be generated.

The legitimacy of political aesthetics could be established easily if there were a simple correlation between art styles and political ideologies. But in fact the relation between them is tremendously complex, at times almost incoherent or paradoxical. The most elaborate treatment of the relation in this book has concerned the classical in its use by, for example, both Jefferson and Hitler. Obviously, if "the classical" is actually a single art style, it correlates no more neatly to republican than to fascist values. But we have seen a number of other examples of all sorts. Hip hop graffiti can be as effective as an advertising style for corporate mega-capitalism as it can be for the teenage hooliganism of the teenage hooligans among whom it originated. But we might point out that part of the effectiveness of graffiti-style visual culture for corporate capitalism is precisely that it still carries the slightly hip charge of yesterday's vandals.

In other words, the meaning of graffiti is both taken up and contradicted by its appropriation for different purposes or by different forces. This is typical of the redeployment of a previously existing style; the meaning is at once the motive for the appropriation and is attenuated, contradicted, or intensified in the appropriation. We might think of the history of a particular style, such as the classical, or reggae music, as a series of loops, in which the style, in being revived, is pushed forward and distorted by, among other things, the new political meanings it generates in a new context.

I resist the claim that art is a language, or that art styles are vocabularies. Language, however, is an art, and vocabularies are art styles. At any rate, the parallel is enlightening within certain bounds. Language changes through time in a million unpredictable ways. Words slowly shift or even reverse their meanings. English is "the same" language now that it was in Chaucer's time, or at least we call it by the same name throughout that stretch. But it has been entirely transformed, and what accounts for its identity through time is precisely the history of these shifts. In addition, the language can be made to reverse its own meanings or elaborate on them right now: if I say "that's great" in a certain tone of voice, I mean precisely the opposite of what I might have meant without the sarcasm.

The primary unit of meaning, in other words, is the specific utterance made on a certain occasion. Most language has various "indexical" elements, elements that gain reference or extension only relative to a particular occasion. Thus "over here," pointing here, means a different place from "over here," pointing there. The tenses of verbs refer to different segments of time depending on when the utterance is produced. "I" means me when I say it, you when you say it, and so on.

I propose that art styles have indexical elements, that their meanings emerge only within the full context in which they are produced. But though "I" has an unstable reference, it has a stable sense: the principle by which its referent is determined is that it refers to the speaker of the utterance in question. The case is (somewhat) analogous in artpolitical style, though here it is better to say that the meaning is always, in being redeployed, being at once taken up and deflected. And insofar as, for example, prose styles are artpolitical styles, the metaphor of art to a language is more than metaphor, and Jefferson's classical prose does not mean the same as Cicero's, of course, but is the product of myriads of these deflections, including a series of transpositions between languages.

In other words, in each redeployment of the classical there is content—meaning—provided by the occasion and context of expression. Even if something is stable—the column, perhaps, or the golden section—the meaning of the column is its meaning here, now, where "here" and "now" begin to bleed off on the edges to the whole temporal and spatial set of the world oriented around that building or piece of writing as its center. Nevertheless, the meaning of the column is also the meaning of the column in its origin in classical antiquity, or else the whole history of meanings generated in it would be senseless. It is important in each iteration that it is an iteration of the same. Each repetition is different, but because it is a repetition, it is a reappearance of the same.

Kierkegaard wrote a whole book on this topic and titled it *Repetition*. One of the elements in it is the story of a young man from Copenhagen who lives for a while in Berlin and then returns to his native city. In order to see whether a true repetition is possible, he goes back again to Berlin, rents the same room he had before, goes to the same theater, frequents the same restaurants, and so forth. The experience is at once disappointing and stimulating: he finds that a repetition is both impossible and inevitable, that he cannot have the same experiences and that he cannot fail to be the person who had these experiences. Now, doing this may strike you as a remarkably perverse exercise. But in fact it is quite typical; we often seek to reproduce experiences we have had before: set out to achieve the same ... relationship, home, vacation, or whatever it may be. Indeed the representation of experiences, for example in snapshots or videos, is precisely an attempt to make a repetition possible, to hold on to something that seems to be receding into an incomparable past. In one sense, such a repetition is impossible, but the attempt at it lends our life whatever comprehensible structure it may have or lends us whatever comprehensible character we may have, a music that is our personhood—and though the routine may be tedious, it is also comforting.

Kierkegaard writes, in what may be termed an emblem of our theme, that "the dialectic of repetition is easy, for that which is repeated has been—otherwise it could not be repeated—but the very fact that it has been makes the repetition into something new" (Kierkegaard, p. 149). In repeating the style of classical Greece or roots reggae, we can more or less genuinely do what has been done before. But we are creating a new and incomparable situation.

We might ask where this leaves the assertion with which this book started: "Not all art is political, but all politics is aesthetic; at their heart political ideologies, systems, and constitutions are aesthetic systems, multimedia artistic environments. The political 'content' of an ideology can be understood in large measure actually to be—to be identical with—its formal and stylistic aspects." I do not withdraw those claims, but I think that we have seen in the case studies that the identity between political and aesthetic systems has to be carefully delineated. I only begin here to suggest how to unwind this relation. And my own interest is primarily in the phenomena, rather than in their reconstruction at the most abstract possible level. Nevertheless, in materialist philosophy of mind, there are token-identity theories and type-identity theories. On the latter, if there is a type of mental state, it is held that it must be identical to an underlying type of physical neural state. So if two people are angry, or if one person is angry at different times for different reasons, then— if anger is a type of mental state—there must be underlying commonalities in the brain states involved that explain the commonalities, explain why they are both tokens of the same type (anger). On the token-identity view (which I hold with some qualifications), though there may not be interesting commonalities in the brain states underlying all the mental incidents we call "anger," there must in each case of anger be a brain state which is identical to that mental state. (The way I'd qualify this is to point out that mental states are identical not to brain states but to [physical] states of the whole organism in relation to the whole environment.) As I said in the section of chapter 1 on totalitarian aesthetics: "Specific totalitarian regimes use specific aesthetic effects: the visage of the dictator, or Riefenstahl's cult of the body and the collective body. We can't understand the specific totalitarian system without understanding its aesthetics. But no specific aesthetic system is identical to totalitarianism in general."

The idea of token identity provides an interesting way to express what I take to be the relation between aesthetic style and political system. We might say that art style and political content are token-token identical. So there is an identity between a certain expression or moment of the classical and Jefferson's republicanism circa 1780. But there is no type-type identity between classicism and republicanism, as can be seen perfectly clearly from the use of classical tropes in imperial or fascist permutations. Garvey's Black Nationalism is inextricable from its aesthetic embodiments at any given moment, and understanding one is understanding both, or at least neither can be fully grasped without the other. Yet what "red, gold, and green" means now is not what it meant then. And more important, what "black" means is not the same. A dictator such as Robert Mugabe can use elements of the same aesthetic vocabulary to express a profoundly corrupt or oppressive ideology, whereas Garvey invented it as the vocabulary of a liberation movement.

And yet if Mugabe is availing himself of the aesthetic resources developed by Garvey, he is also trying to associate himself with Garvey's liberatory values. Perhaps that association is luridly false, and perhaps the vocabulary is selected precisely to disguise or obscure the actual nature of the Mugabe regime. It is, we might say, an ironic, or sarcastic, or merely a lying appropriation of the aesthetic style. The reversals and forks, the loops and erasures, the de- and resignification of an aesthetic style form a single history: fraught, complex, or even chaotic, looping or scribbled as a timeline, subject to incalculable external effects from other styles and political or economic contents. Such things are true also of political systems or ideologies, of course. What "democracy" means to us now is not what it meant to John Adams, for example, who is now accounted a hero of democracy, but who took himself to be opposed to it.

That is, though the Mugabe regime in its distribution of the sensible is token-identical to its aesthetic embodiments, and though similar aesthetic embodiments might at another place or on another occasion have a completely different meaning, there are historical connections among the deployments of a given set of aesthetic gestures or forms. The historical connections are not best conceived of as identities, but they suggest that more can be said, not in terms of types (as in classical = republican), but in terms of unfolding developments, which would include reversal, falsification, irony, as well as faithful attempts to recapture an artpolitical moment or thrust. This is why the disciplinary model of art history is particularly useful, because it can trace the development and multiplicitous uses of a style or its elements over time, as when impressionism develops from a radical overturning of academic art to being itself an academic or conventional style. This changes the look of impressionism, no doubt, but more important, even if the pictures looked the same, the meanings would be different in different contexts, at different moments. The relation of style to meaning and ideology is token identity and historical transformation.

If, as Wittgenstein taught, meaning is use, then what the tropes of punk mean depends on how they are used: if they are used to mean defiance, they means defiance; if they are used as marketing strategies for clothing at Target, then they mean more or less the opposite of defiance. But in fact meaning is use in dialogue with previous uses, or the uses of a term or a trope or image occur in relation to the history of the uses of that term or trope or image. Any given use, that is, is a social-historical-material event/object in a social-historical-material history. You can't understand why Target is using this particular trope, or why it works in marketing, or what it means to the people to whom it is marketed, without sampling the history from which the appropriation emerges and which it betrays and betrays, shows forth and reverses.

Of course the images and rhythms, the architectures and the melodies, typically are changed formally in their reappropriation. A Target punk T-shirt does not look just like what Johnny Rotten was wearing in 1977. Even if it did, it could not mean the same. Jorge Luis Borges wrote a marvelous "story," or rather a parody of a scholarly paper ("Pierre Menard, Author of the *Quixote*"), in which he describes the work of the author Pierre Menard. Menard's masterpiece is a rewriting of *Don Quixote:* a word-for-word identical copy of Cervantes's novel. Menard says of his method: "My solitary game is governed by two polar laws. The first permits me to attempt variants of a formal and psychological nature; the second obliges me to sacrifice them to the 'original' text and irrefutably to rationalize this annihilation" (Borges, p. 51). Borges observes that although the two *Quixotes* are word-for-word identical, they are radically stylistically distinct: "The archaic style of Menard . . . suffers from a certain affectation. Not so that of his precursor, who handles easily the ordinary Spanish of his time" (Borges, p. 53).

That is, although Menard's and Cervantes's texts are word-for-word identical, they are stylistically distinct. Even if Target reproduced some shirt worn by Johnny Rotten down to the last little hole, the shirt could not mean the same as Johnny's did, if nothing else because Johnny Rotten already existed and had a whole career, and because the Target shirt refers to Johnny's shirt in a way that Johnny's shirt could not have referred to itself. If Speer had built a perfect facsimile of Monticello to serve as Hitler's summer home, it would not (of course) mean the same thing, and the design–identity would be precisely a self-conscious appropriation and falsification, a parody or a painfully sincere misunderstanding.

But in fact when Target makes a punk shirt or Speer makes a classical building (and please do not take me to be identifying the politics of Target with fascism), the result does not look precisely the same as its source. Target doesn't want to reproduce the punk moment, or else people would be shopping in thrift shops or out of Dumpsters. Nor does Speer want simply to hark back to Winckelmann; indeed Hitler would have had Winckelmann executed. What Target or Speer is engaged in is an attempt—among other things—to *signify* punk or the classical. They try to concentrate and convey it, try to make it perfectly clear, not merely to produce an instance of it. They are, in what is a very typical artpolitical moment, making punk or classical things in a self-conscious program of simultaneous revival and falsification. In each such moment of self-conscious redeployment, the actual look and sound of things is shifted. Thus Speer's gigantism, for example: he doesn't just want to make a nice classical house; he wants to blow you away with the classicism of it all.

In a way, Speer's architecture continues to signify republicanism or enlightenment values harking back to circa 1780 neoclassicism, which in turn loops back to Renaissance humanism, to Roman republicanism, and to the Greek polis in a series of self-conscious instantiations/falsifications. But of course to be a classicist in 1935 was to be some sort of reactionary, whereas to be a classicist in 1780 was to be in the avant-garde. And in making a claim to the legitimacy of the tradition, the Nazis were of course engaged in a cynical manipulation of world opinion; they were self-consciously both expressing and concealing themselves. The meaning of Nazi classicism, in other words, is not the meaning of classicism. There *is* no meaning of classicism, exactly, only a set of design strategies and signifiers that can be twisted this way and that. But they can be twisted this way only *because* they have been twisted in that.

They have no definite and perfectly codified meaning, no eternal Form they signify. But that doesn't indicate that they're meaningless. Rather they are replete with meanings, saturated with meanings, which is precisely why they can keep being deflected or reversed, miniaturized or gigantized, incorporated or extruded from other styles with great significance turning on each such choice.

If you were going to attempt to formulate a new political ideology, a utopian image of the world, a new manifesto for world revolution or progress, it might seem that you should start with a wholly new style of architecture, a new prose for your manifesto, a new music to bring everyone into your harmony. Such things have happened many times. One thinks of the liberatory language of the dada-style anarchists, or the utopian architecture of Paolo Soleri, or the start-from-scratch transformations of Schoenberg, or the Situationist clothing of Vivien Westwood. And if you could transform our environment by these means, that would, of course, be a transformation of our politics. The new visual or aural or architectural vocabularies would be propaganda for your utopia. Made real, they would also actually be your utopia. But though Soleri might think that his architecture is the very embodiment of a particular social vision—environmentally responsible, designed to bring people into a kind of social cohesion—he could not hold the meaning of his buildings and their design style steady. Soleri intended to create vast complexes called "arcologies": essentially city-sized buildings which would obviate the need for cars and leave most of the countryside uninhabited and unspoiled. What arcologies meant as models of a visionary future and what they would mean as authoritative or gigantical human environments built twenty years ago are completely different. They might serve as symbols of unity or of the profoundest alienation, these meanings depending on each other, or opened up as possibilities together. And then there could be a centuries-long history of permutation, return to purity, decontextualization, and obsolescence, at every moment of which the meaning of the design style would be at stake, or liquid.

We can imagine a history of the arcology in which Soleri's buildings were made according to his designs, and then expanded or enumerated with changes. We could imagine radical movements departing from the classical arcology, and reactionary returns to it. We could imagine baroque and neo-classical arcologies, arcologies inflected by a dozen different political tendencies, ideologies, administrations. We could imagine arcologies imploded or reconstructed. And so on.

So if Paolo Soleri's utopian architecture were to have a built history, he could not—nor could anyone—hold it to a singular meaning. But neither could anyone who was adopting it detach it from its history. The arcology comes loaded with a prescriptive, determinative meaning, but each arcological period would be in a complex relation to that ideology, and with all the others, in an unfolding history. An arcology two centuries into the history of arcologies comes saturated with meanings, and one is working not only to shape materials into forms but also to shape the histories of meaning into something slightly new, or to suggest the next ramification of that history. To appropriate Soleri's radically progressive style in the future might be reactionary or retrograde, but it would also call to mind the history of utopian architecture; it would express and reverse Soleri's vision simultaneously; indeed it could not reverse it without expressing it.

The complexities of the relations of this counterfactual history are a radically foreshortened version of the complexities of our actual architectural or, more widely, artpolitical expressions. They cannot have their essence in the work of one person or movement or moment, because each person's work emerges at each moment within—and takes up its significance within—existing histories, which they drive forward in a loop backward. And the elaborations represent not only excursions and returns but also influences from everywhere, a constant work of synthesis and reinterpretation. Nevertheless, at each point an understanding of the configuration within its history is an understanding of the political configuration in its history. To repeat: inextricable at each node, distinct or of different orders as types.

Finally, this suggests that the aesthetics of politics is comprehensible only in terms of its entire physical-cultural surround, and each surround is comprehensible only in terms of its own surround, including the temporal environment in which it all unfolds. That is frustratingly vague, of course, and in some sense just a version of the insight that every specific phenomenon implicates the whole, that each thing is in that sense a microcosm or fully comprehensible only if everything is fully comprehensible, or in terms of everything: that everything is related to or actually is everything. Leibniz essentially held that each thing was unimaginable without the whole, and the whole unimaginable without each thing. This was, among other things, a profound theological vision. That accounts for the fact that although Leibniz regarded himself as a scientific thinker, his thought was at last extruded from science utterly in favor, for example, of the work of his rival Newton, and that the eighteenth century after Leibniz was obsessed with taxonomy, with making distinctions rather than collapsing them.

Perhaps we have gone too far in making distinctions—for instance, in terms of the subject matters of academic disciplines such as art history and political science—and now the point is not to show how different things are, or even to go back to the Leibnizian idea that each thing is everything and everything each. Perhaps, in the case of style and ideology, and in other cases as well, we should try to show how different things become so intensely and elaborately related that they merge into identity with one another and emerge into difference at every moment.

APPENDIX

Riffing on Political Aesthetics: Suggestions for Case Studies and Research

Here are some suggestions for case studies and research. The idea at this point would be to encourage the greatest possible variety of methodologies: ideologies left, right, close up, or far beyond; taxonomies; potential data, ordering the material in alternative hierarchies; strategic deployment of various traditional scholarly approaches or epistemic standards. This list is an attempt to show the richness and scope of a potential field of inquiry.

1. Charlemagne's standardizations of text and measures
2. the political aesthetics of measurement: "English" versus metric; demographics; big versus little
3. aesthetic aspects of tribal resistance to the state: Ghost Dance, personal war adornments, weapons
4. the aesthetics of weaponry: flint blade to mushroom cloud
5. apocalypse: art, eschatology, and politics
6. political function of festival: Mardi Gras, Rio, Woodstock, VFW hall; the honky-tonk; Navajo/Yoruba/voodoo/hoodoo aesthetics
7. the triumph and the triumphal arch; parades and processions; the funeral as political expression
8. effects of political autobiography: Caesar, Hitler, Malcolm X, Obama
9. satire, humor, and ridicule as political/aesthetic resources

10. identity politics, affirmative action, and postmodern art and architecture
11. poetics of political power: ancient epic, for example
12. political drama: from Aeschylus to Plautus to Beckett and beyond
13. history of the "uniform" in relation to fashion and power
14. symbolic sexualization of politics: Sade, Masoch, concubinage and hierarchy, Kennedy and Marilyn
15. craftwork, manufacturing, and the articulation of domestic spaces (quilting, cabinetmaking, Wal-Mart)
16. the art of Norman Rockwell
17. political implications of pictorial, literary, and political realism: Flaubert, Courbet, and Machiavelli; antirealism and surrealism in politics
18. political poetics of Nature: Lucretius, Aquinas, Voltaire, Wordsworth, Thoreau, Muir, ELF, *The Monkey Wrench Gang*
19. artpolitics of social constructionism and twentieth-century democracy: Mead, Dewey, Foucault, Rorty, Habermas
20. scent, essence, and witchcraft: in imperial Rome, Protestant Europe and America, rococo France, contemporary capitalism
21. cosmetics and propaganda: the appearance/reality distinction
22. artpolitics and medicine: epidemiology and depiction; disability aesthetics
23. monasticism and the political aesthetics of Tibet; Franciscans
24. constructivism and socialist realism: art of Malevich
25. the cult of technology: futurism, Charles Sheeler, design of bridges, interstate highways, factories
26. gay artpolitics: the vogue, cross-dressing, music, fashion, speech and body styles
27. aesthetics of utopia: Plato, Augustine, More, Shakers, Mormons, Oneida (sainthood and silverware); Walden 2, sixties communes (urban and rural); aesthetics of dystopia
28. signage
29. text and image in comic books and graphic novels: Captain America, Maus, Marjane Satrapi, manga (*Lone Wolf and Cub,* Osamu Tezuka, *V for Vendetta*)
30. Bugs Bunny, againsthestatesman
31. modernist architecture and internationalist politics: United Nations, globalization of economies
32. aesthetics of power: coal, nuclear, electric lines and substations, dams, solar
33. how to adorn: a president, an emperor, a king, a dictator, a pope, a zoning board

34. aesthetics of education and childhood as a political arena: the school; toy design; playgrounds; children's television programming and music (Hannah Montana); the politics of Webkinz

35. design and political effects of personal tech: iPod, iPhone, Blackberry; prostheses and implants; cyborg aesthetics

36. animals, design, and politics: breeding horses and dogs and their use in crowd control and law enforcement; cult of the dachshund; birds (divination, eagle, owl, and dove as symbols, the pigeon)

37. cuisine and power: the feast, the formal dinner, anorexia, veganism; aesthetics of farming

38. political uses and implications of the "genius," insider and outsider: Shakespeare, Milton, Beethoven, Emerson, Wagner, Nietzsche, Einstein, Picasso, Oppenheimer, Turing, Pollock, Warhol, Basquiat

39. optics and power: telescope and microscope, Huygens, Galileo, Hubble; political history of perspective; "Mirror of Princes" and mirroring

40. codes: in espionage, internal or secret media of communication, jargons and shorthands

41. standardization and liquification of languages: dictionaries, French linguistic nationalism, Canadian bilingual legislation; artpolitics of slang; speech impediments; universal or limited literacies; barbarian as nonlinguistic versus Chinese, Roman civilization; circulation and restriction of language in slavery; machine languages

42. the bell

43. filth and hygiene in art and government

44. meanings of color: black; red, white, and blue; blue, white, and red; green politics

45. politics of the flower: Wars of the Roses; herbicides, crop eradication, and dandelions; the corsage

46. aesthetics of smoke and fire: tobacco, sacred pipe, smoke signals, fires of an encamped army; aesthetics of pollution, industry; role of the smithy

47. money and aesthetics: gold and other media (shells, jewels); coin and bill design; money and political portraiture

48. vehicle design: Volkswagen, chariot, Model T, tank, the future of the car, covered wagon; aesthetics of the airplane, delivery vehicle; ships and political history; the train; trucking; the hybrid car

49. aesthetics of American slavery/aesthetics of abolitionism: picturing the plantation; plantation architecture; the body of Frederick Douglass; poetics of the slave narrative; John Brown's body in song, visual arts

50. artpolitics of colonialism; raced bodies, bwana; art, architecture, and looting; African mask fad in modernism; primitivism of J.-J. Rousseau/ Henri Rousseau; picturing the indigenous
51. aesthetics of law: Hebrew Bible; sharia; judges' robes; law books as aesthetic objects/texts
52. politics, art, and sport: art of the replay and shooting a game/individual; implications of color commentary

References

Adams, John. *The Political Writings of John Adams,* ed. George W. Carey. Washington, D.C.: Regnery, 2000.

Adorno, Theodor. *Minima Moralia* [1951], trans. E. F. N. Jephcott. London: Verso, 1978.

Ames, Roger, and David Hall. *Focusing the Familiar: A Translation and Philosophical Interpretation of the Zhongyong.* Honolulu: University of Hawai'i Press, 2001.

Ankersmit, F. R. *Aesthetic Politics: Political Philosophy beyond Fact and Value.* Stanford: Stanford University Press, 1996.

Antliff, Allan (1). *Anarchist Modernism: Art, Politics, and the First American Avant-Garde.* Chicago: University of Chicago Press, 2001.

——(2). *Anarchy and Art: From the Paris Commune to the Fall of the Berlin Wall.* Vancouver: Arsenal Pulp Press, 2007

Arendt, Hannah (1). "Excerpts from Lectures on Kant's Political Philosophy." In *The Life of the Mind,* ed. Mary McCarthy, pp. 255–257. New York: Harcourt, 1978.

——(2). "What Is Freedom?" In *Between Past and Future,* pp. 142–169. New York: Penguin, 2006.

Aristotle (1). *Poetics.* Trans. Ingram Bywater. In *The Complete Works of Aristotle* vol. 2, ed. Jonathan Barnes, pp. 2316–2340. Princeton: Princeton University Press, 1984.

——(2). *Politics.* In *The Politics and the Constitution of Athens,* ed. Stephen Everton. New York: Cambridge University Press, 1996.

Ashfield, Andrew, and Peter de Bolla, eds. *The Sublime: A Reader in British Eighteenth-Century Aesthetics.* Cambridge: Cambridge University Press, 1996.

Austin, Joe. *Taking the Train.* New York: Columbia University Press, 2001.

Bailyn, Bernard, ed. *The Debate on the Constitution.* 2 volumes. New York: Library of America, 1993.

Bain, Peter, and Paul Shaw, eds. *Blackletter: Type and National Identity.* New York: Princeton Architectural Press/Cooper Union, n.d.

Barrow, Steve, and Peter Dalton. *Reggae: The Rough Guide.* London: Rough Guides, 1997.

Benjamin, Walter. "The Work of Art in the Age of Mechanical Reproduction" [1935]. In *Illuminations,* trans. Harry Zohn, pp. 217–251. New York: Schocken, 2007.

Bey, Hakim. *TAZ: The Temporary Autonomous Zone, Ontological Anarchy, Poetic Terrorism* [1985]. New York: Autonomedia, 1991.

Blush, Stephen. *American Hardcore: A Tribal History.* Los Angeles: Feral House, 2001.

Borges, Jorge Luis. "Pierre Menard, Author of the *Quixote.*" In *Ficciones,* pp. 45–55. New York: Grove Press, 1962.

Bruni, Leonardo. *The Humanism of Leonardo Bruni: Selected Texts,* trans. Gordon Griffiths, James Hankins, and David Thompson. Binghamton: Renaissance Society of America, 1987.

Burke, Edmund. *A Philosophical Inquiry into the Origin of Our Ideas of the Sublime and Beautiful* [1756]. In *Edmund Burke,* pp. 29–140. New York: Collier [Harvard Classics], 1937.

Calhoun, John. *Union and Liberty: The Political Philosophy of John C. Calhoun.* Indianapolis: Liberty Fund, 1992.

Chan, Wing-Tsit. *A Source Book in Chinese Philosophy.* Princeton: Princeton University Press, 1963.

Chang, Jeff. *Can't Stop Won't Stop: A History of the Hip Hop Generation.* New York: Picador, 2005.

Chytry, Josef. *The Aesthetic State: A Quest in Modern German Thought.* Berkeley: University of California Press, 1989.

Confucius. *Analects,* trans. David Hinton. Washington, D.C.: Counterpoint, 1998.

Cronon, E. David. *Black Moses: The Story of Marcus Garvey and the Universal Negro Improvement Association* [1955]. Madison: University of Wisconsin Press, 1969.

Danto, Arthur (1). *The Abuse of Beauty: Aesthetics and the Concept of Art.* Chicago: Open Court, 2003.

——(2). *The Transfiguration of the Commonplace.* Cambridge: Harvard University Press, 1983.

Debord, Guy. *Society of the Spectacle* [1967], trans. Donald Nicholson-Smith. New York: Zone, 1995.

de Cleyre, Voltairine. "Anarchism" [1901]. In *Exquisite Rebel: Essays of Voltairine de Cleyre,* ed. Sharon Presley and Crispin Sartwell. Albany: State University of New York Press, 2005.

Deleuze, Gilles, and Félix Guattari. *A Thousand Plateaus,* trans. Brian Massumi. Minneapolis: University of Minnesota Press, 1987.

Dewey, John (1). *Art as Experience.* New York: Minton Balch, 1934.

——(2). "Creative Democracy: The Task Before Us." In *John Dewey and the Promise of America,* pp. 227–233. Progressive Education Booklet No. 14. Columbus, Ohio: American Education Press, 1939.

Douglass, Frederick. *Autobiographies.* New York: Library of America, 1994.

Drew Ali, Noble. *The Holy Koran of the Moorish Science Temple of America.* http://www.hermetic.com/bey/7koran.html.

Dryden, John. "A Parallel of Poetry and Painting" [1695]. In *Works of John Dryden,* Volume 2, pp. 324–339. New York: Harper and Brothers, 1844.

Du Bois, W. E. B. (1). *The Souls of Black Folk* [1903]. New York: Penguin, 1989.

——(2). *Writings.* New York: Library of America, 1986.

Eagleton, Terry. *The Ideology of the Aesthetic.* Malden, Mass.: Blackwell, 1990.

Eco, Umberto, and Alastair McEwen. *History of Beauty.* New York: Rizzoli, 2004.

Essien-Udom, E. U. *Black Nationalism.* Chicago: University of Chicago Press, 1962.

Falasca-Zamponi, Simonetta. *Fascist Spectacle: The Aesthetics of Power in Mussolini's Italy.* Berkeley: University of California Press, 2000.

Freedberg, David. *The Power of Images.* Chicago: University of Chicago Press, 1991.

Gadamer, Hans-Georg. *Truth and Method.* New York: Continuum, 1975.

Garvey, Marcus. *The Philosophy and Opinions of Marcus Garvey* [1925], comp. Amy Jacques Garvey. Dover, Mass.: Majority Press, 1986.

Glasper, Ian. *The Day the Country Died: A History of Anarcho-Punk.* London: Cherry Red Books, 2006.

Greenberg, Clement. "Avant-Garde and Kitsch" [1939]. In *Art and Culture,* pp. 3–21. Boston: Beacon Press, 1961.

Habermas, Jürgen. "What Is a People?" trans. Max Pensky. In *The Postnational Constellation,* pp. 1–25. Boston: MIT Press, 2001.

Halliwell, Stephen. *The Aesthetics of Mimesis.* Princeton: Princeton University Press, 2002.

Hariman, Robert: *Political Style: The Artistry of Power.* Chicago: University of Chicago Press, 1995.

Hebdige, Dick. *Subculture: The Meaning of Style.* New York: Routledge, 1981.

Hobbes, Thomas. *Leviathan* [1651]. New York: Penguin, 1968.

Hoffman, Abbie. *Revolution for the Hell of It* [1968]. In *The Best of Abbie Hoffman,* pp. 3–97. New York: Four Walls Eight Windows, 1989.

Hsün Tzu. *Hsün Tzu: Basic Writings,* trans. Burton Watson. New York: Columbia University Press, 1963.

Hughes, Langston. "The Negro Artist and the Racial Mountain" [1926]. In *Modern Black Nationalism,* ed. William Van Deburg, pp. 52–56. New York: New York University Press, 1997.

Hutcheson, Francis. *An Inquiry into the Original of Our Ideas of Beauty and Virtue* [1725]. Indianapolis: Liberty Fund, 2004.

Hyman, John. *The Objective Eye: Color, Form, and Reality in the History of Art.* Chicago: University of Chicago Press, 2006).

Jefferson, Thomas (1). *The Commonplace Book of Thomas Jefferson: A Repertory of His Ideas on Government,* ed. Gilbert Chinard. Baltimore: Johns Hopkins University Press, 1926.

——(2). *Writings.* New York: Library of America, 1984.

Kant, Immanuel (1). *Critique of Judgement* [1790], trans. J. H. Bernard. New York: Hafner, 1951.

——(2). *Observations on the Feeling of the Beautiful and Sublime* [1763], trans. John T. Goldthwait. Berkeley: University of California Press, 2003.

Kierkegaard, Søren. *Repetition* [1843]. In *Fear and Trembling/Repetition,* trans. Howard V. Hong and Edna H. Hong, pp. 125–231. Princeton: Princeton University Press, 1983.

Knight, Michael Muhammad. *The Five Percenters: Islam, Hip Hop and the Gods of New York.* Oxford: One World Publications, 2007.

Lee, Hélène. *The First Rasta: Leonard Howell and the Rise of Rastafarianism.* Chicago: Lawrence Hill Books, 2003.

Lehmann-Haupt, Hellmut. *Art under a Dictatorship.* New York: Oxford University Press, 1954.

Michaud, Eric. *The Cult of Art in Nazi Germany.* Stanford: Stanford University Press, 2004.

Moses, Wilson Jeremiah. *The Golden Age of Black Nationalism.* Oxford: Oxford University Press, 1978.

Mozi (Mo Tzu). *Mozi,* trans. Donald Sturgeon. http://chinese.dsturgeon.net/text. pl?node=579&if=en.

Muhammad, Elijah (1). *Message to the Blackman in America* [1965]. http://www.sev enthfam.com/temple/books/black_man/blk4.htm.

——(2). *The True History of Master Fard Muhammad: Allah (God) in Person.* Maryland Heights, MO: Secretarius MEMPS Publications, 2002.

Panofsky, Erwin. *Renaissance and Renascences in Western Art.* New York: Harper & Row, 1972.

Pettersburgh, Balintine F. *The Royal Parchment Scroll of Black Supremacy* [1926]. http:// www.sacred-texts.com/afr/rps/rps03.htm.

Plato (1). *Republic.* In *Collected Dialogues,* trans. Paul Shorey, pp. 575–844. Princeton: Princeton University Press, 1982.

——(2). *The Statesman,* trans. B. J. Skemp. In *Collected Dialogues,* pp. 1018–1085. Princeton: Princeton University Press, 1982.

Quine, W. V. "On What There Is." In *From a Logical Point of View: Nine Logico-Philo- sophical Essays, pp. 1–19.* Cambridge: Harvard University Press, 1980.

Rancière, Jacques. *The Politics of Aesthetics,* trans. Gabriel Rockhill. London: Con- tinuum, 2004.

Richard, Carl. *The Founders and the Classics.* Cambridge: Harvard University Press, 1994.

Riefenstahl, Leni. *Leni Riefenstahl: A Memoir.* New York: Picador, 1992.

Robinson, John Mansley. *An Introduction to Early Greek Philosophy.* Boston: Houghton Mifflin, 1968.

Rogers, Robert Athlyi. *The Holy Piby* [1924–28]. http://www.sacred-texts.com/afr/ piby/index.htm.

Sartwell, Crispin (1). *Against the State: An Introduction to Anarchist Political Theory.* Albany: State University of New York Press, 2008.

——(2). "The Analytic Turn: An Institutional Account." *Metaphilosophy* 20, no. 3–4 (July–October 1989): 248–266.

——(3). *Six Names of Beauty.* New York: Routledge, 2004.

Scarry, Elaine. *On Beauty and Being Just.* Princeton: Princeton University Press, 2001.

Schier, Flint. *Deeper into Pictures.* Cambridge: Cambridge University Press, 1986.

Schiller, Friedrich. *On the Aesthetic Education of Man* [1795], trans. Reginald Snell. New York: Dover, 1954.

Schmitt, Carl. *The Concept of the Political* [1932], trans. George Schwab. Rev. ed. Chi- cago: University of Chicago Press, 2007.

Shaftesbury (Anthony Ashley Cooper, third Earl of Shaftesbury). *Characteristicks of Men, Manners, Opinions, Times* [1714]. 3 volumes. Indianapolis: Liberty Fund, 2004.

Sontag, Susan. "Fascinating Fascism." In *Under the Sign of Saturn,* pp. 73–107. New York: Picador, 1991.

Speer, Albert. *Inside the Third Reich: Memoirs.* New York: Simon and Schuster, 1970.

Spotts, Frederic. *Hitler and the Power of Aesthetics.* Woodstock, N.Y.: Overlook Press.

Thompson, Robert Farris. *Flash of the Spirit.* New York: Vintage, 1984.

Trimborn, Jürgen. *Leni Riefenstahl: A Life,* trans. Edna McCown. New York: Faber and Faber, 2007.

van Creveld, Martin. *The Rise and Decline of the State.* Cambridge: Cambridge Uni- versity Press, 1999.

Van Deburg, William L., ed. *Modern Black Nationalism*. New York: New York University Press, 1997.

Veal, Michael E. *Dub: Soundscapes and Shattered Songs in Jamaican Reggae*. Middletown, Conn.: Wesleyan University Press, 2007.

Vico, Giambattista. *New Science* [3rd ed. 1744], trans. David Marsh. London: Penguin, 2001.

Vitruvius. *On Architecture,* trans. Frank Granger. Cambridge: Harvard University Press, 1970.

Whitman, Walt. *Poetry and Prose*. New York: Library of America, 1982.

Wilson, Peter Lamborn. *Pirate Utopias*. New York: Autonomedia, 2003.

Wölfflin, Heinrich. *Principles of Art History* [1932]. New York: Dover, 1950.

Wolin, Sheldon. *Politics and Vision*. Princeton: Princeton University Press, 2004.

Index

oratory, 156, 196, 209, 229
Ordway, Nico, 102
organic conception of the state, 132–33, 146, 221, 224, 225
ornament, 7, 19, 49, 50, 61, 70, 73, 138, 147, 198, 204, 210, 228, 232
outhouse, 193
Owens, Jesse, 32

Pablo, Augustus, 171
pacifism, 107, 108
paganism, 16, 205
Paine, Thomas, 209
painting, 16, 17, 19, 71, 77, 84, 141, 192, 195, 202, 204, 219
  graffiti as, 182
  vicious, 85
Palestine, 119
Palin, Sarah, 96
Palladio, Andrea, 65, 221, 225, 227
Panofsky, Erwin, 219, 222–23
Pantheon, 26, 40
Parmenides, 129, 227
patois, 173, 176, 194
patriarchy, 72
patronage, 10, 72, 198
Paul (Church father), 204
peace movement, 194
Pearl Harbor, 190
Peirce, Charles Sanders, 57, 90
Pentagon, 69
people, the, 88–98
People for the Ethical Treatment of Animals (PETA), 108
performance, 209
Pericles, 213
periodization, 193–98
Perry, Lee "Scratch," 169, 171
persona, personae, person, 88–89
perspective, 92, 247
Petit, Philippe, 44
Petrarch, 214, 219
Pettersburgh, Balintine F., 157–58
Pettibon, Raymond, 116–17
PHASE 2 (graffiti artist), 183–84
photography, 27, 28, 30, 31–32, 97
Picabia, Francis, 125
Picasso, Pablo, 124, 247
Picciotto, Guy, 109
pimping, 205
Pink Floyd, 105
Pinnacle, (Rasta community), 161–62, 169
planning, urban, 38, 68–69, 81, 195
Planno, Mortimer, 171

Plato, 2, 13, 23, 28, 52, 56, 62, 67, 75–76, 85, 87, 92, 95, 128, 133, 136, 139, 140, 145, 148, 177, 179, 189, 215, 216, 227, 246
  his aesthetic politics, 129–32, 218
  on music, 135, 137
  See also Neoplatonism
Plautus, 246
pleasure, 70–73, 200
Plotinus, 52
Plutarch, 221, 226
Pnyx, 8–9
poetics, 3, 25, 148, 213, 246, 247
poetry, 3, 19, 39, 51, 62, 129, 131, 146, 178, 192, 194, 213, 230
Poison Girls (punk band), 108
political, concept of, 8–11
political aesthetics defined, 1–2, 10, 11, 235–43
political science, 2, 10, 12, 14, 53, 187–90, 195, 235, 243
  Arendt on, 86
  Calhoun on, 224
Polk, James Knox, 231
Pollock, Jackson, 90, 126, 247
Poor Righteous Teachers (hip hop act), 174
Popper, Karl, 56
popular art, 21
pornography, 72
portraiture, 36, 90, 117–18, 125, 156, 190, 206, 232, 247
postcolonialism, 111
postmodernism, 46, 165, 209, 246
poverty, 55
power, 8–10, 18–19, 21, 35–36, 68, 96, 191, 196, 212, 235, 246
  and beauty, 76
  Hitler's, 38–39
  language and, 175–86
  and resistance as taxonomical principles, 193–94, 197–98, 198–200
  and sublimity, 78–83
Poussin, Nicolas, 214, 221
pragmatism, 57
Praxiteles, 30
Prendergast, Maurice, 123
Pre-Raphaelites, 73, 75
pre-Socratics, 128
primitivism, 110, 216–17, 247
Prince (recording artist), 104
Prince Buster, 164
Professor Griff (hip hop performer), 173
propaganda, 1, 3, 18, 32, 38–40, 49, 103, 246